Understanding Social Lives
Part 2

Understanding Social Lives Part 2

Edited by John Clarke and Kath Woodward

This publication forms part of the Open University module DD102 Introducing the social sciences. Details of this and other Open University modules can be obtained from the Student Registration and Enquiry Service, The Open University, PO Box 197, Milton Keynes MK7 6BJ, United Kingdom (tel. +44 (0)845 300 60 90; email general-enquiries@open.ac.uk).

Alternatively, you may visit the Open University website at www.open.ac.uk where you can learn more about the wide range of modules and packs offered at all levels by The Open University. To purchase a selection of Open University materials visit www.ouw.co.uk, or contact Open University Worldwide, Walton Hall, Milton Keynes MK7 6AA, United Kingdom for a brochure (tel. +44 (0)1908 858793; fax +44 (0)1908 858787; email ouw-customer-services@open.ac. uk).

The Open University, Walton Hall, Milton Keynes MK7 6AA

First published 2014

Edited, designed and typeset by The Open University.

Printed and bound in the United Kingdom.

ISBN 978 178 00 7853 3

1.1

Contents

Preface

Understanding Social Lives, Part 2 is the second module textbook for *Introducing the social sciences* (DD102). As with other Open University materials, *Understanding Social Lives, Part 2* has been produced by a 'module team' of academic and production staff that included the authors and editors named here, but also many others. This wider module team played a key role in shaping the module, the book and individual chapters through successive drafts. Professor Dale Southerton, our external assessor, was a valued source of critical and supporting advice, and we very much appreciate all his careful work on our behalf.

The academic staff at The Open University are unusually lucky in being able to benefit from the expertise and professionalism of the best production and administrative colleagues. Lesley Moore, our Module Coordinator, was a model of efficiency, 'unflappability' and good humour, and provided strong support to the module team. Production colleagues and editors – Melanie Bayley, John O'Dwyer, Katie Belcher and Salia Nessa – did far more than edit and compose this book and the range of online study materials with care, attention to detail and goodwill: they must take a large share of credit for the clarity, coherence and accessibility of this book and all of the other study materials. Thanks are also due to Jo Mack and Roshni Amin, both consummate professionals, whose years of experience ensured the quality of the films and audio materials. Paul Hillery and Howie Twiner, Graphics Media Developers, are due our collective thanks for their creative work on the design and artwork of the book. And last, but certainly not least, thanks must go to Ann Tolley and Eileen Potterton, who worked as Curriculum Managers on *Introducing the social sciences*. They are the best in the business and oversaw the production of this book and the rest of the module with such enthusiasm, efficiency, goodwill and patience that our lives were made much easier than we had any right to expect.

Unusually, perhaps, DD102 builds on its predecessor module – DD101 – through trying to both incorporate what worked on this previous module and improving what worked less well. In this regard, the DD102 module team also owe their thanks to the DD101 module team and particularly to its chair, Dr Simon Bromley, who laid such excellent foundations for our work here.

Understanding Social Lives, Part 2 is divided into two strands of content – 'Connecting lives' and 'Ordering lives' – edited respectively by Kath Woodward and John Clarke. With years of experience at their fingertips, the strand editors worked to shape and refine this text and much of the module besides. We are truly grateful for all their creative efforts, which have made the module far better than it would have been without their invaluable participation.

Georgina Blakeley and Matt Staples
Chair and Deputy Chair of the *Introducing the social sciences* module team

Connecting lives

Chapter 1
Identities

Stephanie Taylor

Contents

Introduction

In many situations, people are required to provide 'evidence of identity', such as a passport, driving licence or student card. To obtain this, they have probably been required to fill out a form similar to the one in Figure 1.1.

3. Sex

Male / Female

4. Age group

Under 18 / 19-25 / 26-35 / 36-45 / 46-55 / 56-65 / over 65

5. Nationality

UK citizen / Other EU citizen / Other Commonwealth citizen / Other

6. Race or ethnicity

Indian / Bangladeshi / Pakistani / Chinese / White (Scottish / Irish / British /

Caribbean) / White and Asian / Black (African / Caribbean) / Irish Traveller /

Other White background / Other Black background / Other mixed background /

Other Asian background / Any other ethnic group

Figure 1.1   Example of a form

Activity 1

Think about how you would complete the form in Figure 1.1.

Would you feel you had much in common with someone who had given the same answer as you for *one* of the questions? What about with someone who gave the same answers for *all* of the questions?

To what extent do you think you would want similar things as the person who had given the same answers for all of the questions? To what extent would you agree about what is important in life?

Only a part of the form is shown in Figure 1.1. There would, of course, be other questions, for example about details of name(s), address, occupation and income. Otherwise, the form is unremarkable. However, it does raise an important puzzle around identity. The form as a whole is about identifying a particular named person – to be distinguished from everyone else – yet, most of the answers connect the respondent to a group or category of people who are the same because they are the same sex, age group, and so on. The double association of identity with difference and sameness is part of its interest for social scientists. This chapter will explore some different identities and the issues they raise for social scientists, including those introduced by the questions in Activity 1.

Section 1 explores some conventional categories of identity, based on both sameness and difference, which interest social scientists as well as politicians and commercial companies. Two of these categories – gender, and race and ethnicity – refer to identities that might seem fixed, whereas the third – class – is perhaps more fluid and changeable. The section discusses whether or not those assumptions are correct. Section 2 outlines two classic approaches that link identities to people's social activities and interactions. Section 3 discusses people in the street, in another country and time, to show how negative identities and identities of difference can separate or disconnect people, and groups, from society. Section 4 returns to everyday identities, which are based on (an idea of) sameness, through shared family, place and nationality. It shows, again, how identities can be actively constructed to create connections. The conclusion of the chapter reviews the main ideas that have been introduced, including the connections between social and personal identities.

1 Identity categories

This section will explore three categories of identities, of both sameness and difference, which connect and disconnect other people and have been studied by social scientists:

- gender
- race and ethnicity
- class.

It might seem logical that sameness connects people. People of the same nationality or age are often referred to as 'groups' within society (as in the term 'age group'), as if they share interests and concerns. Of course, such a group would be too large for everyone in it to be personally acquainted. They resemble the concept of 'group' discussed by the political scientist Benedict Anderson (1983), which is made up of people who read the same newspaper. Each reader imagines all the other people who are reading the news at the same time, seeing the same pictures, responding to the same headlines and stories. This connection and sharing with an 'imagined community' is an essential aspect of the news: a newspaper written for one person would not be a newspaper. The group is imagined by its members as connected by this shared identity and it is imagined by other people. For example, in the UK, politicians are said to think about voters as *Sun*, *Daily Mail* or *Guardian* readers, referring to the views associated with particular newspapers. These therefore become important social identities, even though each group never comes together in any situation in which the members can directly encounter each other.

To say that a group is 'imagined' does not mean that it does not exist at all, but has been invented, like a lie or fictional story that is not 'true'. Instead, the term refers to the importance of people's ideas and beliefs about the world, including people's connections with each other. Imagining can have practical consequences, such as a political party targeting the opinions of the imagined newspaper readers. The categories discussed below are inevitably imagined because they are extremely large. Two of the categories are commonly included on forms like the one in Figure 1.1, but the third category is less openly discussed.

1.1   Gender

The question on the form that asks whether you are 'female' or 'male' invites you to indicate your sex or gender. The sociologist Richard Jenkins has called gender a 'primary' identity (1996, p. 21) and certainly it is very difficult to talk about someone without identifying them as either female or male. The announcement of 'It's a girl' or 'It's a boy' when a baby is born is probably the last time a person is described as 'it'. The identification refers to the baby's body and specifically the outward appearance of the genitalia.

However, there is a minority of people for whom this identification can be misleading because the bodily appearance is ambiguous, especially in a newborn, or because of details of genes and other physical features that are not directly observable. There are also people whose personal sense of **gender identity**, as a woman or man, differs from the identity that is indicated by their bodies. The term 'transsexual' is used to refer to people born apparently one sex but who, from a very early age, feel themselves to be the other sex and seek to undergo sex reassignment surgery to bring their physical body in line with their gender identity.

Gender identity
The identity category usually represented as female/male or woman/man.

Even without these complexities, the bodily differences used to identify a baby as female or male do not indicate much about its future life because it is difficult to generalise across the range of experience of either women or men. In addition, the patterns of difference that do exist, and the experiences of being a woman or a man, vary between different societies. Women and men are always distinguished, but it is difficult to generalise beyond that point. This can be seen if the contemporary UK society is compared with that of the late nineteenth century. Nowadays, few people would accept that women need to be protected because they are physically and emotionally fragile; or that men are insensitive or unemotional or incapable of nurturing. Schools, generally, do not expect girls to be more artistic and practical or boys to be better at maths, although recent research has shown a gender bias in the way that teachers tend to rate white female students' abilities in maths as lower than those of white male students, even when the grades of female students are comparable to male students (Riegle-Crumb and Humphries, 2012). Most jobs and careers are open to both women and men and, legally, they are entitled to equal pay.

In practice, some occupations are dominated by women and others by men – women tend to be paid less and they are more likely to be the main carers of children. But even these distinctions are not absolute.

For example, some occupations, like nursing, have changed from being regarded as a woman's job to one for either women or men, and some women earn a good income and more than the men in their families. All of these points suggest that there is not just one identity for a woman or man, and that the range of possibilities will vary from society to society (including societies of different times). In this sense, gender is not fixed, even though individuals might not regard their own female or male identity as changeable.

Feminists have criticised reductive explanations that link gender back to biology and attempt to explain complex social identities as having a single cause or source: most of the differences between men and women have no basis in biology (just as there is no gene for carrying a handbag or preferring pink to blue!). To emphasise the social aspects of these identities and differences, some social scientists distinguish 'sex', as a bodily or biological identity, from 'gender', as a collective **social identity**. This does not mean that the social identities are less important. Gender difference has become a practical political issue precisely because it refers to both differences (between women's and men's lives) and similarities (such as the problems of low pay and heavy childcare responsibilities that are shared by many women). Nonetheless, the example of gender indicates the importance and limits of group or collective social identities.

In the 1970s and 1980s, an important issue for feminists worldwide was whether their collective identity as women was more or less important than differences of race, wealth and nationality. The issue was one of equality and, in particular, the different identities, and associated experiences and situations, of Western women and women in developing countries, white women and women of other **identities of race and ethnicity**. In trade unions, there was a similar issue of whether a common identity as workers was more important than the different workplace experiences and opportunities of women workers, or black workers or black women. The examples suggest that instead of trying to establish similarities or discuss social issues with reference to just one identity category, it is often necessary to consider the connection or intersection of different identities such as gender and race and ethnicity (Phoenix and Pattynama, 2006; Valentine, 2007).

Gender has been discussed here as an identity of difference (female not male, or male not female), which is tied to the body, yet not fixed by biology. It is both personal and social. The next identity category to be

Social identity
An identity given by connections to other people and social situations (often contrasted with personal identity). Some examples are: *collective identities*, referring to groups or categories of people; *situated identities* given by the immediate situation so liable to change; and *relational identities*, usually given by a two-sided, possibly unequal, relationship.

Identities of race and ethnicity
The category of marked identities that has a historical basis and refers to (imagined) differences of colour, origin, religion, and so on.

discussed is also often included on official forms, but there is much less agreement about the alternatives.

1.2 Race and ethnicity

The terms 'race' and 'ethnicity' are used in many different ways, and often interchangeably. One possible distinction is that race refers to features of the physical body, especially skin colour, and ethnicity refers to language, nationality and culture, including religion (Lewis and Phoenix, 2000). This distinction does not always work in practice. For example, by this definition, my own racial identity is white and I am ethnically an English-speaking New Zealander. However, my racial identity in New Zealand is also 'pakeha' (a Maori term for non-Maori people) or 'European', since for historical reasons 'European' is an alternative term for white skin colour there (rather like 'Anglo' in the USA). A more important point is that I would very seldom describe myself, or be described by other people, in these ways because my identity is 'unmarked' in both New Zealand and the UK; in other words, it is the collective identity that generally goes unnoticed, but is assumed to be normal and vaguely positive, so that other identities become noticeable or 'marked' in contrast. (The exception is my accent, which causes comment in both countries: people in the UK describe it as 'New Zealand', but New Zealanders call it 'British'.) There has been a considerable amount of social science research on race and ethnicity, most of it focused on marked identities. More recently, social scientists have begun to research whiteness as a taken-for-granted, unmarked ethnic identity.

There is an almost infinite range of possible distinctions and terms for racial and ethnic identities. The form in Figure 1.1 attempts to present a fairly full list for the UK today, but it is certainly not complete. This variety occurs because both racial and ethnic identities are situated, having a reference and value that depend on the social and historical context. It might seem logical that, if race refers to the body rather than culture, racial identities will be more fixed than ethnic ones. Nevertheless, different societies have always identified different racial categories (for instance, in nineteenth-century England, the Irish were often described as 'black'). Racial categorisation is generally linked to exaggerated stereotypes, a point that psychologists have studied in detail. There have been political attempts to divide societies according to race (for example, in South Africa under apartheid), but in these situations there have invariably been many people whose category was unclear or disputed. People's bodies vary, but the differences do not separate them neatly into this category or that: there is as much biological variation *within* so-called races as *between* them. Some social scientists put the terms 'race' and 'ethnicity' in inverted commas to emphasise the situated and relational nature of the identities that they refer to.

Racial and ethnic identities are often marked identities that are usually negatively valued. Although, in practice, the categories are difficult to separate, they are usually used to refer to groups of people who appear to share racial and ethnic characteristics. They are to some extent identities of place because they generally refer to some historical movement of people, even though the movement may have occurred generations before. A common aspect of racial and ethnic identities in the UK is that they often position people as recent immigrants to the country in which they were born and grew up. However, in some other parts of the world, such as South Africa, Australia and New Zealand, the marked identity is that of the indigenous people; the white identity is still unmarked, even though it derives from the movements of 'settler' immigrants. This apparent inconsistency is explained by the fact that most racial and ethnic identities in the UK today also refer to former colonial relationships.

The British Empire established unequal identities for both people and places; indeed, differences of identity were essential to the power relationships through which a large part of the world was ruled from Britain as the imperial centre. In both the UK and the other countries I have referred to, the **unmarked identity** is that of the former colonisers. The relational identities of colonisers and colonised peoples were linked to an imagined history involving conquest, cultural superiority, civilisation, economic development, and the achievement of prosperity and order. You may wonder if this history is still relevant. It persists in the continuing associations of racial and ethnic identities with somewhere else, and in racist language and practices by which non-white identities are negatively valued – at its most extreme, a common demand in **racist rhetoric** is that people should 'go home'. Yet, paradoxically, the imagined histories of contemporary British society often 'forget' centuries of connection with India and Africa, not to mention Ireland.

As with gender, racial/ethnic identities are social and relational and cannot be reduced simply to biology. Moreover, there is an almost infinite range of possible racial and ethnic identities, but these are

Unmarked identity
Part of a pair of unequal relational identities in which the unmarked identity is taken for granted as normal, but the marked identity never goes unnoticed and usually carries a negative value.

Racist rhetoric
Speaking or writing, especially for a public audience, which talks about society as divided into completely separate, closed and unequal groups that can supposedly be distinguished by the physical appearance and origins of the people in the inferior group(s).

generally defined in contrast to an 'ordinary', 'normal' or unmarked identity. They are situated identities that cannot be understood or explained adequately without reference to their context and going beyond the immediate situation, for example, to encompass larger geographical and historical phenomena. The third identity category to be discussed in this section is even more difficult to pin down precisely.

1.3   Class

Unlike gender or race and ethnicity, the identity category of 'class' is rarely included on forms, although questions about 'occupation' and 'income bracket' may indirectly refer to class. This section will consider the relevance of class and class identities to contemporary lives. It will discuss what locates people in one class or another, how many class divisions there now are and how freely individuals can move between classes.

Class has been called an 'unspeakable' identity that is seldom discussed. This is probably because it refers to inequalities by which a small number of people occupy superior positions in society, in the same way that the people with first-class train tickets have more comfortable seats in less crowded carriages. Of course, the inequalities of class are part of British social history and have been the focus of many popular television series. These tend to present class as a complicated amalgam of birth, money, accent and style, looking back to the nineteenth and early twentieth centuries to show a drab but spirited working class who are servants to a beautifully-dressed upper class, usually alongside a few less interesting middle-class characters, such as doctors and lawyers.

The audience's enjoyment of these programmes depends a great deal on the assumption that the class system that is being depicted no longer exists. The privilege and injustices of the past have supposedly been superseded by a fairer and more equal contemporary society. There may still be rich and famous people who are higher up the hierarchy, but in theory anyone can now rise to those upper levels through talent and hard work, whatever their background. This is the model of society known as a 'meritocracy'. It emphasises individual freedom and the opportunity to compete and succeed, including through education. This is similar to the discussion you came across in the 'Making lives' strand about the ways in which individuals make their lives, albeit not in circumstances of their own choosing.

A different depiction of a class society is that of the famous theorist Karl Marx. Writing in the nineteenth century, Marx linked class inequalities to people's work and their positions in the economy. Marx argued that capitalist society was divided into two mutually antagonistic classes, the proletariat and the bourgeoisie, or in other terms, the working class, which is forced to sell its labour in order to survive, and the capitalist class, which employs them. For Marx, class is oppositional because it is defined by whether people have to sell their own labour, so in a sense their lives, to their employers. However, the different classes are dependent on each other in order to keep the economy going, like parts of the same industrial machine. The people within each class – the small number of capitalists at the top and the many more workers below – are connected by their shared situations and interests. In contrast to the individual freedom and mobility within a meritocracy, Marx's model emphasises the collective class divisions in society and, in particular, the ways in which a whole class, the working class, is constrained. People's lives and opportunities, or lack of opportunities, are defined by the class that they are born into.

What is of significance here is the extent to which class and class identities still exist in the contemporary UK and, if they do, whether they remain relevant to contemporary lives. We might then ask: what locates people in one class or another? How many class divisions are there? How freely can individuals move between classes? To begin to answer these questions, Activity 2 focuses on one source of inequality: money.

You will read more about inequality in Chapter 9.

Activity 2

Think about the following questions:

- Do you think that people's lives in Britain are improving or getting worse?
- Do you think that people in Britain are becoming more equal?
- Is life getting better for rich people or for poor people?

One aspect of the class system of nineteenth-century Britain was the huge inequalities between the rich and the poor. An early social scientist Henry Mayhew (2008 [1861]), who conducted studies of London in the middle of the nineteenth century, found that many poor people survived (just) by selling small items on the street (such as pies, fried fish or toys), or simply by sweeping an area of road in the hope that the rich people who crossed would 'pay' something for the convenience of keeping their feet clean. We generally assume that these economic differences have been reduced. But how has the difference between rich and poor changed more recently?

One way to approach this is in terms of income, which is literally the money 'coming in' to a household from earnings, investments and interest on savings. On the evidence of income, the answers are that people's lives are improving because incomes increase every year, looking at the UK as a whole. But the increases are not shared out equally. In the 20 years leading up to 2008, when the global economic crisis began, the incomes of the richest people in British society (the top 10 per cent) grew faster than the incomes of the poorest 10 per cent, so inequality increased. The incomes of the richest 10 per cent are about 10 times the average of the incomes of the poorest 10 per cent. Incomes grew fastest of all for the top 0.1 per cent, that is the one thousandth of the population who in 2008, before the crash, received about 4 per cent of the national income – about 40 times their 'fair' share (OECD, 2011).

This evidence of income indicates not only that huge inequalities still exist in Britain, but also that these are becoming greater, not less. They are collective inequalities, between groups. The people within a group, such as the top 10 per cent or the bottom 10 per cent, are perhaps connected by their similar income and the life it makes possible, but the differences between the groups are likely to weaken connections across society as a whole.

Another way to look at economic divisions that relate to class is in terms of the kinds of work that people do (and incomes are of course related to this). A 2002 scheme (in Crompton, 2008) attempted to map contemporary economic class divisions in terms of occupations. It concluded that Britain now has three main classes:

- managerial and professional
- intermediate
- routine and manual.

Crompton adds a fourth class of 'never worked and long-term unemployed' people who do not fit neatly into classifications based on employment (Crompton, 2008, p. 65). However, the three main classes can be further divided into five or eight classes: the picture is complicated because it is not entirely clear where the lines should be drawn and because people can move into different groups by changing their jobs.

Economic divisions are a useful start but most social scientists would agree that they are not sufficient to explain all the differences and identities of class in Britain, partly because they are tied to other kinds of differences. This becomes visible if we consider the enormous changes in economic activity and employment that have taken place in Britain since the middle of the twentieth century. One change was the decline of industries traditionally associated with working-class (male) employment, such as ship building, mining and car manufacturing. Another change was the rise of service industries, such as retail and office work, which are major employers of women. These economic changes inevitably caused significant social change. The impact was heaviest on the working-class communities attached to particular places of industry, such as a shipyard, mine or large car factory. People who had previously been united by their dependence on the same employer, their shared routines and personal familiarity, suddenly lost those connections. In addition, the changes affected the traditional working-class family in which a man was the breadwinner or main earner and a woman was responsible for domestic tasks, and their children were raised with the expectation that they would have similar lives to their parents. This model of the family and its associated lifestyle and gender roles became less commonplace, even if it has not entirely disappeared as an ideal.

On the evidence of these changes, it has been argued that the traditional collective identity of the British working class has now ended. Further evidence cited in support of this claim is that more people now exert more choice in how they live their lives. For instance, more people can now buy their own home (with a mortgage) rather than renting, and go to university as the pathway into their own chosen career. You read in the 'Making lives' strand how people also shape their own individual identities through the ways that they dress and present themselves, although of course they may be constrained by lack of money. One optimistic view, popular with politicians, is that the increase in individual choice means that class has disappeared and Britain is now a meritocracy. Alternatively, and somewhat confusingly, this individualism is sometimes equated with being middle class. In other words, the working class are defined as sharing a collective identity whereas middle-class people present themselves as independent individuals. Therefore, the alternative argument goes, everyone is now middle class.

Against this, there is an argument that collective class identities persist in an updated form, continuing to connect people through sameness to others in their own class and recognisable difference from other classes. For example, in 2012 the artist Grayson Perry made a series of tapestries (see Victoria Miro, 2012) supposedly depicting the contemporary working, middle and upper classes, the differences evident in their lifestyles, in the ways they dress and decorate their homes and spend their leisure time, despite all the choice supposedly available to them.

To review the arguments so far, the economic evidence indicates that Britain is indeed a divided and unequal society. Economic change produces social change, but the question that remains is whether class differences and class identities are primarily economic, given by income and occupation. In other words, is a sudden rise in earnings or a change of job sufficient to produce a change of **class identity**, or is something more involved?

Class identity
A group or collective identity that links economic inequality and social differences, including superior or inferior status and differences of family background and lifestyle.

Many social scientists argue that to understand class in Britain today, we need to look more closely at people's lives, their beliefs and their own sense of who they are. The sociologist Andrew Sayer argues that class identities are not merely a matter of lifestyle difference, but are tied to ideas about 'what is of value, how to live, what is worth striving for and what is not' (Sayer, 2005, p. 6). This kind of 'morality', Sayer suggests, is likely to be deep rooted and personal, acquired as part of people's upbringing and difficult to change. For example, it may influence how children are brought up. Is it more important for them to prioritise their schoolwork or be free to play and develop friendships? Sawyer suggests that how that question is answered is one indicator of different class values, moralities and identities, all of which affect people's opportunities.

To illustrate the continuing importance of class, Sayer discusses the example of entry to a particular career. Logically, becoming a medical doctor should be a popular career choice, given that this is a prestigious professional occupation, which is likely to be well paid and satisfying. However, class operates on the choice in subtle ways. On the practical side, entry will require good educational qualifications and obtaining these will seem easier, and *be* easier, for ambitious young people whose family income supports their education, and whose moralities encourage them to study hard and be competitive. The selection panels of medical schools will be impressed by applicants who already look like the kind of people who become doctors, which is probably more likely if their family and close friends do in fact include doctors. On a more personal level, those same young people will find it easier to imagine themselves in medical careers. In contrast, someone from a different background might feel arrogant and even disloyal for aspiring to a medical career if no one they know well has done anything similar. The example shows that the social and personal aspects of class identities are difficult to separate. Class is linked to some of our most personal values and to emotions, like confidence and embarrassment. Most importantly, the example shows that class still matters because it is based on economic and social inequalities, *and* it functions to maintain and perpetuate those inequalities. In the words of the sociologist Rosemary Crompton, class 'persists as systematically structured social and economic disadvantage, which is reproduced over the generations' (Crompton, 2008, p. 5).

The discussion has now addressed most of my initial questions about class. I have argued that class and class identities do still exist in Britain today, and they matter for people's lives. Class is complex. It is economic and social, collective and personal. The personal aspects, given in large part by family background and upbringing, are perhaps the most difficult to change since they include people's deeply held values and beliefs about the right way to live. The other question that I posed earlier, about the number of classes, now seems relatively unimportant. Most people, if asked, would probably say that there are three main classes in Britain: the upper, middle and working classes. However, many other categories are also distinguished, such as upper- and lower-middle class, underclass, and there is a huge range of associated terms like 'professional', 'white collar', 'blue collar', 'posh', 'common' – you can probably think of others. Clearly, a neat two- or three-class model is not sufficient to encompass all the possible distinctions.

The more important point is probably that class rests on a situated distinction between superior and inferior, better and worse, like the classes on the train. Class is not only about sameness and difference, but also about status. The issue is that people are being judged and classified (the word from which 'class' derives). This is probably why class continues to be an 'unspeakable' identity and why many people would like to deny that it still exists.

You came across the term 'status' in Chapter 5 of *Understanding Social Lives, Part 1.*

Some social scientists suggest that this judging is now played out in the kind of reality television programmes in which an expert guides people in matters of lifestyle and taste. The sociologists Beverley Skeggs and Stephanie Lawler argue that these programmes are about contemporary class identities (see for example Skeggs, 1997; Lawler, 2005). The expert's identity is unmarked in that it is presented as normal; the sociologists describe it as middle class. The people in the programmes who are being marked as inferior because they apparently don't know how to eat or dress properly, or how to decorate their homes or bring up their children, are working class. The programmes invite viewers to position themselves with the middle-class expert, against 'them', the working class. The programmes therefore reinforce existing class differences and a hierarchy of superior and inferior class identities.

This can also be seen in two new variations on a working-class identity: 'chavs' and 'neds'. The psychology researcher Robert Young interviewed young people and found that they associate 'chav' and 'ned' identities with socio-economic disadvantage, and also with particular types of social behaviours that are judged as 'wrong' from a middle-class perspective. These behaviours include: low educational achievement, heavy drinking, and a 'tough' masculinity of violence and law breaking (Young, 2012). These claims repeat points already noted in this section, that class is economic and social, and that it is linked to values or morality. In addition, the claims show how class identities are difficult to pin down with a factual description: the behaviours that Young's interviewees list are not exclusive to people of a similar background, nor are they shared by everyone from, say, a particular group defined by income or occupation.

The importance of these identities is that they mark some other people as inferior. However, the political writer Owen Jones notes a further, rather subtle, twist. The new 'chav' class identity is linked to the meritocracy model of society. It suggests that this particular group is at the bottom because of their own behaviour, because they do not make the effort needed to rise higher (Jones, 2012). The description therefore simultaneously identifies chavs as a collective and blames their *individual* behaviour for keeping them in an inferior position, denying that there are external constraints on them as a class or that their lives, life chances and identities are at least partly determined by their starting places in society. This kind of contradictory double negative, of inferiority and blame, has in fact been common in descriptions of lower classes. In contrast, people in superior or upper classes are often

The term 'life chances' was discussed in Chapter 5 of *Understanding Social Lives, Part 1*.

presented as privileged by their situations, but also somehow deserving to be at the top of society, for instance because they are especially intelligent, beautiful or charming, at least as they are presented in historical television series.

Summary

- Section 1 has discussed three categories of identity. Each refers to sameness and difference.

- Two of the categories – gender and race, and ethnicity – are often assumed to be fixed identities of the body. However, these are social identities that vary according to how people are situated in particular social and historical contexts, including the historical connections between different countries.

- The third category – class – refers to inequalities. Class identities are often believed to be changeable, or even to have disappeared from contemporary British society. Nevertheless, social scientists have argued that class persists as an identity that is both personal and social, referring not only to economic and social differences, but also to status. The effect of class is to increase or limit people's opportunities, so that class differences are reinforced and perpetuated, sometimes under new names.

2   Identities in everyday life

The previous section discussed some common categories of identity. The remainder of the chapter will discuss the ways that identity is encountered in everyday life. To assist these discussions, this section introduces two ways of understanding society that centre on identities.

The sociologist Erving Goffman (1959) studied everyday behaviour. He suggested that in every situation of ordinary life, people behave in ways that will tell others who they are, what they're doing, and what they expect and want to happen. Social life is an ongoing series of interactions that centres on identities, and people have learnt the skills of presenting themselves in these interactions to manage the impressions they give to others. In Goffman's view, social behaviour is 'dramaturgical', like a theatrical play – people are actors, trying to give their best possible performance and make their lives work as they wish. People actively connect with others through the identities that they claim and perform.

Goffman's work has been criticised because it seems to assume that there is a 'real me' who is the actor behind the roles; in other words, it retains to some extent the concept of an individual identity that pre-exists connections with other people. However, his work remains influential because of two other ideas, which have also been developed by other social theorists:

1   Goffman suggests that to understand the bigger picture of society, social scientists should look at the details of ordinary social life, including how people connect with others through identity.

2   Goffman focuses on what people *do*, suggesting that identities are performative and relational, given by people's behaviour and actions.

At the simplest level, this is a matter of definitions: a person who gardens is a gardener; the cook is the person who prepares the food; a singer is someone who sings. But this is also the way in which we encounter identity in daily life. People don't usually walk around with labels saying who they are, although in some jobs they do wear uniforms or name badges. In most situations, identities are understood in terms of what people *do* rather than what they *are*.

This is evident in everyday situations. For example, the shop assistants inside a shop will usually be recognisable, even if they are not wearing uniforms or name badges, for example from where they are (perhaps behind the till) or what they are doing and, more subtly, from the way they look at other people, seeking eye contact, or from the confidence with which they move around the shop. Other people, the ones who are shopping, will approach the shop assistants to pay for goods or ask for information, setting up the relational identities of shop assistant and customer. All of this will happen smoothly and almost automatically; if there is an interruption, for example if one customer mistakes another for an assistant, then there will probably be a brief apology.

These ways of practising or performing identity operate in every context of life. People connect with each other and take up identities relationally through what they do: your friend greets you as a friend and talks to you in a 'friendly' way; the senior person at work is the one who can ask others to do certain things and expect the request to be taken seriously. The notion of performance is now widely used in the social sciences, associated with the work of a number of theorists, with some variations.

The sociologist Harold Garfinkel (1967) suggested, like Goffman, that the best way to study society is to look at the practical activities of people's ordinary lives. People are endlessly engaged in doing things. For example, in the street they are engaged in walking, stopping, looking, looking away, passing each other, queuing, and so on. Garfinkel suggests that social life is in constant motion, yet it is not chaotic because people have the skills and knowledge to create and maintain social order in each situation, mostly without thinking about it. If the order is broken, for example if people bump into each other or someone takes the wrong place in a queue, then there are ways to repair it, perhaps through comments and apologies. Social life proceeds rather like an endless slow dance because as members of society people have the commonsense knowledge and skills to keep it going. This occurs almost automatically, although people notice immediately if normal behaviour is interrupted (or 'breached', in Garfinkel's terminology) without being repaired.

The notions of performance and interaction can be applied to the study of specific identities, as the next sections will discuss. Goffman's and Garfinkel's work offers a way of understanding society and its connections from the bottom up, as fitting together and perpetuated by the multiple actions and reactions of people going about their everyday lives. This is a 'moving picture' of society. Life continues mostly without people being led, controlled or directed from above. However, the orderliness must not be exaggerated since social life is not, of course, always harmonious. The orderly dance of ongoing social life sometimes breaks down and it is sometimes maintained through inequalities and exploitation.

Summary

- Goffman and Garfinkel describe how social identities are made through people's behaviour and actions (performance). They explain how social identities change in different situations.

- Relational identities, given by the relationships between people, can be fixed (for example parent–child) or situated and therefore changeable (for example shop assistant–customer). Relational identities can also be unequal, negative and exploitive (for example mugger–victim).

- Garfinkel's notion of 'social order' explains how society and social activities keep on going (most of the time) without breaking down or becoming chaotic. However, an orderly society can be unequal and unfair.

3   The Street People

The previous sections have discussed identities of sameness and difference. This section will discuss a social group that was encountered in everyday life and imagined to have a very negative identity – the Street People of New York.

Figure 1.2   Homeless people on the streets of New York, 1980s

In the 1980s, the writer Jonathan Raban visited New York. At that time, there were record numbers of homeless people living on the streets of the city and he noticed the negative ways in which other people described them: 'long-term mental patients discharged from hospitals … crack addicts, thieves, alcoholics, hobos, the temporarily jobless, the alimony defaulters, rent-hike victims' (Raban, 1991, p. 78). These separate identities came together into one larger identity: the Street People. Raban suggested that this identity should have capital letters because it was used like a national or tribal identity, 'like the Indians in an old Western' (Raban, 1991, p. 78). This was, of course, a relational identity, although only one identity in the relationship, the Street People, was named; the identity on the other side of the relationship was not.

■   How do you think that other identity could be described? (I will return to this question.)

Out on the street, Raban experimented with performing each of the two identities. First, he set himself to walk and look ahead, like most of the people on the pavements:

> I straightened my shoulders, focused on an imaginary point in the far distance, and marched, swinging my arms like a marathon walker. Almost immediately, I started to acquire Manhattan tunnel-vision. The Street People moved from the centre to the periphery of the frame; within a minute or two they became virtually invisible – bits of stationary furniture, on a level with the fire hydrants and the trashcans.
>
> (Raban, 1991, p. 79)

An important part of this performance was to keep moving, as he found when he stopped and sat down. He was, of course, still the same person, but for the moving people he was now performing the identity of a Street Person:

> On West 22nd at Broadway I found a vacant fire hydrant, and settled on it, as into an armchair, like the Street People did, to watch the crowd file past. Everyone moved with the same stiff clockwork action; everyone wore the same boiled look on their face. As they approached my fire hydrant, they accelerated slightly from the waist down, locked their eyes into the horizontal position, and swept by, giving me an exaggeratedly wide berth. I tried making eye contact, and managed to catch a few pairs of pupils off-guard; they swerved away in their sockets, as quick as fish.
>
> It was interesting to feel oneself being willed into non-existence by total strangers. I'd never felt the force of such frank contempt – and all because I was sitting on a fire hydrant.
>
> (Raban, 1991, pp. 79–80)

Identity work
The performance of identity in talk, practices and behaviours, including how the individual positions him/herself.

Raban's small 'experiment' is an example of **identity work** and it may remind you of the ideas of Goffman. It shows the ways that certain street identities could be performed, at least in the particular situation of Manhattan in the 1980s. However, it also shows how relational identities are not necessarily chosen, but can be imposed or conferred by one person on another. When Raban sat down, he took an **identity position (or subject position)** as one of the Street People. This could be seen as his choice, although of course most of the Street People didn't have a choice about where to live. But the other people also positioned him in a certain way – very negatively – as deserving contempt and hardly more important than a piece of street furniture, like a rubbish bin.

You may also have noticed how the Street People were seen by others as somehow the same rather than as individuals with different histories. This is part of the nature of group or collective identities. It is interesting that Raban compared them to a nation, another collective whose members are also assumed to have things in common. Think about how nationalities are referred to as 'the Italians', 'the Brazilians', and so on. The commonsense assumption that *all* Italians or *all* the people of another nationality are somehow similar is sometimes turned into a political argument: that they *should* be similar and any difference is potentially problematic.

The negative collective identity of the Street People was attributed to them by other people, as a label. Psychologists use the term 'label' to refer to a negatively valued identity which, once given, sticks to a person and is difficult to escape: for example, 'labelling' someone as mentally ill has a negative effect in itself. Of course, it is possible that their poverty and the experience of living on the streets had made the Street People in New York similar in some ways. At the most practical level, having no fixed address can make life very difficult in contemporary society and the ways that they were treated may also have helped to constitute the Street People as a group or collective: Raban says that he 'felt the force' of other people's negative attitudes and this kind of positioning probably had consequences.

Nonetheless, it is unlikely that they initially claimed the identity: 'we are the Street People'. It is an example of a negative identity given to one group of people by others. I asked you to describe the identity on the other side of the relationship. Different answers are possible. I suspect that all are more positive than the Street People's identity and less specific than Raban's description of 'long-term mental patients', and so on. As with marked versus unmarked identities, the 'other' people are perceived as the problem.

Identity position (or subject position)
A temporary identity giving a particular view of the world and the relationship to people in other positions. People can position themselves or be positioned by others.

Othering
The social process through which the difference of other people is marked and their negatively valued identity becomes established.

Such '**Othering**' can also explain some of the ways in which global divisions are understood. The expressions 'the Orient' and 'the mysterious East' are rather old-fashioned now, but advertisements and films still play with stories of hot foreign countries in which a visitor encounters exotic people who are dangerously attractive. The relational and contrasted identities are Western (that is, the rich countries of Europe and North America) and Eastern (the rest of the world, but especially poorer countries that were formerly colonies of the West). The Western identity is the unmarked identity.

The cultural theorist Edward Said (1978) suggests that this 'Orientalism' arose in a process of Othering: people in the rich and powerful West liked to think of their own societies as normal by contrasting them with poorer countries in which they imagined that life was immoral and disorganised, and therefore also rather exciting in contrast to the West. This might sound like a silly but harmless way of thinking. However, as Said argues, it can have serious consequences because it positions the West as superior to other countries. For example, a Western government's intervention in another country's politics and economy might seem justified if the poorer country's authorities are believed to be incompetent and corrupt.

Summary

- The example of the Street People shows an identity of difference that disconnects a group from society.

- Raban's experiment illustrates active identity work through which people are connected and disconnected in everyday life, as described by Goffman and Garfinkel.

- The relational identities of groups can be unequal, negative and exploitative.

- The unmarked identity of a powerful group is positive and normal without being very specific, in contrast to the negative and marked identity of the groups positioned as 'others'.

- This 'Othering' can occur at a global level, as in the relational identities of the (poor) East and (rich) West, described by Said.

4   Origins and family

4.1   A family photograph

Where people live seems to say something about who they are. The negative identity of the Street People came partly from images of streets as dirty and dangerous, and it is often assumed that people who live in the same place have some collective identity, for example as: 'Scousers', 'Brummies', 'Weegies', 'northerners', 'southerners', or just 'locals'. It is also assumed that most people have a link to some particular, original place, which has further implications for their identity. We may ask new acquaintances where they grew up or came from, as if that tells us something more about them than where they live now. Identities of race and ethnicity often involve an imagined link to some (other) place of origin. This emphasis on origins is not really logical because everyone has connections to a number of places. People may have moved several times during their own lifetimes, and in most UK family histories there was at least one big move during the nineteenth and twentieth centuries, from the countryside to the city or from one country to another, in search of better opportunities or simply a safe place to live. Nevertheless, people researching their family history look back to find their 'roots', as if every family had some single original home. This section will look at how family provides identities and life courses that carry certain values. It will show how everyday life practices can reinforce some of the taken-for-granted ideas that people hold about what is normal.

It might seem obvious that a family is a known rather than an imagined group, but in the idea of origins we can see how the distinction is not clear-cut. For example, the geographer Catherine Nash has researched North Americans, Australians and New Zealanders, exploring links to Ireland in their family histories (Nash, 2003). She suggests that they seek an 'imaginative repossession' of 'a land of rolling green fields and cottages' (Nash, 2003, p. 189) and may also want to make contact with the Irish relatives they have traced. This can create tensions if they visit people in Ireland who perhaps have less interest in ancestral connections and a different, more limited, imagined family.

Figure 1.3   The Taylor family in Auckland in 1932

Figure 1.3 is a photograph from part of my own family history. It was taken in 1932 and shows three generations. A family carries certain relational family identities within it, such as parent and child, wife and husband, brother and sister. You can probably work out quite easily which people in this family are the grandparents, or first generation; which are the second generation of adult children, with husbands and wives; and which are the grandchildren who are the third generation. The newest grandchild, and the first child of his parents' marriage, is being held by his father. The grandparents, the newest grandchild and his proud father are posed in the centre, showing the continuity of the family line. The baby's mother is the woman sitting on the ground in the central position. The family identities are also relational identities of gender (father/mother, brother/sister, and so on) and age or seniority (parent/child, grandparent/grandchild).

The photographer, a neighbour, has arranged his subjects according to the conventions of the time. Nevertheless, a posed photograph of this kind can be seen as a kind of performance of identity. It represents the family but also helps to construct it: for example by including the new baby and his parents in their new identities as mother and father, in the family led by the grandparents. The people in the photograph are dressed up in 'good' clothes and I suspect that the occasion was the christening of the baby, so it was one of the milestones in a family history and probably the first time the baby had been included in a family group. The photograph makes a statement of identity ('we are the Taylors'), while reinforcing established ideas of what a family should be and established values or statuses for different identities, including class identities. Copies of the photograph were probably framed and displayed in various homes; this was an everyday practice and functioned as a further statement of family identity.

The arrangement of people in the photograph indicates the values attached to certain identities. Seniority is important, as are the heterosexual couple relationships through which children are to be raised to carry on the family. The women sitting on the ground on either side of the baby's mother were both unmarried. In a photograph that celebrates a certain version of the family, in which heterosexual couples become parents, it is clear that these unmarried women have a marginal position. They are less important than their parents and married siblings, standing above them; less important than their sister-in-law, in the centre, who has recently become a mother. The photographer has posed them in almost the same position as the two children, as if they, too, have not yet grown up. As a child from the next generation of this family, I was aware of the different status of these unmarried sisters. They led very different lives but both remained 'Miss Taylor' throughout their lives and when I was a child the title seemed to me rather sad (although they were not unhappy).

Because I grew up within a family, the succession of generations in which children become parents seemed to me the normal course of life. Now I can see this photograph as a selective presentation of this normality, reinforcing the idea that there is one kind of family and a certain life course in which children grow up to marry and have their own children. This is a celebration of heterosexual identities and behaviour, and a lifestyle centred on heterosexual couples. It reinforces 'heteronormative' values because gay identities are excluded and there is no clear forward narrative for a life that is not based on coupledom and parenting. There is also no place in the photograph for childlessness, adoption or divorce, although these too were of course part of the experience of the family.

4.2   Reinforcing normality

Photography is now much cheaper and easier than in 1932, and families have greater numbers of photographs, many of them digital and most are less formally posed. However, when the geographer Gillian Rose (2003) studied the practices around family photographs at the beginning of the twenty-first century, she found some similar kinds of identity work taking place. Photographs were taken to commemorate important events and milestones in family life, including many of the 'first' occasions in a child's experience, such as the 'first bath, first visitors, first outing, first smile, first solid food, first tooth, first shoes, first swim, first plane flight, first wedding and first birthday party' (Rose, 2003, p. 14). Some of the milestones were probably different from those celebrated in 1932 but a similar version of the normal family was constructed in the displays of photographs, which Rose found in people's homes and in careful arrangements in their family albums.

The psychologist Jerome Bruner (1991) suggests that people understand their lives and the things that happen to them by organising them into fairly conventional narratives, such as stories, histories, explanations, and so on. This organising, again, reinforces ideas about what is normal in a society and it also 'repairs' breaks or breaches. Some of the people Rose studied arranged their photograph displays to bring together successive generations of relatives, even if they had not all met in person, and sometimes to cover over gaps created by emigration, divorce and death. The sociologist Janet Finch (2007) suggests that this kind of display may be particularly important for contemporary families, which are different or have changed their relationships. The Taylor family photograph (Figure 1.3) did this kind of repair in order to create new connections over time and distance. The grandparents and their children had emigrated to New Zealand from England about 20 years before the photograph was taken. The three children in the photograph, the boy, girl and the baby, were the first generation to be born in a new country, the first to be New Zealanders rather than English. The photograph is taken in the garden of the family house in Auckland (visible on the right of the photograph; the neighbour's house is behind them). The house was then fairly newly built; it is now in one of the oldest suburbs in the city. Although they were the first people to live in this house, it acquired the kind of status as the centre of family life and the site for special celebrations that traditionally belongs to a much older building, as if other generations of the family had lived there before.

The photograph therefore constructs a connected family history that extends halfway around the world. The arrangement of the photograph can be seen to construct a history backwards from this day, a narrative of family and origins that repairs the break created by emigration. It is also a photograph of hope, constructing a future for the family with a new generation to take it forward. This may have had a special importance since one of the two adult sons (the baby's father) had survived a serious illness as a child and the other had been to war and returned safely. It is a photograph with subtle but definite classed meanings, of respectability and (moderate) affluence. It functions as a claim that this family, like so many others making the same migration at this time, was successfully moving upwards, from the UK working class to the New Zealand middle class.

Finally, in the same way that it constructs a certain family history, the photograph can also be seen as a part of the construction of a particular colonial and racialised national history and identity. This family was part of a migration from the British Isles that changed the meaning of 'New Zealander'. In the nineteenth century, that identity belonged to the indigenous Maori. After 1859, the majority of the people living in New Zealand were white (Belich, 1996, p. 228). By presenting this family as belonging here, in this house and garden, the photograph reinforces a version of the national history in which New Zealand begins with colonisation and the settlement of immigrants from the UK. In this history, the normal identity for a New Zealander is white and English-speaking, not brown and Maori-speaking. In the twenty-first century, after further immigration, the New Zealand identity is changing again. The white identity is being challenged, both by Maori and by recent immigrants from other parts of the world, including South-East Asia, although it still remains the majority and unmarked identity in many situations.

Summary

- Identities of family and origins connect people to groups and places, real and imagined.
- Representations of families, for example in photographs and stories, can be part of the performance of identities and can reinforce ideas of what is normal, marginalising or excluding some people and experiences.
- Personal family identities are linked to social identities.

Conclusion

This chapter has explored identities and the ways in which they connect people to each other, to places and to the ongoing activities of everyday life that make up society. Some identities are fixed or very difficult to alter, whereas others are situated and transient, changing as people's activities and relationships alter. People actively claim and perform some identities, for example in their interactions with other people, while other identities are attributed to people and may be difficult to challenge or change. Identities can be positive or negative. Collective identities refer to difference as well as similarity. Relational identities can involve an imbalance of power and a lopsided, damaging connection, as with winner and loser. Class identities are oppositional and unequal, defining people through contrasts and judgements about who is better or worse.

You came across the term 'personal identity' in Chapter 8 of *Understanding Social Lives, Part 1*.

Many people feel that they have a unique personal identity ('who I am'), which is separate from the social identities given by situations, relationships and membership of groups, imagined or real. However, the chapter has shown that social identities can also be personal: class identities of inequality are linked to some of our most private emotions (confidence, embarrassment), and the marked identity of a group will impact on the group members' feelings and life experiences. On the other hand, some of people's most personal identities, like the primary identity of gender, are also social identities that vary from one society to another. Many social scientists therefore believe that all identities are ultimately social and people are fundamentally social beings, shaped by society through their positions and life experiences, often in ways that they may not immediately recognise.

References

Anderson, B. (1983) *Imagined Communities: Reflections on the Origin and Spread of Nationalism*, London, Verso.

Belich, J. (1996) *Making Peoples: A History of the New Zealanders*, Auckland, Allen Lane.

Bruner, J. (1991) 'The narrative construction of reality', *Critical Inquiry*, vol. 18, pp. 1–21.

Crompton, R. (2008) *Class and Stratification*, Cambridge, Polity Press.

Finch, J. (2007) 'Displaying families', *Sociology*, vol. 41, no. 1, pp. 65–81.

Garfinkel, H. (1967) *Studies in Ethnomethodology*, Englewood Cliffs, NJ, Prentice Hall.

Goffman, E. (1959) *The Presentation of Self in Everyday Life*, Harmondsworth, Penguin.

Jenkins, R. (1996) *Social Identity*, London, Routledge.

Jones, O. (2012) *Chavs: The Demonization of the Working Class*, London, Verso.

Lawler, S. (2005) 'Disgusted subjects: the making of middle-class identities', *Sociological Review*, vol. 53, no. 3, pp. 429–46.

Lewis, G. and Phoenix, A. (2000) '"Race", "ethnicity" and identity', in Woodward, K. (ed.) *Questioning Identity: Gender, Class, Ethnicity*, London/Milton Keynes, Routledge/The Open University.

Mayhew, H. (2008 [1861]) *London Labour and the London Poor*, Ware, Wordsworth Editions Ltd.

Nash, C. (2003) '"They're family!": cultural geographies of relatedness in popular genealogy', in Ahmed, S., Castaneda, C., Fortier, A.-M. and Sheller, M. (eds) *Uprootings/Regroundings: Questions of Home and Migration*, Oxford, Berg.

Organisation for Economic Co-operation and Development (OECD) (2011) *Divided We Stand: Why Inequality Keeps Rising – An Overview of Growing Income Inequalities in OECD Countries: Main Findings* [Online]. Available at http://www.keepeek.com/Digital-Asset-Management/oecd/social-issues-migration-health/the-causes-of-growing-inequalities-in-oecd-countries_9789264119536-en#page1 (Accessed 22 February 2014).

Phoenix, A. and Pattynama, P. (2006) 'Intersectionality', *European Journal of Women's Studies*, vol. 13, no. 3, pp. 187–92.

Raban, J. (1991) *Hunting Mister Heartbreak*, London, Pan.

Riegle-Crumb, C. and Humphries, M. (2012) 'Exploring bias in math teachers' perception of students' ability by gender and race/ethnicity', *Gender and Society*, vol. 26, no. 2, pp. 290–322.

Rose, G. (2003) 'Family photographs and domestic spacings: a case study', *Transactions of the Institute of British Geographers*, vol. 28, pp. 5–18.

Said, E.W. (1978) *Orientalism*, Harmondsworth, Penguin.

Sayer, A. (2005) *The Moral Significance of Class*, Cambridge, Cambridge University Press.

Skeggs, B. (1997) *Formations of Class and Gender: Becoming Respectable*, London, Sage.

Valentine, G. (2007) 'Theorizing and researching intersectionality: a challenge for feminist geography', *Professional Geographer*, vol. 59, no. 1, pp. 10–21.

Victoria Miro (2012) *Grayson Perry* [Online]. Available at http://www.victoria-miro.com/exhibitions/_429/ (Accessed 3 March 2014).

Young, R. (2012) 'Can Neds (or Chavs) be non-delinquent, educated or even middle class? Contrasting empirical findings with cultural stereotypes', *Sociology*, vol. 46, no. 6, pp. 1140–60.

Chapter 2
Bodies, places and rules

Kath Woodward

Contents

Introduction

Chapter 1 introduced the discussion of the connections and disconnections between personal and social worlds with the example of filling in a form to provide evidence of personal identity. The form had some of the most frequently used categories – sex, age, nationality, and race and ethnicity. Disability is another category that often appears on forms and brings another important dimension of identity – bodies – which connect and disconnect personal and social worlds.

Other categories on the form (such as sex and age) may be socially defined, but they too involve bodies. This chapter adds another connection to the discussion of identities, and how they link personal and social worlds, by showing that identities are also embodied. Bodies may be the concern of biology and medical science, but bodies connect people to society, and matter to social scientists too. Sport is an area of social life where bodies and their practices are really important. Your body might determine whether you win or lose, or even if you can take part at all.

This chapter, however, is less interested in each separate social category, but more interested in how different social categories, such as class, gender and disability, combine together as part of the process of creating opportunities and inequalities in sport. Indeed, one identity not usually asked for on forms is that of social class, yet this chapter will explore how enduring class inequalities are.

The chapter starts by considering what is social about bodies and then moves on to the field of sport to explain its relevance. Next, the chapter turns to examining the claims made about the legacy of the 2012 Olympics and Paralympics, and the evidence used to support these claims. Of particular interest here is the supposed legacy of the Olympic Games for the deprived communities of East London, and the extent to which social class still matters both in sport and wider society.

Finally, the chapter turns to two case studies that offer instructive examples of the connections and disconnections between bodies and society in the case of disability and gender.

1   Bodies

Activity 1
When do you tend to think about your body?

Being conscious of your body – or parts of it – is most likely to be when you are in pain or discomfort. Bodies are the site of pleasurable feelings but pain, whether acute, as in an injury, or chronic, as in long-term conditions like arthritis, is what draws attention to physicality. Another occasion might be when your body doesn't do what you want it to do – you can't reach something because you are not tall enough or strong enough. You may have a disability that reminds you of your physicality and what your body can and cannot do. Bodies make up who people are and how they are seen by others. Images of attractive bodies draw attention to the less-than-perfect bodies of most people, which creates a contemporary concern with improving physical appearance. Keeping fit may be a healthy activity but that too reminds people of their bodies. If you do sport, you will constantly be reminded of your body and what it can and cannot do. Sport is all about bodies.

There are clearly similarities between bodies: everyone is born, breathes, eats, sleeps, feels pleasure and pain, and of course, dies, but bodies are different too. Bodies make each individual different from others and are an important part of identity.

■   Everyone is not the same – but what are the differences and which ones matter?

Differences between bodies, for example in terms of body size, health and well-being, can be about physical characteristics but they are often social. The more affluent you are, the better access you have to high-quality food, warmth, good hygiene and health care. Such social factors create healthy bodies that actually look different: taller, fitter, more upright, clear skin. Some bodies, and consequently some people, can also be more valued than others in society.

Sometimes it is difficult to separate the physical aspects of bodies from those that are social. For example, there are visible differences between the bodies of women and men, older people and younger people, white people and black people, and sometimes between **people with**

disabilities and those who are able-bodied, but do these differences explain or justify social inequalities such as pay differences? Social scientists ask questions about why having a particular sort of body might mean you earn less than someone else with a different body. Some bodies are deemed more attractive than others and appear on television and in popular culture, and are financially rewarded. What counts as an attractive body changes over time. In contemporary Western society, the promotion and consumption of products that claim to make you more attractive and younger looking have led to a concern about managing well-being through '**body projects**' (Shilling, 2013), which suggest that you will be happier and even more successful if you work on your body by getting down to the gym, following (often bizarre) diets or trying cosmetic surgery or other expensive cosmetic enhancements.

Physical fitness clearly matters more in some areas of society than others. For example, professional athletes are often defined by their physical capacities. As this chapter shows, however, the connections and disconnections between bodies and selves, and between **embodied selves** and society, are not always obvious or straightforward. Bodies come in different shapes and sizes but social values play an important part in making some bodies more valued, and seen as more attractive, than others. Some people depend on having fit bodies, which can perform in particular ways, for their livelihood. In sport, you have to be fit and bodies are central to the connections between people, their personal world and understanding of themselves and society.

Activity 2

Think about work – paid and unpaid – and the sorts of job that involve physical labour. Is work that is associated with bodies given a high status or highly paid? Does it depend on who does them?

I think the answer would be that in many cases work and jobs associated with bodies are not highly regarded activities, whether paid manual labour or unpaid domestic housework. Some jobs demand physical skill and effort, such as those associated with the now greatly reduced heavy manufacturing industries, but they are largely not those with the high wages. Other manual labour may include risk but this has not been well rewarded traditionally, although skilled jobs involving

People with disabilities
A recent term favoured by policy makers and officials because it is intended to put people first and is therefore seen as more positive than the term 'disabled people'. For others, however, it makes disability an individual issue and individual and ignores societal factors which 'disable' people.

Body projects
Activities that result from people's preoccupations with looking younger, being fitter and more healthy, as well as worrying about physical and mental well-being in contemporary society.

Embodied selves
Are made up of physical bodies and individuals who are connected to the wider society, where the body that each person has is inextricably connected to who they are and how they are seen by others.

some risk have been better rewarded than more routine heavy lifting, for example in factories. There are some exceptionally highly paid sports stars but this is only the elite. Apart from the celebrities of popular culture, high remuneration goes with the good fortune of inheritance or the jobs that are more associated with minds than bodies.

Mind and body separation

Often called 'Cartesian dualism', it suggests that mind and body are distinct from each other, as expressed in 'mind over matter' where your rational mind can tell your body what to do and take control.

The **separation of mind and body,** as developed by the French philosopher René Descartes (and often called the Cartesian separation of mind and body), has led to a devaluing of bodies, with the activities of the mind being privileged in a number of ways, not least its links to rational thought over raw emotion and mindless physicality. The rational selves can take control over their lives and are not subject to the irrational demands of the body. The rational self is often associated with the Enlightenment, which is a tradition of thought arising in the seventeenth century that stressed the possibility of organising social life around reason.

The mind/body separation is based on two assumptions:

- minds and bodies are separate
- minds are superior to bodies.

The mind/body split has been challenged by subsequent thinkers, from Karl Marx through to more modern times, when social scientists and philosophers have argued that mind/body dualism is a false dichotomy, and the brain is part of the body and not separated from the material world. Rather than conscious decisions being what happens in the mind, mind, body and society are all connected parts of the same process, and the mind is not superior to the body. This is important when one considers that the mind/body split has often been used to distinguish between 'rational' men and 'irrational' women, or between the working classes with only their physical labour to sell and the middle and upper classes who can rely on their reason. Feminists such as Raia Prokhovnik (2007) have emphasised how 'women, other races and places, the working class, those with disabilities, animals, children, the mentally ill, and prisoners have all been classed as less than rational' (Prokhovnik, 2007, p. 13). These inequalities are brought out very forcefully in sport.

Summary

- Bodies are an important part of what is involved in connecting social and personal worlds, and are thus part of the process of social science inquiry.

- Differences between bodies are both physical and social, but social values play an important role in valuing some bodies more than others.

- Sometimes bodies and minds are seen as separate, and minds are valued more highly than bodies.

2   Why sport?

Sport is a part of everyday life and popular culture, and of social relations and divisions. As the cricketer and writer Ed Smith observed (2009), sport is not just a reflection of social life; it also contributes to making lives through the ways in which people are connected to each other and to different places. Sport not only reflects the connections and disconnections of everyday life, it makes some of them too. Social divisions of gender, class, race, ethnicity and disability are key elements of the world of sport.

■   What does sport mean to you?

You may be a fan or a follower and have some traditional loyalties that occasionally emerge, for example in supporting a national team, or you might take part in sport at some level, perhaps just occasionally to keep fit or maybe more competitively. Sport can be a part of family life and traditional kinship networks that bring people together. When people talk about 'the team', they say 'we' in a collective identity with what Benedict Anderson called the 'imagined community' (1983) of the nation or the team. Sport invokes passionate feelings, sometimes related to the politics and culture of fragmented communities, for example as expressed in the long-standing hostilities between Celtic and Glasgow Rangers football supporters. If you have children, you may support their participation in sport, not least for health reasons. Even if you do not actually follow sport, it is unlikely that you know nothing about sporting stories and sports celebrities because of the following:

You came across the concept of the 'imagined community' in Chapter 1.

- Sport is a large part of the economy and patterns of consumption. Sport is big business. For example, Sport England (2013a) calculated that in 2010 sport and sport-related activities generated £20.3 billion of **Gross Value Added (GVA)** – 1.9 per cent of the total for England. This placed it above sectors such as insurance, telecoms services, legal services and accounting.

Gross Value Added (GVA)
A measure of economic output for individual parts of a national economy.

- Sports stars occupy huge areas of media space, not only on the sports' pages.
- Sporting mega events, like the Olympic Games, are hard to ignore. If you were in the UK in 2012, it would have been very difficult to not know that the Olympics and Paralympics had come to London.

Sport also raises some key issues about inequality.

2.1   Sporting inequalities

Sport does not always involve an equal playing field. In fact, it rarely does, in spite of the claims, for example by the Olympic Movement, that sport, particularly the Olympics and Paralympics, provide equal opportunities across the globe. Sport involves competition and not everyone can access the resources that are required to be successful in competitive sport.

The culture of amateurism surrounding sport in the contemporary UK can be seen to have privileged the very wealthy and upper-class amateurs who can devote themselves to sport without having to earn a living, rather than promoting grass-roots participation. The Olympics have been the site of struggle for equality not least in relation to the participation of:

- women, who were excluded from the modern games, which started in 1896

- black and minority ethnic people, who were allocated their own separate 'Anthropology Days' in 1904

- **disabled people**, whose fight for inclusion led to the establishment of the Paralympics in 1947.

Some sports are associated with particular classes, like polo, which is associated with the upper classes, and golf, which is distinctively middle class and requires not only expensive equipment, but often membership of a club and access to the networks that can get you in. Other sports, like football, have stronger working-class roots, for players and spectators. Pierre Bourdieu called this the 'distinction of taste', where social class is seen as defined by cultural as well as economic aspects of social life (Bourdieu, 1984). Bourdieu argued that there are three different sorts of capital in a capitalist economy – economic, cultural and social (he included symbolic capital as an additional factor that shapes class position). In sport, especially those sports associated with working-class people and those with very little economic or cultural capital such as educational qualifications, all that a person may have is **physical capital**.

In a sport like boxing, with its strong tradition of the participation of migrant, black and minority ethnic, traveller and gypsy young men, all that participants have to invest is their bodies. Think back to the mind/body split mentioned earlier and its assumption that minds are superior to bodies. This suggests that those who can only invest physical capital

disabled people
Favoured by many activists, this term reflects how people are disabled by ideas and arrangements in society. It literally means 'people who are discriminated against' although this insight is not obvious in the wording so the term can sound negative. Hence policy makers and officials prefer the term 'people with disabilities'.

Physical capital
An embodied version of cultural capital, which is often associated with working-class people who lack other sorts of capital and have only their own bodies to invest.

– who do not have cultural capital like education or cultural networks, or financial and economic capital – are not only different from those who do, they are less valued. Boxing is a sport that has offered some a route out of poverty and does not require financial or educational investment or access to privileged networks, such as those needed to gain access to more privileged sports clubs.

Different social factors, such as class, gender and disability, are all part of the process of creating opportunities and inequalities in sport. These factors intersect to generate disconnections as well as opportunities and new connections for athletes, which also offer insights into how the wider society is made and remade. Intersection means that the different elements combine and work together. For example, people are connected and disconnected by gender, but gender is also connected to social class and to race. The experience of bringing up children on your own is very different for working-class women, who do not have the resources to pay for support and childcare, from that of more highly-paid middle-class women, although they share some of the particularities of gender. The different connections overlap and work together.

As Chapter 1 showed, people have several identities, for example as a woman, as a white person and as a university lecturer, which bring out the intersection of different social divisions such as gender, ethnicity and class. Societies are made through these connections, disconnections and intersections, which people living in a particular society recognise.

Summary

- Sport connects people to each other and to places, but it also creates disconnections.

- Competition in sport is linked to mass entertainment, consumption and opportunities for profit on a large scale, as well as reflecting and creating social inequalities.

- Different inequalities cross over and combine; embodied difference and inequalities intersect with social factors.

- Physical capital provides an explanation for some of the inequalities in sport – between different sports and between the people who take part in them – as well as showing how bodies are social.

3 Olympics and Paralympics: legacy claims and evidence

The ideals of the Olympic Movement apply to the Olympics and Paralympics. These ideals are distinctive to the Olympic Movement, as is the Olympic motto 'faster, higher, stronger', or as is often used, the Latin *'citius, altius, fortius'*. There are three Olympic values – friendship, respect and excellence – and four Paralympic values – determination, inspiration, courage and equality. It is the last value, equality, that is of particular interest here.

The siting of the 2012 Olympic Games in five East London boroughs – Newham, Tower Hamlets, Hackney, Waltham Forest and Greenwich – was not a coincidence. Since Charles Booth first completed his survey of the social conditions of every street in London in 1889 (Booth, 1902–03), East London has been home to some of the poorest communities. Some would argue that little had changed by 2012. London's geography shows remarkable class continuity in its division between the affluent West End and poor East End. Since the nineteenth century, East London has been home to the city's working classes who laboured in the docklands and manufacturing industries there. The area's proximity to employment and relatively cheap accommodation also attracted different groups of new migrants. When the docks closed in the 1970s, the area suffered all the consequences of major job losses as it de-industrialised. Subsequent regeneration attempts, such as the London Docklands development in the 1980s, Canary Wharf in the 1990s and the building of the new Jubilee underground line in 2000, were patchy in their success, and created '... an area that is socially polarized, containing pockets of relative affluence within an area that has a high concentration of relative poverty and deprivation' (MacRury, 2009, p. 5).

East London contains some of the most deprived communities in the contemporary UK. Since 2004, Hackney, Newham and Tower Hamlets have been among the most deprived English boroughs according to the **Index of Multiple Deprivation (IMD)**. There is, then, a stark contrast between the 'conspicuous-consumer-like excessiveness of the global spectacular' of the Olympic Games and its location in the most deprived boroughs of London (MacRury, 2009, p. 39). Given the scale of deprivation, much was made of the Olympics' ability not just to regenerate this area, but to produce its convergence with the rest of

You came across Charles Booth in Chapter 1 of *Understanding Social Lives, Part 1*.

Index of Multiple Deprivation (IMD)
This is a composite index of deprivation, the scores of which reflect seven sets of statistics: income, employment, health, education and skills, housing, crime, and living environment. The index is relational; the average scores are ranked by English local authorities of which there are 354. The lower the ranking, the higher the level of multiple deprivation.

London. The aim of convergence was a key part of the legacy of the Olympic Games, which meant that 'within 20 years the communities that host the 2012 Games will have the same socio-economic chances as their neighbours across London' (cited in MacRury, 2009, p. 66).

Writing in 2014, it is difficult to evaluate the legacy of the Olympic Games when 'legacy' is judged to need a 20-year time period to bear fruit. It is possible, however, to judge the progress made so far and to consider some of the existing evidence. This section will focus on two main areas:

- the creation of employment
- the provision of housing for existing East London residents.

In a later section, the aim of the Olympic Games to increase participation in sport as part of its legacy will also be examined.

3.1   East London legacy

The ability to move residents of the host boroughs into employment was central to the goal of convergence. However, unemployment within the host boroughs is still among the highest in the region and resident employment rates are currently 5.5 per cent below the regional average (House of Lords, 2013, p. 69). There is slightly more promising evidence that local residents gained employment during the construction phase of the Olympic Games. For example, out of a workforce of 6243 on the Olympic Park in September 2010, 23 per cent were from the five host boroughs and Barking and Dagenham, and a quarter of these claimed previous unemployment. Of those working on the Athletes' Village, 29 per cent of the workforces were from the five host boroughs and Barking and Dagenham, 15 per cent of whom claimed previous unemployment (Clarke and Holborough, 2011, p. 50).

Yet, these figures do not speak for themselves. It is unclear, for example, if these figures include long-term residents of the boroughs or whether they include workers who moved to the area specifically to gain this employment. It is also unclear how many of these jobs lasted more than six months or led to further opportunities, such as apprenticeships. Remember also the distinction at the start of this chapter between mind and body, and the undervaluing of work that relies on manual labour. There are question marks, therefore, over not only the extent to which the employment opportunities provided by the Olympic Games are long lasting, but also the extent to which they enable economic inequalities to be overcome and convergence with other parts of London to occur.

A survey of 140 residents in Newham conducted by the London School of Economics (LSE) found considerable disillusion over the legacy of the Olympic Games for local residents:

> Residents expressed general frustration over the difficulty of tapping into economic activity developed by the Olympics. Residents resented that they had been promised economic benefits, which ultimately had not materialised. Few knew of someone who had received training or a job through the Olympics, and those that had said the jobs were temporary and low paid. Some residents complained that contracts had not been awarded locally and business owners in the area that we spoke to during the Olympic period said that the Games had been disappointing and sometimes devastating for their business.
>
> (LSE, 2012, p. 4)

Inequality in unemployment can produce inequalities in housing. Housing-related deprivation in East London includes homelessness, overcrowding and poor housing conditions. In March 2012, the five host boroughs plus Dagenham and Barking had 7989 households living in temporary accommodation with 2253 of these being in Newham alone (cited in Watt, 2013, p.103). In April 2011, 103,944 households were on the local authorities' housing waiting lists across these six boroughs (cited in Watt, 2013, p. 103).

The Olympic Games aimed to create new homes for existing residents in East London. The original figure of 4000 new homes was scaled back in the wake of the credit crunch to 2800 units (MacRury, 2009, p. 70). In total, 2818 properties are available in the former Athletes' Village, renamed East Village. In August 2011, 51 per cent of the site was sold to a partnership of Qatari Diar, the real-estate arm of Qatari Investment Authority, with the housing to be marketed as private rental accommodation (House of Lords, 2013, p. 63). The remaining 1379 properties will be 'affordable housing', but only 675 of these are social housing (Watt, 2013, p. 104).

Regardless of how social housing is defined, it is clear that these numbers are not enough to meet the needs of existing residents, given the high numbers on the waiting lists. Moreover, much hinges on what is 'affordable' to the residents of East London. The definition of an affordable home changed in April 2012 under the coalition government to no more than 80 per cent of the local market rent (an increase of 10 per cent), which makes it harder for existing residents to access 'affordable' homes (DCLG, 2012). As Anne Power (2012) claims, the 'affordable' rents for the new homes in the East Village 'will be unaffordable to Newham's poorest households. As one third of all children in the borough live in workless households, their families will almost certainly be excluded. This is all the more likely as house prices in the host boroughs, while historically lower than the London average, had begun to increase as a result of the Olympics' (House of Lords, 2013, p. 68).

In addition to East Village, the aim is to build five additional neighbourhoods within the Olympic Park that would create a further 6684 homes, 35 per cent of which would be designated as affordable housing. In addition to the problematic definition of 'affordable housing', there are also concerns over the definition of a 'family home' and the number of bedrooms required, as many families in the boroughs surrounding the Olympic Park are multigenerational and require more than the three bedrooms of a 'typical' family home (House of Lords, 2013, p. 65). Thus, Watt concludes that: 'It is clear that the Olympic housing legacy will be limited for *existing* working class East Londoners' (Watt, 2013, p. 104, original emphasis).

3.2   Sporting legacy

Another area in which claims for legacy were bold was in the area of health, through a large-scale and sustained increase in sport and physical activity participation. This was particularly ambitious for two main reasons:

- There is no evidence that previous Olympic Games have been successful in this area (McCarthy and Synnott, 2012, p. 307).
- The relative health inequalities for communities in East London are stark. A dramatic visual representation of this is provided by the London Health Observatory (Figure 2.1), which illustrates the drop in average life expectancy of one year for every second tube station that is further east from Westminster to Canning Town (cited in McCarthy and Synnott, 2012, p. 304).

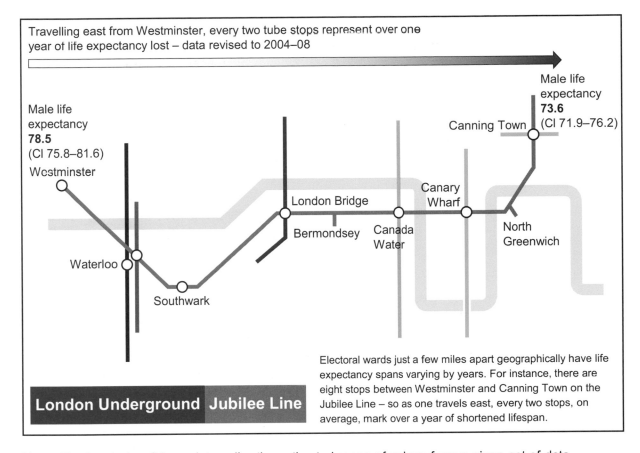

Travelling east from Westminster, every two tube stops represent over one year of life expectancy lost – data revised to 2004–08

Male life expectancy **78.5** (CI 75.8–81.6)
Westminster

Male life expectancy **73.6** (CI 71.9–76.2)
Canning Town

Waterloo

Southwark

London Bridge

Bermondsey

Canada Water

Canary Wharf

North Greenwich

Electoral wards just a few miles apart geographically have life expectancy spans varying by years. For instance, there are eight stops between Westminster and Canning Town on the Jubilee Line – so as one travels east, every two stops, on average, mark over a year of shortened lifespan.

London Underground Jubilee Line

Note: CI refers to 'confidence interval' – the estimated range of values from a given set of data.

Figure 2.1   Visual representation of health inequalities in East London (Source: analysis by the London Health Observatory of Office for National Statistics (ONS) and Greater London Authority (GLA) data for 2004–08, cited in McCarthy and Synnott, 2012, p. 304)

The previous Labour government's legacy action plan aimed to get two million more people active by 2012. However, the coalition government dropped the physical activity target and data from the Active People Survey (APS) (Sport England, 2013b), which is the instrument chosen to measure this legacy outcome. Nevertheless, the data from this survey shows some increase in participation, although this is uneven across age, gender, disability and class.

Sport England's main criterion for the measurement of sporting outcomes is based on the percentage of adults (aged 16 and over) playing sport at moderate intensity for at least 30 minutes at least once a week, measured by the APS.

Activity 3

Looking at Figure 2.2, has the previous Labour government's target of getting two million more people active by 2012 been met?

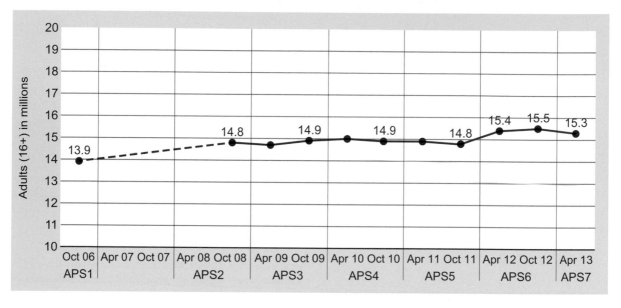

Note: results for the rolling 12-month period to the date shown on the chart. Dotted line due to the 12-month gap in fieldwork between APS1 and APS2.

Figure 2.2   APS data on participation in sport, October 2006–April 2013 (Source: Sport England, 2013c)

Figure 2.2 shows that during October 2012 (APS6), 15.5 million people played sport at least once a week compared to 13.9 million in October 2006 (APS1). This represents a 1.6 million increase, but not the previous government's target of a two million increase.

Data from Sport England also shows that the increase is variable across different social factors. For example, in October 2006 (APS1), 38.9 per cent of men played sport once a week compared to 29.8 per cent of women (Sport England, 2013c). By 2012–13, these percentages had increased to 40.1 per cent for men and 30.5 per cent for women. Thus, male participation (1.2 per cent) had increased slightly more than that of women (0.7 per cent). In terms of age, the prospects are perhaps more alarming. Sport England (2013c) reported that 3.856 million 16–25 year olds (54.7 per cent) played sport once a week, but that this age group had been 'flat lining' (with rates of 54 per cent in 2011 and 2012), although they claimed that this group is now showing signs of growth.

With regard to disability, there is also some sign of increasing participation. During the period April 2012 to April 2013, 1.67 million people with a long-term limiting illness or disability (18.2 per cent) played sport once a week. This result is a 353,100 increase from 2005–06 (Sport England, 2013c). Whether this increase is enough to support the claims made for widening participation for athletes with disabilities as well as extending the popularity of the Games for spectators, however, is uncertain.

In the words of Sir Philip Craven, International Paralympic Committee (IPC) President, in 2013:

> In my opinion, 2012 was the greatest year yet for the Paralympic Movement with London 2012 propelling Paralympic sport into the mainstream and new audiences engaging in a new generation of household-name athletes.
>
> (IPC, 2013)

How could Craven's claims be supported? One of the main sources of evidence to support the success of a sporting mega event would be quantitative evidence of the numbers of people involved. The IPC produced a report in July 2013 (*The Annual Report 2012*), which included an overview of the IPC as an organisation, key financial figures for the organisation and a look at all nine sports under IPC management, as well as overall numbers of participants:

> A record-breaking 4,237 athletes from 164 countries took part in London 2012 – an event that drew 2.78 million spectators and 3.8 billion cumulative TV viewers in more than 115 countries.
>
> (IPC, 2013)

In order to know how record breaking these figures were, it is necessary to know that there were 3951 athletes from 146 countries in the 2008 Beijing Olympics. The report also states that:

In addition, one of the year's biggest milestones was the signing of the IPC/IOC Co-operation Agreement, which means that the 2018 and 2020 Paralympic Games will be held in the same city as the Olympic Games.

(IPC, 2013)

This statement provides evidence that the Paralympics are increasingly on a par with the Olympics. This claim of equal status with the Olympics is supported by an increase in the amount of intervention required by its governing body:

Advances took place in classification, anti-doping, sports science and medical procedures, and the IPC expanded its reach on social media and ensured its sponsors activated and extended their partnerships.

(IPC, 2013)

The reference to social media is an important measure of the opportunities for wider participation and connecting people and places that internet technologies afford. Social media provide a measure of the scope and range of interest in the Paralympics – the London Paralympics were called the 'digital Olympics'. What evidence supports this claim? The IPC produced the following figures for online access to the Paralympics:

- nearly two million people visited www.paralympic.org
- 130 per cent growth of IPC's official Facebook group
- four-figure growth of athletes' Facebook fan pages
- 50 per cent increase in followers of @paralympic
- close to nine million views of videos featuring London 2012 sporting action or ceremonies were uploaded on YouTube
- over 300,000 views of behind-the-scenes videos provided by the athletes' Samsung Bloggers.

(IPC, 2013)

This evidence relates to people watching the Olympic Games or following them, not actually taking part. Not many people can be elite athletes of course and the claim being made about the increased popularity of the Paralympics is based on the idea that the more visible athletes with disabilities are, the more ordinary such sport practices might become, so that others will be encouraged to take part. Identities are made through the relationship between how I see myself and how others see me, which links personal and social worlds, and connects embodied selves to the social world. The visibility of the Paralympics and of athletes with disabilities is an important source of evidence that sport, and the Games in particular, can offer equal opportunities and be socially inclusive. This visibility is also about bodies and the different sorts of bodies that are made visible and represented in the media. At the start of this chapter, I referred to two aspects of inequality that are apparent in sport: I claimed that not all bodies are equally valued and that one indicator of inequality is the lack of visibility of some embodied selves.

Nevertheless, the impact of the popularity of the Paralympics for athletes with disabilities who are not in the elite category remains uncertain. A survey by the Sport and Recreation Alliance (SRA) in October 2012 (SRA, 2012) reported two-thirds of the respondents claimed that:

> … they did not have suitably trained staff to cater for disabled participants, whilst 3 in 5 lacked the appropriate equipment. The same survey showed 89% of clubs reporting no change in the number of disabled people joining, with 86% noting no change in the number of enquiries from disabled people and 96% reporting no change in the number of disabled people volunteering in their clubs.
>
> (cited in House of Lords, 2013, p. 32)

The SRA's October 2013 Sports Clubs survey claimed that only 35 per cent of clubs had access to appropriate equipment for disabled people (House of Lords, 2013, p. 32).

Perhaps the most durable inequality, however, is that of class. Table 2.1 shows that there was very little (statistically insignificant) increase between 2005–06 and 2012–13 in the numbers of those participating in sport among those classified as lower supervisory/technical/routine/

semi-routine/never worked/long-term unemployed, while those classed as managerial/professional had increased their participation from 40.1 per cent to 41.3 per cent. This is particularly disappointing given the lower starting participation rate in 2005–06 of 26.9 per cent for those in the lower socio-economic category.

Table 2.1   APS data on adult participation in sport by socio-economic group, October 2005–April 2013

One session a week *	APS1 (Oct 2005–2006)		APS5 (Oct 2010–Oct 2011		APS7Q2 (Apr 2012–Apr 2013		
	%	Number	%	Number	%	Number	%
NS SEC1–2 (managerial/professional)	40.1	4 462 100	41.4	4 812 000	41.3	4 903 800	Increase
NS SEC3 (intermediate)	32.3	1 244 000	32.4	1 303 700	34.4	1 415 900	Increase
NS SEC4 (small employers/own account workers)	32.4	920 200	32.3	958 400	32.7	992 400	No change
NS SEC5–8 (lower supervisory/technical/ routine/semi-routine/never worked/long-term unemployed)	26.9	3 450 200	26.6	3 564 800	26.6	3 639 900	No change

Note: *At least four sessions of at least moderate intensity for at least 30 minutes in the previous 28 days

(Source: Sport England, 2013c)

Recent research has demonstrated the relationship between social class and elite sport. While there were some notable successes for state-educated athletes in the 2012 Olympic Games, such as Jessica Ennis, Bradley Wiggins, Andy Murray, Victoria Pendleton and Mo Farah, 'athletes who attended independent schools were more than five times over-represented among Team GB medal-winners relative to their proportion in the population' (Smith et al., 2013, p. 2). Moreover, 36 per cent of British medal-winners in the 2012 Olympic Games were privately educated, although the private sector represents only 7 per cent of the UK school population (House of Lords, 2013, p. 39). Opportunities to succeed in sport reflect class divisions in wider society. Moreover, these are exacerbated in certain sports where access to first-class facilities and infrastructure are essential. Sports such as rowing, sailing and equestrian events are dominated by privately educated competitors. The selling-off of school playing fields is likely to have an adverse impact on facilities in the state education sector. The bulk (10,000) were sold off under Conservative governments between

1979 and 1997, but their sale continued under New Labour (1997–2010) when 226 were sold. Between May 2010 and June 2013, the coalition government sold off a further 50 playing fields with 19 of these applications, perhaps surprisingly, approved since the August 2012 Olympic Games (Hope, 2013).

While education opportunities are important, other non-educational features of social background also influence the chances of likely success in elite-level sport. Birthplace, for example, is important. Research produced by *Channel 4 News* (cited in Smith et al., 2013, p. 3) showed that the richest areas of the UK – notably the south-east and parts of London – contributed 30.3 per cent of Team GB's athletes while few were born in the most deprived areas of the UK. Birthplace relates to another source of class-related inequality highlighted by Smith et al. (2013), namely, childhood socialisation. The authors claim that a predisposition to succeed in sport is shaped by families during childhood and youth. Middle-class families have more time and resources to devote to their children's development in extra-curricular activities than do working-class families. Thus, they conclude that 'the class-related patterns evident in the social profile of medal winners are expressive of broader class relations in Britain associated with prevailing economic inequalities' (Smith et al., 2013, p. 3).

This also raises questions over the ability of the Olympic Games to achieve their promises of increasing young people's participation in sport. A focus on the provision of sporting opportunities in schools is, Smith et al. (2013) argue, unlikely to have much of an impact on the persistent inequalities within sport, as these inequalities are already well established in wider society prior to sport participation and they are unlikely to be changed by it.

Moreover, following the Olympic Games, even the provision of sporting opportunities in schools is under question. A survey of teachers carried out by The Smith Institute in 2013 reported that more than a third of teachers (34 per cent of primary and 35 per cent of secondary school teachers) reported a decrease in sports participation since the coalition government abolished the ring-fenced funding for the School Sports Partnerships Programme (The Smith Institute, 2013). The main reasons mentioned by those who indicated a fall in participation levels were a lack of funding and resulting time pressures. This had an adverse effect on the ability of schools to run sports clubs, competitions and events, which resulted in fewer participation opportunities.

Summary

- The claims of government and sporting bodies are supported by evidence, for example of increased numbers of participants and spectators, but the figures do not speak for themselves.

- Claims are made and challenged, for example about legacy, because of financial inequalities and lack of resource (such as the closure of many sports clubs).

- One of the most durable inequalities in sport is that of class.

- Bodies and their representation are connected, as is claimed by the Paralympic Movement about increased viewing, so that athletes with disabilities become part of the mainstream of society.

4   The rules of the game: supporting claims

Rules can be written or unwritten. As the discussion of Erving Goffman's (1959) work on a dramaturgical model of identity showed in Chapter 1, the roles that people take up are similar to parts in a play, which have already been written but may be subject to some negotiation, and rules tend to be assumed rather than stated (Goffman, 1959). What is noticeable is when the rules are 'breached', in Harold Garfinkel's (1967) terminology, and people often only realise what the rules are when someone breaks them. There is little chance of this in sport because the rules are written and enforced through rigid mechanisms, although they are frequently challenged and there are ever more sophisticated mechanisms for adjudicating, such as third umpires or video referees. Referees and umpires refer to the rule book produced by sporting governing bodies. Sport is full of rules – about what you can do, where you can do it and how.

Changes take place, however, through modifications of the rules and regulations that govern behaviour. Sometimes the rules are changed in response to people breaking them. Rules can be challenged. Rules and regulations often describe and define the roles that people have, and the type of person they are, for example by allocating people to categories. Rules also define and categorise bodies. In sport, this could be categories of disability or those related to age, such as under-21 or veteran, or the gender categories of men and women, which are not always as obvious and given as they might at first appear. Almost all sports are divided into men's and women's competitions. Bodies might at first appear to be a part of life that is largely unchanging, apart from the development of skill, speed, stamina and strength, and not subject to social forces, but bodies and the connections between bodies, selves and society contribute to an understanding of society over time. Bodies are involved in the connections between personal and social worlds.

A major claim in this chapter is that bodies and embodied selves, which are the identities that connect people, their bodies and the social world, cannot be reduced to biology or anatomy. Social forces are part of the process of making and remaking embodied selves too. The Olympics and Paralympics demonstrate some of the ways in which society is made and remade through organising bodies of sport, such as the Olympic Movement, which explicitly states that the body practices of sport have social implications: sport is international and can promote full participation in social life.

4.1   Who is in the Paralympics? Rules of classification

Rules in sport apply to who plays in which competitions as well as what happens on the field. The Paralympics, like the Olympics, have different events, competitions and sports. The Paralympics, however, also have competitions organised around the different disabilities that athletes may have. Rather as boxing is organised into weight classes, the Paralympics are structured around categories of disability. How is Paralympic status decided?

Every athlete competing at the Paralympics has gone through an evaluation, conducted by authorised, technical officials called 'classifiers', who are appointed by the international governing body of that particular sport. It is a long-term process that takes place at all major events, before and during competition.

A mathematical formula known as Raza is applied to each athlete's throw or jump distance to calculate a point score. It works a bit like a handicap in golf and is designed to create as fair and equal a competition as possible so that the athlete with the least impairment does not receive an unfair advantage. The algorithm was established by tracking a number of athletes' performances over a range of years.

The following example from the sport of cycling illustrates in more detail some of the connections between athletes' bodies and the Paralympics governing body. The following extract is taken from the regulations classifying Paralympic sports.

IPC classification of Paralympic athletes

Athletes with physical and visual impairments are eligible to compete in the sport. There are four classes. In the H, T and C classes, the lower the athlete's class number, the greater the impact on their ability to cycle, i.e. a C1 cyclist has a greater impairment than a C5 cyclist.

B – athletes with a visual impairment who compete on a tandem bicycle with a sighted pilot on the front

H1–H4 – athletes with an impairment that affects their legs who compete using a handcycle

T1–T2 – athletes with an impairment that affects their balance who compete using a tricycle

C1–C5 – athletes with an impairment that affects their legs, arms and/or trunk but compete using a standard bicycle

(IPC, 2007)

Different categories are organised around different body parts in relation to the particular sport of cycling, which shows that the IPC acknowledges the connections between bodies and machines, in this case bicycles and the sporting environment, for example by including tandems for B athletes, handcycles for H1–H4 and tricycles for T1–T2. Athletes can compete because of these categories and it is the social system of classification that makes the Paralympics possible. These groups also involve technical modifications. Bodies and things – technologies – are connected, often so closely that the mechanical aid becomes part of the person.

4.2   Changing technologies, changing times

Technological innovations have greatly improved athletic performances in the Paralympics. The example of 'Blade Runner', the name given to the white, South African runner Oscar Pistorius, is an example of the making of a person in whom technology and flesh merge. Pistorious's nickname even recognises his high-tech identity as a **'cyborg'**. Feminist scholar Donna Haraway (1991) uses the concept of a cyborg to describe the ways in which it becomes impossible to separate embodied people from the technological aids that have increasingly become a part of everyday life. 'Blade Runner' draws on the title of the science fiction film *Blade Runner* and its concerns with the relationship between the human and non-human (*Blade Runner*, 1982). Haraway's arguments are more far-reaching and she extends them well beyond science fiction and into everyday life.

Cyborg
A concept used to challenge the boundaries between what is human and what is not and to show that, for example, machines and technologies are part of embodied selves; technological interventions are not added on to people, but become part of who they are.

Activity 4

Think about the ways in which technologies are part of your embodied daily life.

If you have any kind of disability, it soon becomes obvious how technologies are part of your everyday embodied life. The technological aid that I think of first is glasses, without which I could do very little – for others it might be contact lenses or something less visible like a pacemaker, stent or a hip joint replacement, as one of the myriad of technological interventions in the bodies of people in the contemporary world. My mobile phones, tablet and laptop carry the photographs that record my life, contain my diary and connect me to others.

Oscar Pistorius is dependent on aids for mobility. He is a double amputee who lost both legs below the knees when he was a baby and ran on shock-absorbing carbon fibre prosthetics, called 'cheetah blades': designed by the Icelandic company Ossur, they store and release energy in order to mimic the reaction of the anatomical foot/ankle joint of able-bodied runners. He had competed in two able-bodied athletics meetings in 2007, but the International Association of Athletics Federations (IAAF) ruled in January 2008 that his prosthetics qualified as technical aids, which were banned because they were seen to afford an unfair advantage to the athlete. In July 2008, however, he won the right to be eligible to compete at the Olympic Games in Beijing against able-bodied athletes. In the end, he failed to qualify for the 2012 Olympics, but ran in the Paralympics.

You came across the term 'case study' in Chapter 8 of *Understanding Social Lives, Part 1*.

The Oscar Pistorius case study raises questions about the rules and regulations that are in place to combat discrimination, but which also construct categories of person, for example by disability. Not only are bodies categorised, as in the Paralympic cycling example above, connections between technologies and bodies are also regulated. This example shows how regulatory bodies such as the IAAF can set the boundaries and show which connections are allowed and which would be considered unfair enhancement. Pistorius's experience as a competitive athlete challenges the parameters of the natural body and what might be legitimate means of increasing body competences and achievements in sport, and demonstrates the connections between embodied selves and society more widely.

Figure 2.3   Oscar Pistorius

The advances in science and technology, which Haraway (1991) has collectively called **technoscience**, have played a big part in the transformation of bodies and embodied selves. Technoscience offers much more than superficial changes, whether in health care or cosmetic surgery, which is also used by the affluent to offset the effects of ageing in far more radical ways than the use of cosmetics on the surface of the body. Embracing technologies as Haraway does means that people are not reduced to a natural body, and new connections, and thus new opportunities, are possible.

Technoscience
A concept used by Haraway to explain cyborgs as the mixing of human beings, science and technology, and the breaking down of boundaries between nature and culture, which has implications for challenging other divisions that appear to be natural.

Sport is a highly competitive field, which is marked by divisions between women and men and between able-bodied and disabled athletes, with a strong emphasis on the capacities of the athletic body, especially that of elite athletes. The example of Pistorius also demonstrates the power of representation in making sense of bodies, and the connections between representations and lived experience.

One sport that has increased in popularity since the 2012 Paralympics is wheelchair basketball, with British wheelchair basketball claiming a 25 per cent increase in participation in their clubs (IPC, 2013). This increase can at least partly be attributed to the popularity of the sport on television during the Olympic Games.

Figure 2.4   Wheelchair basketball at the 2012 Paralympics

Wheelchair basketball offers new connections between able-bodied athletes and those with disabilities. Yet, athletes with disabilities observe that they achieve more media coverage and public recognition in the mainstream sport than they do at, for example, the Paralympics. This is why Pistorius sought to compete with able-bodied athletes. Sarah Storey, the Paralympic medallist, received much more media coverage when she competed in the Commonwealth Games in Delhi in October 2010 than she ever had before in the Paralympics, even though she had won two gold, three silver and a bronze medal for swimming. Athletes with disabilities may still feel that they are competing in an under-valued space, which is disconnected from the mainstream of sport.

While the Paralympics are based on values of courage, determination, inspiration and equality, it could indeed be the last value that is the most problematic, as is illustrated in competitions where some athletes clearly benefit from more advanced technologies than others. For example, in the 100 metres on 8 September 2008, there was a stark contrast between the rudimentary blades of Vanna Kim, a 40-year-old Cambodian who had lost his legs in a landmine in 1989, and those of Oscar Pistorius.

Figure 2.5   Mixed wheelchair basketball

4.3   Sporting intersections

Disability is not experienced in a vacuum. Bodies and their practices in sport connect to society in many different ways, for example bringing together different social relations and social inequalities. Pistorius's case illustrates the mix of factors, such as ethnicity, social class and gender. Pistorius's white ethnicity is another connection that demonstrates the intersection of disability with ethnicity, as well as gender and class. Pistorius's whiteness is a factor that intersects with his privileged class position and investment in masculinity. These factors are not simply added together; they reinforce each other and are connected. Disability is not experienced in the same way by every athlete – or every person. Social class and ethnicity can make a big difference and can increase or reduce the impact of inequalities. As Chapter 1 pointed out, whiteness, as a taken-for-granted, unmarked ethnic identity, is no longer assumed and left without discussion (Ware and Back, 1992); whiteness in relation to masculinity has to be considered in its specific contexts.

Sport is a field that is strongly marked by gender and gender differences. For example, within the field of sport, the dominant discourse is that of competitive, physically competent masculinity. Think about big sporting events such as the World Cup in football. In sport, the default position is masculine. The 'World Cup' is the men's competition, but gender is unstated. When women compete in football, rugby or cricket, they do so as women and largely receive less media coverage (Markula, 2009).

Disabled people are usually grouped with women and other marginalised groups, such as disaffected young people, in policies that promote sport (Woodward, 2009); they are the outsiders and not the representatives of these networks of masculinity, which Connell calls **hegemonic masculinity** (Connell, 2005). Here, Connell is combining masculinity as a set of cultural and social qualities and practices associated with men and hegemony, which literally means leadership – or dominance either by an individual or a state. Hegemonic masculinity is a concept developed by Connell to explain some of the ways in which masculinity is valued over femininity and men are valued more than women in many societies. Not all men are the same and some groups such as gay men or men with disabilities may not be part of the dominant masculinity.

Hegemonic masculinity is a cultural and social dominance that involves networks of privilege. The values of hegemonic masculinity, such as leadership, strength, courage and honour, connect to make a cultural norm, a set of qualities that is valued very highly. In sport, this usually means that men's sport is valued more than women's, sometimes because it is faster, more aggressive and more exciting. Different social systems and organisations are connected – such as the press, journalists, fans, athletes, trainers, managers, promoters – all of whom invest in the support of this culture that tends to marginalise and exclude others – such as women, gay men and men who do not engage in hegemonic masculinity. Connell's conceptualisation of hegemonic masculinity sees heterosexual men as entrenched in a system of **patriarchy**, although Connell argues that, even though they are the main beneficiaries of the system, they could change their oppressive practices (Connell, 2005).

Connell has more recently argued that, for example through challenges and political action, what was called hegemonic masculinity is changing and is responsive to local and global shifts. What is useful about the idea is that it shows how different elements in society are connected, for example television and media, films, schools and sports clubs (many

Hegemonic masculinity
This attempts to explain the social dominance of a particular sort of masculinity, which has practices and cultures traditionally associated with men, but is not restricted to men. This culture is so dominant that women may attempt to copy its practices in order to gain access to power.

Patriarchy
A social system in which adult men have power, particularly over women, and occupy dominant positions, for example in government and in industry and commerce.

golf clubs were only recently compelled to include women as members on an equal footing with men since the Equality Act 2010). These connections are part of the process of making and remaking society. Race, ethnicity, class and disability also intersect within these processes of connection and disconnection.

Hegemonic masculinity is also racialised and ethnicised, and these dimensions of social life intersect with others such as disability and sexuality. Athletes with disabilities can achieve a higher media profile if they too invest in this competitive, assertive version of masculinity. The idea is also useful for understanding connecting lives because bodies are part of the network. Having a male body is not the only factor but hegemonic masculinity is based on particular interpretations of body practices, for example as aggressive and forceful, such as tackling in sport. In order to compete successfully, women too have to invest in this gender identity and this version of masculinity, which is defined as:

- accepting and admiring physical prowess and aggression
- dominating qualities of leadership
- embodying particular versions of honour
- a lack of emotion and empathy with others.

Hegemonic masculinity means taking control and being strong; it is not associated with being a victim or vulnerable. This is considered below in relation to gender in the case of the South African runner Caster Semenya, who came from an impoverished family in a disadvantaged black community in South Africa.

4.4   Gendered connections: gender verification

Gender is important in connecting people in sport and more widely in society. Gender is also a source of difference, which is often linked to inequalities. In Western societies, there may be recognition of more fluid gender categories, including transgender, but in sport, regulatory bodies aim to identify two: competitions are for women or for men. Gender identities in sport are seen as a matter of scientific verification by regulatory bodies, which appears to mask all the social factors that are implicated. Mixed competitions in contact sports are discouraged. Even in football, according to Football Association (FA) regulations, mixed games are discouraged after the age of 13. The vast majority of sporting competitions are single sex, especially in the case of contact sport and at the highest levels.

As was shown in the case of Oscar Pistorius, athletes with disabilities can be seen as trying to gain unfair advantage through technological aids. When an able-bodied athlete's gender is called into question, it is often seen as men trying to gain advantage by trying to pass as women, sometimes combined with performance enhancement through pharmaceutical intervention; testosterone can boost performance, especially in some sports. Again, this suggests cheating, although bodies are more complicated.

Intersex and a range of different forms of development mean that not everyone conforms neatly to the clear genetic and physical criteria that the regulatory bodies of sport deploy. Intersex is complex because it is used to describe individuals who do not conform to the prescribed two-sex model, especially in terms of reproductive and sexual anatomy. Bodies are different and some babies are born with the external characteristics of one sex but the internal features of the other; sometimes it is ambiguous. The condition is not that uncommon – it is estimated that 1 in 1660 babies are born without clear XX or XY chromosomes (Fausto-Sterling, 2000).

Sex and gender
Some social scientists distinguish between sex as biological, physical and genetic, and gender as social and cultural, suggesting that sex is relatively fixed whereas gender can be changed by doing things differently.

The South African 800m athlete Caster Semenya is an example of how an individual's experience can demonstrate wider issues about the relationship between **sex and gender**, and how societies are made. Semenya's gender was called into question in August 2009 at the World Athletics Championship in Berlin, when she won the 800 metres. She was suspended from competitions until a decision could be made about whether or not she was a woman, and thus whether she could retain her medal and compete as a woman. Semenya's physical appearance led other athletes to question whether she was a woman, leading the IAAF to instigate gender verification tests. Semenya's photograph appeared in media coverage, generating comments about her athletic physique.

The debate, especially in the media, invoked expert scientific and medical commentary as well as claims of unfair practice. Her body was described as 'manly' and with a 'strikingly musculature physique'. The South African sports authorities noted class differences and inequalities. If Semenya had come from an affluent country like the USA her treatment might have been different. Similarly, if she had been white rather than black, she might also have been treated quite differently. In all the debates, there was heavy dependence on the expert testimony of medical authorities, not only in accessing the certainty of gender identity. Gender testing has a long history in sport, even though compulsory tests were abandoned at the Olympics in 1992. Tests have changed from those based on the embodied features, which those accorded expert status can see, to DNA and chromosomal tests and the current more complex panoply of procedures that includes psychological testing. There is recognition of social and psychological factors, which were emphasised in Connell's (2005) concept of hegemonic masculinity.

Activity 5

Make a list of ten characteristics that you see as female and ten as male. How many of these are biological? Would these aspects constitute a definition of being female or male?

This activity is not quite as easy as it seems! How many of the features that you identified were linked to body parts or to genetic make-up or maybe to reproductive capacities? How many apparently biological categories are less obvious? Being able to bear and feed a baby are clearly female characteristics, but not all women can. There are transgender people who are legally male, but become pregnant and give birth, those who may externally appear to be male but retain the uterus and ovaries with which they were born. Even reproductive sex is not quite as clearly biological as it might seem at first, not least because of the interventions of reproductive technologies. Body size and strength are not necessarily reliable features. What about people who do not conform to cultural stereotypes, such as dress and ways of walking and sitting, but nonetheless see themselves as female or male? There are also psychological characteristics that are particularly associated with one sex or the other in the two-sex model. This exercise might demonstrate the difficulties of separating cultural and social expectations from bodies and biology, which are not the same thing.

One way of finding out more about what people think at a particular time and in a particular place is to ask them, as the psychologist Sandra Bem did in the USA in 1970. Bem constructed a sex role inventory based on people's responses to a set of questions about gender characteristics. It was based on a model of two sexes, but allowed for four groups: masculine; feminine; androgynous; and undifferentiated (Bem, 1993 [1971]). People were asked to rate themselves on a scale of 1 (almost never) to 7 (almost always) according to 60 stereotypical gender characteristics, including the characteristics shown in Table 2.2.

Table 2.2   Gender characteristics from Bem's study

Self-reliant	Reliable	Warm
Yielding	Analytical	Solemn
Helpful	Sympathetic	Willing to take a stand
Defends own beliefs	Jealous	Tender
Cheerful	Leadership ability	Friendly
Moody	Sensitive to others' needs	Gullible
Independent	Truthful	Inefficient
Shy	Willing to take risks	Acts as leader
Conscientious	Understanding	Childlike
Athletic	Secretive	Adaptable
Affectionate	Makes decisions easily	Individualistic
Theatrical	Compassionate	

Were any of the characteristics in Table 2.2 on the list you made for Activity 5? Things may have changed. Bem's findings were largely seen as reliable, although they relate to how people describe themselves, which does not guarantee accuracy. The majority of people rated themselves according to the appropriate stereotype for their ascribed gender, which tells us something about the connections between people and culture, and among people. The possibility of a mix of characteristics is interesting as is the power of cultural connections.

Performativity

The concept used by Butler (1990) to explain how, for example, sex is made through a set of social practices and values. Performativity means that sex is not shaped by body parts, but by what people do and how they do this.

Goffman (1959) suggested that people perform roles that are largely already written, which could apply to gender roles. Judith Butler (1990) goes further and argues that by acting in certain ways, the role or identity is actually made. Butler applies this to sex as well as gender through her concept of **performativity**. 'Performativity' means that something is made real and given substance and authenticity by being performed. Thus, what is called 'sex', which includes a whole set of characteristics, as was applied to Caster Semenya in the press coverage, is not fixed by biology before birth, beyond some anatomical features and reproductive capacities. Sex and gender are acted out every day, and it is those actions or performances which we call 'sex'. Butler is making quite a radical claim. In sport, bodies and social context are mixed, for example loss of body fat, muscle tone and competitive, assertive, even aggressive body practices and comportment all undermine what can be seen as feminine, but result from engaging in sporting practices. For example, Semenya's raised levels of testosterone demonstrate connections between bodies and practices; doing competitive sport raises testosterone levels.

Bem's (1993 [1971]) inventory supports the claim that people identify with norms. Bodies in sport are also shaped by sporting practices. Women athletes may feel compelled to present themselves as conventionally feminine in order to avoid such prejudice because sport is often characterised by stereotypes, for example of heterosexuality and masculinity. Similarly, in Bem's inventory, few men described themselves as 'always childlike' and the category was dropped in later versions. Gender stereotypes also change over time and in different places. Gender identities are made and remade through the interconnections between the inner worlds and lived bodies of individuals, and the social worlds people live in, and are always situated within the wider field of social systems, values and practices.

Bem's categories (1993 [1971]) demonstrate the connections and disconnections between people and culture in the making and remaking of society. These categories change as you might have noted when listing your own ten key aspects of men and of women, when what seems to be about bodies and appears fixed, turns out to be social and cultural, and can change. Women athletes have to perform their femininity, through comportment and appearance, even when they, through the body practices of their sport, necessarily have very different bodies from their female, non-sporting counterparts. Men too are caught up in the same connections and disconnections, as is illustrated by the homophobia that is prevalent in sport. Male athletes may feel compelled to reassure their fans – and their team mates – that they are heterosexual by the constant presence of a female, preferably conventionally attractive, partner.

Summary

- Rules and regulations play a key role in connecting people in the making and remaking of society.

- Bodies are another element in the intersections of class, disability, ethnicity and gender, which make society through connecting lives.

- Disability is experienced in different ways in sport because of social as well as embodied factors, as the case of Oscar Pistorius showed.

- Social factors include inequalities and differences showing how different bodies are unequally valued.

- Gender classification is central to sport, and gender verification testing shows the importance of social factors and rules and regulations in producing social relations.

- The concept of embodied selves combines bodies and social relations, and mind and body.

5 Conclusion

This chapter has developed the work on identities in Chapter 1 to explore further the connections between personal and social worlds, and between different aspects of that social world by adding bodies to the set of connections and disconnections through which society is made. The concept of embodied selves adds bodies to the discussion in this strand and is used to connect minds and bodies, and show how bodies are part of the processes involved in making and remaking society.

Connecting lives are experienced through people connecting to social worlds through their actions and activities, including embodied activities such as those that take place in sport, which prioritises bodies and body practices. Even bodies are socially made and remade, although there are different claims made about the extent to which bodies and embodied selves are socially constructed, and the extent to which bodies set the limits on what people can do and the opportunities and choices they have. Technological interventions create new connections and new opportunities, as claims about the cyborg show. Objects and technologies, like minds and bodies, become one and it is difficult to disentangle the connections. Disability may appear to be part of physical make-up, but, as the chapter has shown, disability is classified by social organisations and experienced in connection with particular places. The ways in which people are connected to categories may be based on their bodies in sport, but the categories are social and socially defined.

There are also disconnections and the rules do not always fit bodies, or bodies cannot be categorised and do not fit the rules, and rules have to change. Bodies can change, for example through practices like training, through different classifications and through technoscience. Bodies are not fixed.

Sport reflects and creates differences and inequalities. Athletes with disabilities play sport in different competitions from able-bodied athletes, but sometimes these connections are disputed, as in the case of athletes like Oscar Pistorius who ran in the Olympic qualifiers and the Paralympics. Athletes with disabilities may be part of the place where they live and their situation, rather than just connected to their own bodies.

This chapter also highlighted the enduring importance of social class, not just in terms of questioning the limited promise of the legacy of the 2012 Olympic Games for the deprived communities of East London, but also in highlighting how class often intersects with other social factors, such as gender and disability, in making and remaking differences and inequalities.

The chapter has claimed that sport is:

- social
- not an equal playing field.

It has offered evidence of the connections between bodies and the body practices of people who take part in sport, and the intersection of social forces like class, ethnicity, race, gender and the categorisation of disability.

References

Anderson, B. (1983) *Imagined Communities: Reflections on the Origin and Spread of Nationalism*, London, Verso.

Bem, S.L. (1993 [1971]) *The Lenses of Gender: Transforming the Debate on Sexual Inequality*, New Haven, CT, Yale University Press.

Blade Runner (1982) Directed by Ridley Scott [Film]. Hollywood, CA, Warner Brothers.

Booth, C. (1902–03) *Life and Labour of the People in London*, London, Macmillan.

Bourdieu, P. (1984) *Distinction: A Social Critique of the Judgement of Taste* (trans. R. Nice), Cambridge, Cambridge University Press.

Butler, J. (1990) *Gender Trouble: Feminism and the Subversion of Identity*, London Routledge.

Clarke, L. and Holborough, A. (2011) *Olympic Sites: A Celebration of Olympic Values*, CLR News, 2 [Online]. Available at http://www.clr-news.org/CLR-News/CLR%20News%202-2011.pdf (Accessed 26 November 2013).

Connell, R.W. (2005) *Masculinities*, 2nd edn, Berkeley, CA, University of California Press.

Department of Communities and Local Government (DCLG) (2012) *Definitions of General Housing Terms* [Online]. Available at https://www.gov.uk/definitions-of-general-housing-terms (Accessed 27 November 2013).

Fausto-Sterling, A. (2000) *Sexing the Body: Gender Politics and the Construction of Sexuality*, London, Basic Books.

Garfinkel, H. (1967) *Studies in Ethnomethodology*, Englewood Cliffs, NJ, Prentice Hall.

Goffman, E. (1959) *The Presentation of Self in Everyday Life*, Harmondsworth, Penguin.

Haraway, D. (1991) *Simians, Cyborgs and Women: The Reinvention of Nature*, London, Free Association Books.

Hope, C. (2013) 'One school playing field sold off every three weeks since coalition was formed', *The Telegraph*, 13 December [Online]. Available at http://www.telegraph.co.uk/education/keep-the-flame-alive/10516870/One-school-playing-field-sold-off-every-three-weeks-since-Coalition-was-formed.html (Accessed 3 March 2014).

House of Lords (2013) *Keeping the Flame Alive: The Olympic and Paralympic Legacy*, Select Committee on Olympic and Paralympic Legacy, Report of Session 2013–2014, House of Lords, London.

International Paralympic Committee (IPC) (2007) *Classification Code* [Online]. Available at http://www.paralympic.org/Classification/Code (Accessed 3 March 2014).

International Paralympic Committee (IPC) (2013) *Annual Report 2012* [Online]. Available at http://www.paralympic.org/news/ipc-s-annual-report-2012-showcases-record-breaking-year (Accessed 3 November 2013).

London School of Economics (LSE) (2012) *The Olympic Legacy, Headline Findings*, LSE Housing and Communities, London.

MacRury, I. (2009) *London's Olympic Legacy*, London East Research Institute, London.

Markula, P. (2009) *Olympic Women and the Media: International Perspectives*, Basingstoke, Palgrave Macmillan.

McCarthy, S. and Synnott, E. (2012) 'Regeneration and the role of the London 2012 Olympic and Paralympic Games', *Journal of Urban Regeneration and Renewal*, vol. 5. no. 4, pp. 303–10.

Power, A. (2012) *The Olympic Investment in East London Has Barely Scratched the Surface of the Area's Needs* [Online]. Available at http://blogs.lse.ac.uk/politicsandpolicy/archives/26022 (Accessed 24 January 2013).

Prokhovnik, R. (2007) 'Rationality', in Blakeley, G. and Bryson, V. (eds) *The Impact of Feminism on Political Concepts and Debates*, Manchester, Manchester University Press.

Shilling, C. (2013) *The Body and Social Theory*, London, Sage.

Smith, A., Haycock, D. and Hulme, N. (2013) 'The class of London 2012: some sociological reflections on the social backgrounds of Team GB athletes', *Sociological Research Online*, vol. 18, no. 3, pp. 1–5.

Smith, E. (2009) *What Sport Tells Us About Life: Bradman's Average, Zidane's Kiss and Other Sporting Lessons*, London, Viking.

Sport and Recreation Alliance (SRA) (2012) *Olympic and Paralympic Legacy Survey* [Online]. Available at http://www.sportandrecreation.org.uk/policy/research/olympic-and-paralympic-legacy-survey (Accessed 3 March 2014).

Sport England (2013a) *Research* [Online]. Available at http://www.sportengland.org/research (Accessed 24 November 2013).

Sport England (2013b) *How the Active People Survey Works* [Online]. Available at http://www.sportengland.org/research/about-our-research/active-people-survey/ (Accessed 3 March 2014).

Sport England (2013c) *Active People Survey 7* [Online]. Available at http://archive.sportengland.org/research/active_people_survey/active_people_survey_7.aspx?show=true (Accessed 26 November 2013).

The Smith Institute (2013) *School Sport Participation and the Olympic Legacy* [Online]. Available at http://www.smith-institute.org.uk/file/School%20Sports%20Participation%20Survey.pdf (Accessed 3 March 2014).

Ware, V. and Back, L. (1992) *Out of Whiteness, Colour Politics and Culture*, Chicago, IL, University of Chicago Press.

Watt, P. (2013) 'It's not for us', *City: Analysis of Urban Trends, Culture, Theory, Policy, Action*, vol. 17, no. 1, pp. 99–118.

Woodward, K. (2009) *Embodied Sporting Practices: Regulating and Regulatory Bodies*, Basingstoke, Palgrave.

Chapter 3
Connecting people and places

John Dixon and Steve Hinchliffe

Contents

Introduction

Conversations among people meeting each other for the first time often start with the question 'where are you from?', as if the answer to this question will reveal something about the kind of person they might be. This comes from the assumption that identity is somehow connected to the place where people currently live or their place of origin. When individuals meet others from places with which they also have some association, this can help to break the ice and create a sense of connection among people meeting for the first time. This suggests that people living within one place share a collective identity or a sense of common belonging.

Yet, the sense of shared connection that places can engender often hides a set of disconnections and the ways in which people, ostensibly living together cheek by jowl within the same block of flats or street, the same neighbourhood or city, are separated from each other. In the same way that places can shape the **identities** of those who live there, people can also shape places, for better or worse, through the ways in which they relate to each other, their activities and their ways of living together or apart.

Identities
You learnt about making identities through connections in Chapter 1 of *Understanding Social Lives, Part 1*.

This chapter looks at how diverse people live together in the shared spaces of cities. The stakes are particularly high given that the majority of the world's population now lives in cities – as of 2010, more than half of all people lived in an urban area. By 2050, it is estimated that this proportion will increase to seven out of ten people (WHO, 2013).

In Section 1, we look at some of the ways in which British society in particular has changed in the past two centuries, as more and more people started to live in large towns and cities. In Sections 2 and 3, we introduce the idea of divided cities before exploring a case study of Belfast to look at how divided populations can live together better. Finally, in Section 4, we question the usefulness of the concept of **social capital** to understanding how to make better places.

Social capital
The value, in terms of happiness and potential economic prosperity, of social connections and networks.

As you read the chapter, it is important to keep in mind that a main issue being addressed is the relationship between who people are, and where and how they live. You have already learnt that identities are made partly through relations with and connections to others. In this chapter, the focus is on the disconnections that arise from differences between people, and how the binary between 'us' and 'them' can become so entrenched that different forms of segregation become a way of coping with these differences.

1 Urban experiences

1.1 Urbanisation and industrialisation

In 1800, four-fifths of the British population lived in small villages. By 1830, half the population lived in towns. In this time of rapid change, many people in Britain, or coming to live in Britain, moved to the rapidly growing towns and cities. The reasons for these migrations were undoubtedly complex but, briefly and crudely, changes in farming (particularly the loss of common access land through changes to landholding practices) and the growing importance of manufacturing and trade to the British imperial economy meant that a living wage was more likely to be made in a city than in the countryside. In nineteenth-century Britain, **urbanisation** and industrialisation proceeded hand in hand.

In order to give a sense of the scale of these changes, it is useful to examine the available data on where people lived and how this changed over the course of the nineteenth century. This is not as straightforward as it sounds. Where people lived was often difficult to determine exactly. The numbers involved and the difficulty in defining the boundaries of rapidly growing towns meant that counting and classifying people as 'rural' or 'urban' were difficult operations. The population census, which started in 1801, had to deal with these and other difficulties. One of the first attempts to collect together the uneven census data on urban populations and, in turn, to give shape to modern urban studies, was Adna Weber's *The Growth of Cities in the Nineteenth Century: A Study in Statistics*, published in 1899.

Urbanisation
The growth of cities, including the increase in the number of people living in cities, the changes in how they live, and the experiences of living in an urbanised society.

Activity 1

Look at Table 3.1, which uses Weber's quantitative data on urban growth. Describe in your own words how the total population of England and Wales changed between 1801 and 1891.

In comparison, how did the population of large towns (of over 20,000 people) change in the same period? What about the smallest settlements (of under 5000 people)?

Table 3.1 Estimates of the populations of different sized settlements for England and Wales, 1801–91

Classification of settlement by population size	1801	1851	1891
Over 20 000	1 506 176	6 265 011	15 563 834
10 000–20 000	389 624	800 000	2 362 376
5000–10 000	418 715	963 000	1 837 054
Under 5000	6 578 021	9 899 598	9 239 261
Total population	8 892 536	17 927 609	29 002 525

Source: Weber, 1899, p. 4

There are various ways of summarising quantitative data in a table like this, but it is important to not simply repeat what is in the table. Instead, try to offer a descriptive overview, looking for patterns or trends in the data. So, for example, a good way of describing the total population change is to say that in the first half of the nineteenth century, the population of England and Wales doubled from nearly nine million to almost 18 million people. By the end of the century, it had nearly doubled again to just short of 30 million. Meanwhile, the population living in large towns increased over ten-fold in the same period (from 1.5 million to over 15 million). It went from being a relatively small proportion of the population (1.5 of nine million is 17 per cent of the population) to being over half of the population by 1891 (54 per cent of the total population living in the largest settlement category). Finally, the number of people living in the smallest settlements increased relatively slowly in the first half of the century and then actually decreased by the end of the century.

Looking at some of the detail of the census data for individual towns, it is possible to find some particularly intense periods of change. Between 1821 and 1841, the populations of towns and cities grew at unprecedented rates. Populations in Glasgow, Cardiff, Belfast, Sheffield, Birmingham and Leeds grew by over 40 per cent in this 20-year period. In some cities, growth was even more spectacular: Manchester's population grew by 71 per cent between 1831 and 1841 alone. Most of this population growth was in the centre of cities, with many people housed in appalling conditions. But cities also spread out, with farmland and country estates giving way to suburban housing for the growing middle classes. So towns and cities grew in terms of the number of people living there (their population), the density at which people lived (the number of people per square mile/kilometre), and their built-up area or spatial extent. These changes of *where* people lived were accompanied by changes in *how* they lived – for example, how they made a living and the kinds of acquaintance they made. Indeed, urbanisation involved more than a physical change in the population and where it lived, it also referred to the subtle and sometimes momentous changes in the ways in which people lived their lives. The social changes and new experiences that accompanied this incredible period of growth and movement prompted one historian to describe Manchester in the 1830s as the 'shock city' of its time (Briggs, 1990).

■   Why do you think the word 'shock' is used to describe a city?

When social scientists talk of shock cities, they are suggesting:

• that the speed of change was rapid, occurring not within people's lifetime but within a few years. (Imagine living in a city that nearly doubled in size within ten years!)

• the word 'shock' suggests a significant, almost traumatic, change in people's daily lives.

The mass movement from the countryside to the city in nineteenth-century Britain was a process of largely **internal migration**, which was often just as disruptive to people's existing connections as international migration could be. Some of these disruptions included the tendency to live closer together and at greater densities than had been the case in the countryside. People may have had to deal for the first time with living and moving among crowds and strangers. Some of the new urban dwellers may have found that established ways of doing things were now being brought into question. People, it is often said, knew their place in the countryside, whereas the possibility existed in rapidly growing towns and cities for changing some of the make-up of society. Another change was that for many people (though by no means all) the place of work became separate from their place of dwelling. There were also significant changes to how people made their living. People were less likely to be employed on the land, growing food. Instead, they were more likely to be employed in manufacturing and services. Factory employment involved long hours, all year round.

Internal migration
Moving from one place to another within the same country.

However, these observations are rather casual and general, and we need to look in some more detail to see whether or not they are justified or hold for different cities, and apply equally within those cities. Social scientists tend to develop particular approaches in order to avoid making general arguments that are unsupported by evidence. We have already come across one way of doing this, typified by Weber's (1899) use of data. Looking at data over a period of time allowed us to say some general things about changes to how and where people lived in the nineteenth century (though only in England and Wales). Another approach is to make case studies. A case study involves social scientists focusing their attention on a particular issue, place or event and looking at it in detail. It may involve tracing something over a period of time. It may involve looking at how one issue, person, place or event is connected to other issues, people, places and events.

1.2   Nineteenth-century Manchester

In order to acquire more detail on the experience of urbanisation in the nineteenth century, so that we can think more about its effects on how people live today (in particular, their possible disconnection from each other), we can look at accounts from the period. One famous account of nineteenth-century Manchester paints a story of a polarised and divided city. Friedrich Engels, who worked as a clerk in Manchester in the early 1840s, and who would go on to co-author the *Communist Manifesto* with Karl Marx (Marx and Engels (1998 [1848]), wrote in detail about Manchester's uneven social geography. Through his long-term direct contact with the workers of Manchester, Engels described the horrors of urban industrial life. He graphically referred to 'women made unfit for childbearing, children deformed, men enfeebled, limbs crushed, whole generations wrecked, afflicted with disease and infirmity, purely to fill the purses of the bourgeoisie' (Engels, 1969 [1845], p. 194).

Industrial capitalism
A form of capitalism that was associated with: a large investment of private money in machinery and plant; the ensuing changes in the speed and scale of production of goods; and the ways in which workers tended to become specialised within one part of the production line. It also involves a division between workers on the one hand and the owners of factories, or capitalists, on the other.

In *The Condition of the Working Class in England* (Engels, 1969 [1845]) (in which he wrote about Manchester and also, in spite of the title, about cities and towns in Ireland and Scotland), Engels was primarily concerned to analyse the workings of a form of economic activity, **industrial capitalism**, which produced and entrenched class distinctions in industrialising nations.

One of the ways in which Engels investigated capitalism was to focus on two kinds of street. The first kind was the street where many of the workers and urban poor lived. These were the people who were often employed in the new factories, were paid a pittance and easily laid off when economic conditions made production less profitable. In these streets, there were:

... usually one- or two-storied cottages in long rows, perhaps with cellars used as dwellings, almost always irregularly built. These houses of three or four rooms and a kitchen form, throughout England, some parts of London excepted, the general dwellings of the working class. The streets are generally unpaved, rough, dirty, filled with vegetable and animal refuse, without sewers or gutters, but supplied with foul, stagnant pools instead. Moreover, ventilation is impeded by the bad, confused method of building of the whole quarter, and since many human beings here live crowded into a small space, the atmosphere that prevails in these working-men's quarters may readily be imagined.

(Engels, 1969 [1845], p. 60)

Relatively new terraces (Figure 3.1), being built in an area that was known at the time as 'Manchester's New Town' (also known as 'Irish Town'), were often no better.

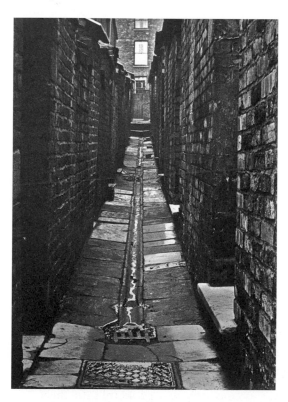

Figure 3.1   Densely packed urban housing built in mid nineteenth-century Manchester

Engels noted how, in these recently built slums, the terraced houses were characteristically arranged in three rows (see Figure 3.2). The houses in the first row each had a back door and a yard, and commanded the highest rent. Behind these lay a narrow alley and then two rows of back-to-back houses (having their rear walls in common). The third row faced a street, while the middle-row houses opened only onto the alley. The middle-row houses commanded the lowest of the three rents. Here, ventilation and sanitation were at their worst and the risk of cholera and other infectious diseases was considered to be greatest.

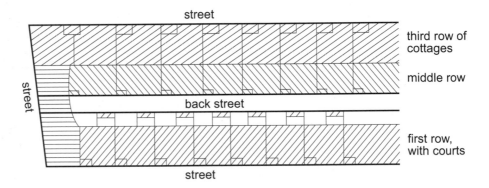

Figure 3.2   Engel's sketch of working-class row housing (Source: Engels, 1969 [1845], p. 89)

The second kind of street that Engels focused on was the thoroughfare, which brought middle-class commuters into the town centre. Famously, Engels remarked on just how effective these streets were at bypassing, or failing to reveal, the urban squalor that lay around them (see Figure 3.3):

> Outside, beyond this girdle [of unmixed working people's quarters], lives the upper and middle bourgeoisie, the middle bourgeoisie in regularly laid out streets in the vicinity of the working quarters … ; the upper bourgeoisie in remoter villas with gardens … in free, wholesome country air, in fine, comfortable homes, passed once every half or quarter hour by omnibuses going into the city. And the finest part of the arrangements is this, that the members of this money aristocracy can take the shortest road through the middle of all the labouring districts to their places of

business without ever seeing that they are in the midst of the grimy misery that lurks to the right and the left.

(Engels, 1969 [1845], p. 79)

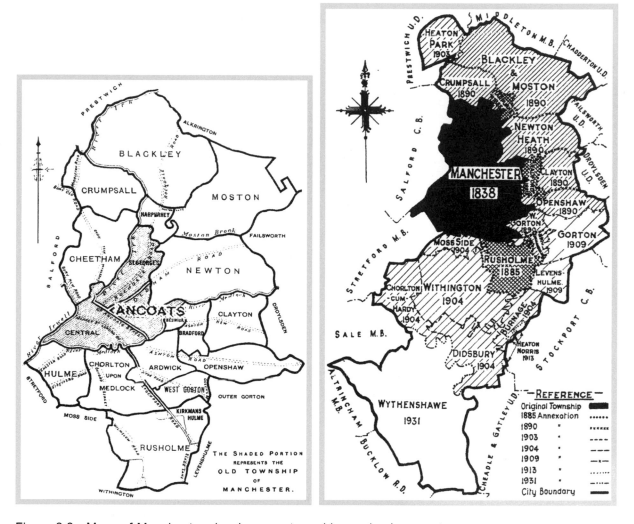

Figure 3.3   Maps of Manchester showing area townships and subsequent growth of the city. The main routes into the city are marked on the left-hand map. The original township contained most of the lower-class housing (Source: Platt, 2005, pp. 50, 315)

Shop fronts, walls and raised sections afforded a physical and mental barrier that, according to Engels, allowed the beneficiaries of urbanisation and industrialisation to remain untroubled by the sights, smells and sounds of the poor and unemployed. Engels saw these conditions, both the poverty and the ability of some to shield it from view, as symptomatic of a greater predicament that lay in the very ways in which society was organised.

Activity 2

Think about your experiences of cities that you know or have visited. Do you think that cities are still divided like this, with the relatively well-off able to ignore the plight of the poor?

Your answer will depend on the cities with which you are most familiar, and you may want to ask others about what they think. Our sense is that it is still fairly easy for the relatively well-off to move around a city without being confronted by poverty. Certainly in Manchester, the residential pattern that was in place by the 1850s – that of concentric circles with the poorest living in the inner ring surrounded by a solid mass of working-class terraces, and then an outer ring of middle-class suburban villas – remains largely unchallenged. Regeneration officers in the city 'still refer to the "doughnut" shape of the city, recognising that in relative terms the position of class-based residential segregation remains unchanged, although their purpose is to develop mixed housing in order to alter it' (Blakeley and Evans, 2013, p. 10). Moreover, the roads and train lines into Manchester run along the same routes now as they did in Engels' day, so the same areas are bypassed and may still be shielded from view. The same could be said for Edinburgh and Glasgow, for Cardiff and Swansea, Newcastle and Sheffield, where the remodelling, historical restorations and general tidying of city centres is seldom matched by investment in outer suburbs.

You read about similar divisions between producers and consumers of goods in Chapters 5 and 6 of *Understanding Social Lives, Part 1*.

Another aspect of this ability 'not to see' social polarisation is perhaps more developed today than in Engels' time. For a lot of the wealth that is enjoyed in places like Manchester is not simply produced by an underclass in the city's poorer areas – it is, and always has been, a wealth made possible by the activities of people elsewhere. So, while Manchester's factories are now mostly silent, the goods that people buy in Manchester's shops are being manufactured in places where poor working conditions and poverty are as rife as they were in nineteenth-century Manchester. Just as 'Cottonopolis' (as Manchester was known in the nineteenth century, owing to its wealth being derived from the finishing of textile goods) could be implicated in the production of poverty in India through the operations of the British Empire and its colonial relations with cotton plantations, so can the cultural and consumer excitement of 'Madchester' (a name given to Manchester during its revival in the 1990s and later as something of a hedonistic party city) be linked to poverty elsewhere. The brightly illuminated high street shops full of goods from all over the world tell us nothing of the conditions of the working people who made those goods possible. The poverty felt in southern China or India, for example, is arguably even more shielded from view than was the case in Engels' analysis (despite a much expanded mass media today).

Figure 3.4   Twenty-first-century slums in Mumbai

In this section, we have looked at urbanisation in a nineteenth-century British industrial city using some historical evidence and accounts to describe and start to analyse the changes that occurred in where and how people lived in nineteenth-century Britain. For some observers, such as Engels, Manchester's urbanisation was **alienating** and disruptive. Engels recognised that urbanisation, and the economic changes that allowed it to occur, also produced great inequalities. The leafy suburbs and the thoroughfares that Engels described capture some of the uneven geography of the growing cities. Cities may have been shocking, but the shock was not necessarily experienced equally or evenly.

Alienation
The detachment or disconnection of people from the world or from a place. The term is sometimes used to imply a loss of identity.

Summary

- Urbanisation describes the growth of cities, the changes in where and how people live, and the experiences of living in an urbanised society.

- Urbanisation went hand in hand with industrialisation, as people flocked from the countryside to the cities to work in factories and mills.

- Both urbanisation and industrialisation involved a disruption to people's lives, and their existing connections to each other and places.

- Urbanisation and industrialisation produced great inequalities within and between cities.

2 Divided cities?

In the previous section, we saw how class divisions may shape the human geography of the city, as illustrated by Engels' account of how the design of thoroughfares in Manchester allowed the rich to insulate themselves from the poor. This example points to a broader feature of urban life. Cities must typically accommodate an extraordinary diversity of people. Indeed, urbanisation creates environments that can best be characterised as 'mosaics' – rich patchworks of different individuals, groups, places, activities and behaviours shaped by differences and inequalities. This raises a range of important social, political and practical questions: how and in what ways can diverse people connect to each other? How can people live together peacefully? How can common public spaces and resources be shared?

In this section, we consider one response to this problem of creating common ground among different and unequal groups of people, which seeks to establish systems of segregation. In simple terms, segregation erects social and spatial boundaries between groups, creating relations of both connection and disconnection. Residents enclosed within a common, bounded territory tend to feel connected to one another by bonds of solidarity, common identity and belonging. At the same time, they tend to feel disconnected from communities lying 'beyond' by relations of social division, distance, and sometimes inequality.

Segregation may result from formal processes of urban planning and state intervention, informal practices implemented 'from below' by ordinary residents, or a complex combination of the two. It may arise through the organisation of residential spaces (who lives where?), educational spaces (who learns where?) or employment spaces (who works where?). It may arise, too, through routine behaviours within so-called 'everyday life spaces' (Schnell and Yoav, 2001), as illustrated by divisions within activities of leisure and recreation (see for example Dixon and Durrheim, 2003). In some places, segregation may come to dominate people's lives with far-reaching consequences.

The most notorious examples have occurred in societies that have employed legal systems of segregation. In cities in South Africa during the apartheid era or the southern states of the USA during the Jim Crow era, for example, formal laws of racial segregation determined where citizens could live, what schools they could attend and where they could work. Segregation laws also governed the most banal aspects of everyday life. 'Petty apartheid' legislation regulated with whom South Africans could sit on public transport, go to the beach, hold hands or enjoy a kiss. Jim Crow's legislation required black and white Americans to drink from separate water fountains, use separate toilets and enter cinemas through separate entrances. Books such as A.J. Christopher's (1994) *The Atlas of Apartheid* or Massey's and Denton's (1993) *American Apartheid* have explored in detail the nature and legacy of segregation in these societies.

Segregation, however, has become a feature of urban life in many cities. The geographer Mike Davis (1990) describes Los Angeles (LA) as a city where the wealthy inhabitants of large parts of west LA can, riots notwithstanding, easily ignore the poverty of east and southern LA through bypassing them on raised freeways and interstate highways. This is one of the clearest examples of the ways in which the wealthy are able to keep poverty 'out of sight' for most of the time. In other cities, some people are choosing to voluntarily segregate themselves from others – usually on the basis of income or race – by living in gated communities. In such communities, fences, gates and security staff keep the inhabitants separated from others. Research in England in 2003 found more than 1000 such communities with more being planned as young professionals in particular were attracted by such places (Atkinson, 2003).

It is noticeable, however, that it is not the self-segregation of the middle classes on the basis of education or income, but the self-segregation of Muslim communities that causes concern among policymakers and is more commonly reported in the media. This was particularly apparent in the summer of 2001 following disturbances in a number of towns in the north of England, particularly Burnley, Oldham and Bradford, and even more acute following the London bombings in July 2005.

Riots
You will read in detail about riots and ways of interpreting them in Chapter 8.

The official investigations into the 2001 disturbances (for example, the 2001 Cantle Report) accepted, uncritically, the characterisation of Bradford's Muslim community as self-segregating. This was a concept that had appeared in the Ouseley report on Bradford written just prior to the riots (Flint, 2009, p. 260). The Cantle Report in turn introduced the concept of parallel lives, according to which contact between different ethnic communities was minimal. Those critical of the concept of parallel lives, however, argued that economic inequalities and marginalisation were the main issues and not ethnic segregation (Samad, 2013, p. 276). Moreover, Samad provided a more nuanced picture of segregation than that of the official investigations. He claimed that although housing enclaves along ethnic and religious lines existed in Bradford, such residential patterns resulted not from self-segregation but from racism in the housing market, reinforced by white migration and flight. His research also showed that newly arrived migrants were the most likely to live in neighbourhoods among the same ethnic and religious groups, while established Muslims were more evenly spread, with a significant number living in neighbourhoods that were mixed in ethnic and religious terms (Samad, 2013, p. 278).

What is significant here is the ways in which some differences come to matter while others do not. Samad emphasises that:

> ... the segregation debate focuses almost exclusively on working-class Muslims and Whites, and ignores middle-class segregation in housing and education: white concentrations in middle-class gated communities, for example, go unmentioned.
>
> (Samad, 2013, p. 277)

Moreover, ethnic minority segregation appears of most concern when linked to Islam. For example, the highest density of any ethnic minority in the country is the Indian concentration in Leicester, yet this is rarely perceived as problematic. In contrast, the Pakistani concentration in Bradford or the Bangladeshi enclaves in Tower Hamlets, which are both lower in density, are perceived as problematic (Samad, 2013, p. 277). In short, it is the intersection of certain differences and inequalities – class, ethnicity and religion – that are perceived as problematic.

In the remainder of this section, we want to consider a city where historically the lines of division have been sectarian rather than racial, and have arisen not from formal segregation laws of the kind used in South Africa and parts of the USA, but as a complex outcome of political policies, urban planning and social conflict. That city is Belfast, Northern Ireland's capital. Belfast makes an interesting case study because it has become an international symbol of the problems that segregation may create. Moreover, since the end of Northern Ireland's transition to shared government, it is also a city seeking to move beyond its divided and violent past. Politicians, urban planners and community groups are currently trying to transform Belfast's segregated landscapes in order to build a more integrated city.

2.1   Living together apart: the sectarian geography of Belfast

Following the War of Independence with Britain from 1919 to 1921, the partition of Ireland in 1921, as a result of the Government of Ireland Act in 1920, led to the creation of an independent Irish Republic in the south and a British-controlled Northern Ireland (see Figure 3.5). Northern Ireland's territorial boundaries were drawn by the British government in order to incorporate as much as possible of the large Protestant population of Ulster who had opposed Home Rule in the wake of partition in favour of union with Britain.

At the heart of the politics of Northern Ireland is a divided population. In simplified terms, a majority in Northern Ireland, although they represent only a minority in Ireland as a whole, regard themselves as British and want Northern Ireland to remain a part of the United Kingdom. This majority of Unionists, and their radical form, the Loyalists, are also predominantly Protestant. A sizeable minority within Northern Ireland, 44 per cent according to the 2011 census, define themselves as Irish and Catholic, although an increasing number of people do not see themselves as belonging to either category. The Catholic Nationalists, and their radical form, the Republicans, would prefer to be ruled by a single, Irish authority. Both the Protestant majority and the Catholic minority, however, are not static: the size of the majority and minority fluctuates over time. Moreover, both within and outside this majority and minority, other majorities and minorities based on, for example, gender, age, sexual orientation, disability, race and ethnicity, coexist. The percentage of the population of Northern Ireland that belonged to minority ethnic groups in 2011 has more than doubled since the 2001 census. To talk of the Catholic or Protestant communities is to talk in terms of Benedict Anderson's (1983) imagined communities (introduced in Chapter 1): people within these communities are connected to each other through a shared identity and shared ideas and beliefs, even though they are not personally acquainted.

Sectarian segregation in Belfast has a long history. Its current formation, however, reflects most directly events that began around the late 1960s and lasted roughly three decades, during a period now known euphemistically as 'The Troubles'. Influenced by similar movements in the USA, in the 1960s the Nationalist/Republican communities began a

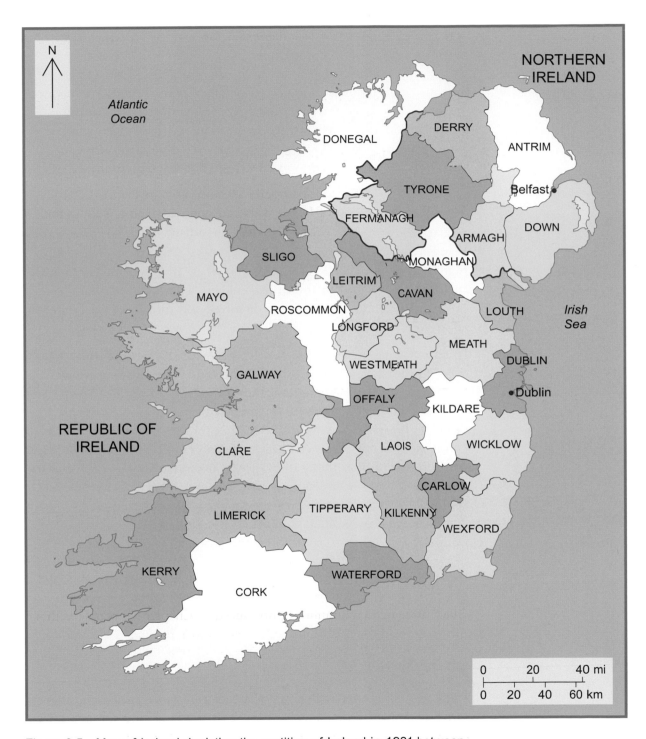

Figure 3.5   Map of Ireland depicting the partition of Ireland in 1921 between an independent Republic in the south and a British-controlled Northern Ireland

series of civil rights marches demanding an end to discrimination against Catholics in the political, economic and social spheres. Specifically, Catholics demanded police reform and a fairer voting system to end Unionist domination of the political system in Northern Ireland, where Unionist Party control of the parliament at Stormont from 1922 to 1972 was matched by Unionist control of 85 per cent of local councils (Tonge, 2001, p. 634). Political discrimination was reinforced by discrimination in education, housing provision and employment.

The increasingly harsh response by the police, and ultimately the British military forces, to the civil rights movement led to a spiral of violence that marked the beginning of 'The Troubles'. The last big civil rights march on 30 January 1972 became known as 'Bloody Sunday', following the killing of 14 civilians by British soldiers. Later in 1972, the Northern Ireland parliament was dissolved and direct rule was imposed from Westminster.

In an influential series of studies, the geographer Frederick Boal, among others, showed how patterns of political violence in Belfast, which emerged in the late 1960s and gathered momentum in the 1970s, polarised the city's Catholic and Protestant communities (see for example, Boal, 1982), setting in motion a process of segregation that continued into the 1980s (Doherty and Poole, 1997) and beyond. When confronted with the (threat of) violence, many families living in Belfast retreated to areas of the city that had historically served as ethnic and religious heartlands – places where they felt relatively secure, protected and insulated from sectarian conflict. Of course, as Doherty and Poole claim: ' … the precise pattern of what is safe and what is unsafe depended on each family's ethnic affiliation, with the Protestant mosaic largely a reverse image of the Catholic one' (Doherty and Poole, 1997, p. 532).

Figure 3.6 shows the distribution of Catholic and Protestant residents across different areas of Belfast, providing a snapshot of residential segregation in the city. West Belfast is inhabited mainly by Catholic residents, with most neighbourhoods containing fewer than 20 per cent Protestants. East Belfast displays precisely the opposite pattern, with most neighbourhoods containing fewer than 20 per cent Catholics. The more affluent south of the city is somewhat more integrated, with several areas containing a more balanced mix of Catholic and Protestant residents. Perhaps most interesting is the 'patchwork' pattern lying to the north of the city in which several mainly Protestant or mainly

Catholic neighbourhoods are located in close proximity to one another,
yet remain separated by a range of symbolic and material barriers.

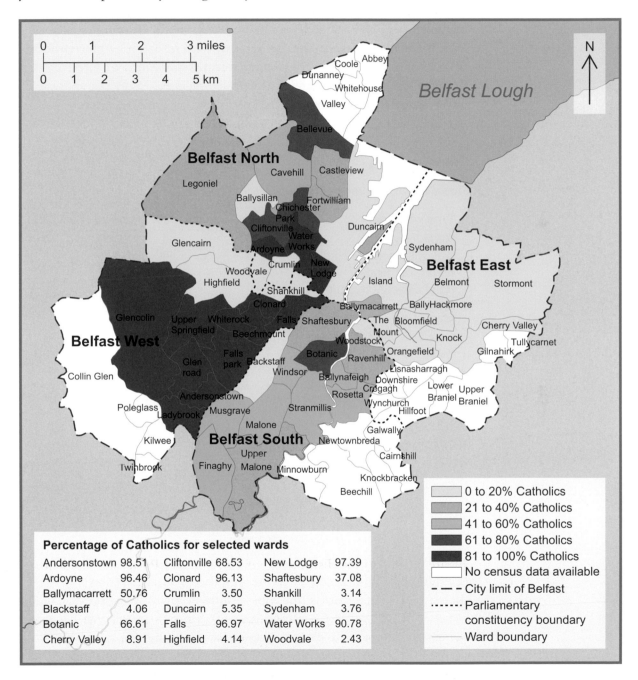

Figure 3.6   Residential segregation in Belfast (Source: Northern Ireland
census 2001, in NISRA, 2014)

The first 'peace walls' were constructed by the British Army in 1969 as a temporary military response to sectarian disorder (Byrne et al., 2012, p. 4), but they soon multiplied throughout the city in places dividing neighbouring Catholic and Protestant communities. Terminology is important here. 'Peace walls' is the term used in everyday conversation (Byrne et al., 2012), but it is a euphemism for all kinds of interface barriers that keep communities apart (see Figure 3.7). In the spring of 2011, research carried out by the Institute for Conflict Research (Jarman, 2012) identified and classified the various types of 'defensive architecture' in Belfast. The report identified 99 barriers classified into the different types represented in Table 3.2.

Table 3.2   Categories of barriers

Type of barrier	Total	Central	East	North	South	West
Metal fence	35	5	1	18		11
Wall with metal fence above	23	3	4	8	1	7
Buffer with fence	14	4	3	3		4
Road closed with pedestrian access	12	1		10		1
Solid wall	8		2	5		1
Gate with vehicle access	7	1				6
Total	**99**	**14**	**10**	**44**	**1**	**30**

Source: Belfast Interface Project, 2013

Activity 3

Look at Table 3.2 and try to identify the most common type of barrier and the least common type of barrier. Try also to identify the areas of Belfast that have the highest and lowest number of barriers.

Despite the common use of the term 'peace wall' to refer to the barriers in interface areas, the most common form of barrier is actually a metal fence; the least common type of barrier is a road that has gates, which are occasionally closed. The area with the most number of barriers is North Belfast (defined in the report as the area north of Crumlin road and west of Belfast Lough). The area with the least number of barriers is South Belfast (defined in the report as east of the Dublin railway line, south of the city centre and west of the River Lagan). This reflects the residential segregation depicted in Figure 3.6.

Perhaps one reason for the widespread use of the term 'peace wall' is
that the barriers were designed to curb intercommunity violence and
increase the possibility of peaceful coexistence. By dividing neighbouring
Catholic and Protestant communities, government officials and city
planners employed the commonsense idea that 'good fences make good
neighbours'. This perception is shared by residents living in interface
areas. A 2008 survey found 'strong agreement that the walls serve to
help residents feel safer by keeping the communities separated' (cited in
Macaulay, 2008). This logic of division gradually spread throughout the
city, sometimes with rather bizarre consequences. In 1999, in an article
published in *The Observer*, Henry McDonald noted wryly that: 'One
"wall" in north Belfast even cuts through a huge public park [Alexandra
Park] designed by the Victorian city fathers of the last century, creating
Protestant trees and Catholic trees; Protestant grass and Catholic grass;
Protestant flowers and Catholic flowers' (cited in Geography in
Action, 2013).

Figure 3.7   Interface barrier, Belfast

Walking in and around this part of the city quickly reveals the extent to
which sectarian divisions have, quite literally, become part of the urban
landscape. Interface barriers signify the boundaries between
neighbouring communities (Figure 3.7); flags and street painting declare
residents' allegiances to Unionist or nationalist causes (Figure 3.8); wall
murals celebrate the collective history, identity and political values of
particular groups (Figures 3.9 and 3.11).

Figure 3.8   Flags and street painting, Belfast

Figure 3.9   Republican wall mural, Belfast

Given this abundance of territorial symbolism, it is perhaps unsurprising that residents tend to avoid areas associated with members of the other community. For example, most residents of the Ardoyne in North Belfast have never ventured into Protestant enclaves such as Duncairn or the Shankill. Correspondingly, most residents of Duncairn or the Shankill have never ventured into Catholic enclaves such as the Falls or the Ardoyne. Relations in North Belfast, in short, demonstrate how systems of segregation allow people to 'live together apart' (Falah, 1996).

Summary

- Urbanisation brings diverse groups of people into new relations of proximity, connection and disconnection.

- Segregation can occur on the basis of a range of differences, for example income, education, race, ethnicity or religion, but some of these differences come to matter more than others.

- The dynamics of segregation and integration shape social life in cities, including people's sense of who they are and where they belong.

- Segregation between groups can create both connections and feelings of belonging, and disconnections and feelings of fear and separation.

- In Belfast, segregation, based on sectarian differences, separates neighbourhoods by a range of symbolic and material barriers, so people live closely together while remaining apart.

3   Segregation and urban experience in Belfast

3.1   Landscapes of isolation

Perhaps the most damaging consequence of segregation is its influence on everyday relationships between members of different communities and, by implication, on the attitudes they hold towards one another. By creating landscapes of isolation, segregation reduces the opportunity to meet members of other groups, to get to know them better, and establish bonds of connection and friendship across group lines. Moreover, once established, segregation encourages behaviour that creates further segregation, setting in motion an insidious cycle that persists across generations and spreads to other settings. For example, in their research on 'race' relations in the USA, Braddock (1980) and Braddock and McPartland (1989) demonstrated how lack of interracial contact in schools perpetuates lack of contact in later life and across other contexts such as the workplace. Dawkins (2005) has similarly demonstrated that lack of parental contact with other 'race' groups shapes where children later want to live, encouraging residential choices that maintain segregation.

This cycle of isolation shapes relations between Catholics and Protestants in Northern Ireland (for example, see Hewstone et al., 2005), with residential segregation underpinning many other kinds of division. Although integrated schools exist, over 90 per cent of Northern Irish children attend effectively denominational schools that contain few, if any, members of the other religion. More than 50 per cent of Protestants and 75 per cent of Catholics have friends drawn exclusively from the same religious group as themselves; and fewer than 10 per cent of married couples are in 'mixed' relationships. What are the consequences of these multiple forms of isolation for how residents perceive and relate to one another in a city such as Belfast?

Katharina Schmid and colleagues (2008) have addressed this question. Their study was based on a tradition of research known as the 'contact hypothesis' (Allport, 1954), which proposes that regular interaction with members of other groups tends to reduce intergroup prejudice, particularly when it occurs under favourable conditions (for example, participants are of equal status). Research in this field suggests that contact tends to diminish negative responses such as anger, fear and hatred, and increase positive responses such as empathy, forgiveness and trust (for a review, see Pettigrew and Tropp, 2011).

More specifically, Schmid et al. (2008) explored the social and psychological consequences of living in segregated versus mixed areas of Belfast. To do so, they conducted a survey with 958 residents of four neighbourhoods of the city, matched for social class, levels of unemployment and past history of sectarian violence:

1 a mainly Protestant estate in east Belfast

2 a mainly Catholic estate in west Belfast

3 a more mixed estate in north Belfast

4 a more mixed neighbourhood in south Belfast.

Participants drawn from these four areas were asked to complete a questionnaire that measured, among other things, their:

- experiences of positive intergroup contact – for example, 'When you have had contact with Protestants/Catholics in the past, how often have you been made to feel welcome?'

- levels of prejudice towards members of the other group – for example, 'I feel "extremely favourable/warm" or "extremely unfavourable/cold" towards Catholics/Protestants'

- desire to act offensively to members of the other group – for example, 'How often have you felt a desire to hurt Protestants/Catholics?'

- sense that members of the out-group posed a threat to their safety – for example, 'I worry about being physically attacked by Catholics/Protestants'

- perceived exposure to violence – for example, 'Have you ever been injured due to a sectarian incident?'.

Out of a much more complex analysis, we wish to extract a few simple findings. First, above and beyond the effects of living in different kinds of neighbourhoods, self-reported experiences of positive contact were associated with lower levels of sectarian prejudice and a reduced desire to act 'offensively' towards members of the other community. Second, as Table 3.3 illustrates, living in segregated versus mixed neighbourhoods was in itself associated with various kinds of intergroup experiences and attitudes.

Table 3.3   The effects of living in segregated versus mixed areas in Belfast

Intergroup experience/ attitude	Mixed neighbourhood	Segregated neighbourhood
Experiences of positive contact	3.6	2.8
Prejudice	4.4	4.8
Desire to act offensively	1.1	1.2
Fear of physical attack	1.7	1.6
Exposure to violence	0.24	0.15

Note: the figures in Table 3.3 are group averages. In each case, residents' attitudes and experiences have been measured on five-point scales, with lower scores indicating less of the intergroup experience/attitude.
Source: adapted from Schmid et al., 2008

3.2   Landscapes of fear

As noted already, Boal and others showed how segregation in Belfast arose, at least in part, in response to political conflict, encouraging residents to withdraw to their 'own' areas. In so doing, it created 'comfort zones' (Hargie et al., 2006) of real or imagined security. As this term suggests, one of the most powerful emotions underlying segregation is fear – fear of encountering others, fear of being targeted for abuse or violence, and fear of feeling vulnerable or 'out of place' in environments associated with others. This theme is captured in Table 3.3, based on Schmid et al.'s (2008) survey. This table suggests that people living in more 'mixed' environments have more positive experiences of intergroup contact and, perhaps as a result, lower levels of sectarian prejudice. At the same time, however, such residents also express greater fear about potential sectarian attacks and a greater sense of being exposed to sectarian violence (albeit that we are dealing with small differences here).

The irony is that, once established, boundaries between groups may not alleviate these fears. To the contrary, anxieties over what lies beyond the 'peace wall' often persist, intensifying the impulse to extend structures of segregation and to avoid encounters with others. Under such circumstances, ironically, boundaries may become their own antidote.

We now consider studies conducted by Leonard (2007) and Bairner and Shirlow (2003). Leonard (2007) explored how children in north Belfast understood 'risk' as they used and navigated the local environment. As part of her analysis, she asked children to draw maps of their local environments and to discuss their everyday movements through them. She found that they often evaluated environments as risky when they were located close to an interface area or when they had to walk through public spaces perceived as 'shared' by both Protestant and Catholic communities.

Relatedly, Bairner's and Shirlow's (2003) survey of over 1800 Belfast residents explored the role of sectarian boundaries in shaping adults' use of public facilities intended to benefit the whole community. Their results were revealing. Approximately two-thirds of users said that they would not visit a facility located within an 'out-group' area: 84 per cent because of fear of attack or abuse and a further 12 per cent because they simply did not want to interact with members of the other community. Interview accounts drawn from their work suggest that certain places have themselves become associated with the emotion of fear (and also, rather disturbingly, of disgust). Below are two such accounts in which a Catholic resident and a Protestant resident try to explain why they would not visit a leisure centre located in the territory of the other group:

> Go up there. Are you mad. Like why? Like why go up there? They would have you for supper. You just couldn't. Like imagine being in the showers and seeing them with their big fat guts and tats [tattoos]. Like they are scum. Not right in the head. Dangerous people even.
>
> (Catholic male, 35 years, in Bairner and Shirlow, 2003)

> How could we go there? They would attack us because we are Prods. Look it's also this way. Go to the leisure centres in Catholic areas and what do you see? Nothing but filth. Their centres aren't the cleanest. Their places are like them. They could do with a good wash.
>
> (Protestant male, 32 years, in Bairner and Shirlow, 2003)

It is important not to dismiss these fears either as simple exaggerations of the 'real' situation in Belfast or as crude symptoms of sectarian prejudice. Although Belfast is not a dangerous city in some kind of general or comparative sense, it is difficult to dispute that sectarianism has fuelled, directly or indirectly, many acts of violence in the city. Moreover, perhaps revealingly, the targets of such violence have disproportionately drawn from one subgroup of the wider population: young men living in highly segregated, working-class environments. Gender, class and religion have interacted in complex ways with social geography to shape the expression of violence in the city.

Many kinds of evidence could be advanced to support this claim. We offer you one to think about. Exploiting recent advances in geographic information system (GIS) technology, Mesev et al. (2009) have recently visualised the spatial distribution of violence in Belfast in a way that provides a grim conclusion to this section (see Figure 3.10). Between 1966 and 2007, 974 sectarian murders were committed in Belfast: 667 of the victims were Catholics; 307 were Protestants. Around 80 per cent of victims of both communities were murdered within areas of the city that were highly segregated (over 90 per cent Protestant or 90 per cent Catholic) and economically deprived. A third was murdered within 250 yards of a 'peace wall' or interface boundary and around two thirds within 500 yards.

The map on the left in Figure 3.10 represents the frequency of murders in specific locations of the city; the right-hand panel represents how this distribution relates both to patterns of sectarian segregation and to the location of interface barriers. With regards to the latter, note how thicker lines, indicating greater numbers of deaths, are clustered in and around the interface areas and also tend to fall within highly segregated areas.

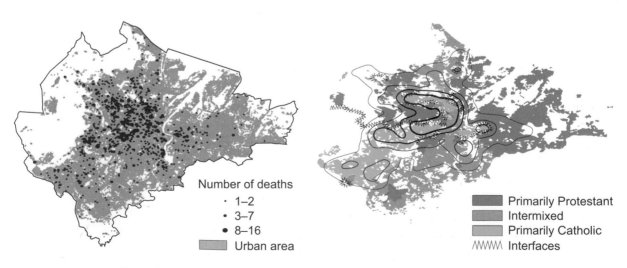

Figure 3.10   Spatial distribution of sectarian murders in Belfast, 1966–2007

3.3 Landscapes of identity

Segregation functions not only as a way of regulating fear of others in Belfast or limiting the opportunity for intergroup contact. By creating an environment in which the differences between 'us' and 'them' are highly visible and part of the everyday environment, it also shapes residents' sense of group identity. After all, our sense of 'who we are' is often bound up with our sense of 'where we are from' and 'where we belong'. In establishing a clear 'home' space, segregation may thus serve the ostensibly 'positive' function of enhancing perceptions and feelings of 'groupness', including a sense of collective pride, attachment to place and community loyalty.

In Belfast, such feelings are both reflected and intensified by processes of 'territorial personalisation' (Greenbaum and Greenbaum, 1981) by which group norms, values and history are expressed through the design and decoration of the local environment. Wall murals, such as those illustrated by Figures 3.9 and 3.11, represent a dramatic example of this process. Over the past century, many of the hundreds of murals painted on walls in Belfast and other Northern Irish cities have been connected, albeit in complex ways, to processes of group identification. For example, murals have often been painted to commemorate group achievements (such as military victories), lament suffering or injustice faced by members (such as imprisonment) or encourage collective activism (such as support for paramilitary groups). In this way, murals reveal the intimate relationship between places and identities.

Murals, however, have a darker side, and are thus the source of opposition as well as pride. Their meanings and consequences are not always as easy to interpret as they first seem. Whereas some community members identify strongly with murals and view them as valuable expressions of group culture and values, others regard them as an attempt to foist a single, homogenous identity on a more diverse collection of people. These communities are after all imagined communities. Moreover, many murals express themes that are experienced as intimidating, violent or unnecessary, even by members of the very communities that they are designed to engage. Look again, for instance, at Figure 3.11, which was produced by a paramilitary group, the Ulster Defence Association (UDA), and depicts a member of its armed wing, the Ulster Freedom Fighters (UFF). Here we find Unionist 'colours' (red, white and blue) mingled with militaristic symbolism

Figure 3.11   Loyalist wall mural, Belfast

(a gun-carrying, balaclava-wearing soldier), and accompanied by a message of political defiance. The motto of this organisation is '*Quis Separabit*', which hearkens back to the organisation's military roots. It means – no irony intended – 'who shall separate us?'.

Summary

- Segregation affects everyday connections between members of different communities and perpetuates a 'cycle of isolation' across generations.

- Residential segregation underpins many other kinds of division in education, friendships and relationships, employment and leisure.

- Fear is a key emotion underpinning segregation and boundaries – both physical and emotional – between communities can intensify, rather than alleviate, fear.

- Segregation shapes residents' sense of identity, which is often manifested visually and territorially in flags, murals and other forms of street painting.

4   Making better places

In this section, we explore different initiatives designed to make Belfast a better place to live. Places, as this chapter has shown, have their particular mix of people, activities, connections and disconnections, which make their identity. The identity of a city depends on how various people and activities relate to one another – making some kinds of connection and disconnection possible, but not others. Making better places requires attending to this complex mix. One approach to building integrated, rather than segregated, communities has involved a contested concept in social science termed 'social capital'. We will look at this concept in greater detail to see if it helps us to engage with making better places, but first we turn to developments in Northern Ireland.

4.1   A changing Belfast?

As Northern Ireland moves towards a new post-conflict era, the murals that represented overtly martial expressions of political identities are gradually being replaced with alternative representations, of which Figure 3.12 is an example. In 2006, the local government launched a programme called 'Re-imaging Communities', which aimed to move the city's visual landscape, including its 'muralscape', beyond traditional sectarian and paramilitary themes and towards more 'positive' themes (see Hill and White, 2011). This initiative has involved, for example, the removal of a number of murals of the kind represented by Figure 3.11. It has also led to several attempts to produce new kinds of murals, the images of which emphasise residents' common identity as Northern Irish rather than their sectarian identities as Catholic and Protestant, Nationalist and Loyalist. Such murals are designed to appeal to members across communities by celebrating Northern Irish sportsmen such as Rinty Monaghan (see Figure 3.12) or by depicting images emphasising the need to overcome sectarian divisions such as peace symbols or anti-sectarian marches.

In 2008, ten years after the implementation of the Good Friday Agreement and only one year after the historic power sharing in government that began in May 2007, a mural, *Painting from the Same Palette*, was unveiled at the University of Massachusetts Amherst in the USA (Figure 3.13). What was unusual about this mural was that it was painted by Danny Devenny, a former IRA prisoner and famous Republican muralist, and Mark Ervine, a famous Loyalist muralist.

Figure 3.12 Transforming Belfast's visual landscape: a new painting by Daniela Balmaverde (shown)

The two artists continued to work together on a series of murals depicting the Beatles to celebrate Liverpool's term as Capital of Culture in 2008.

Although the success of such interventions in changing ordinary people's experiences of the city has yet to be fully determined, this attempt to adapt a medium that is historically associated with the spread of sectarianism is a welcome development.

In a similar vein, other structures of segregation that are discussed in this part of the chapter are now being systematically dismantled. Initiatives such as the 'One Belfast' project aim, among other goals, to create common public space, encouraging the city's residents to interact with members of the 'other' community and to share public resources such as parks and leisure centres. Moreover, in 2012, in a historical reversal of the idea that 'good fences make good neighbours', Belfast City Council announced plans to gradually dismantle the 'peace walls' spread throughout the city, including the 'peace wall' gate that divided Alexandra Park referred to in Section 2.1. Although surveys conducted with residents who live in areas divided by such barriers suggest that the majority do not support their immediate removal, it is possible to detect a sea change in public discourse about this form of segregation, both in Belfast and other areas of Northern Ireland. Debates about whether the walls should come down are being replaced by debates

Figure 3.13   *Painting from the Same Palette* was unveiled at the University of Massachusetts Amherst in the USA

about when and how they should come down. Whatever challenges remain, the society seems to be moving towards a resolution of the problem identified by Poole and Boal in the early years of 'The Troubles':

> ... the long-term task of attempting to achieve social integration between the two religious groups is clearly rendered extremely difficult by the lack of residential mixing which would provide at least one opportunity for people from the two sides of the religious fence to meet and interact in a non-violent way. Without such residential and social mixing, there is little contact between the two religious groups but a high level of contact within each group, thus consolidating each group's solidarity and conformity and accentuating the differences, both actual and perceived, between the two groups.
>
> (Poole and Boal, 1973, pp. 2–3)

4.2   Social capital

One thing that often characterises better places is the degree to which people feel able to form friendships, meet others for social activities (such as football, bingo or chatting in a pub), or gather support in times of need. In short, it is the connections or bonds between people living in an area that are sometimes used to say whether or not it is a good place to live. Not that these bonds have to be too tight – people tend to like to be both private and public; they don't want to feel suffocated. Rather, they are ties that can be used when necessary or when desired. A term developed in the social sciences to capture some of this sociability is 'social capital'. The term generally refers to two elements:

- a set of norms and values, relating primarily to trust and cooperation
- the networks of groups and organisations that operate in that part of society, which is neither family, nor market, nor state.

(Blakeley, 2002)

The term has a long history and has been used to refer to different ideas, but relevant here is the way it was reworked and popularised by the American sociologist Robert Putnam (1993, 2000), particularly in a book about American cities where life, he argued, had often become alienating. The book's title, *Bowling Alone* (2000), communicates some of the pathos of its subjects. In these cities, the amount of social capital had decreased to almost nothing. In the case of Britain, in contrast, levels of social capital had not declined as significantly, yet Hall reported that 'the decline in social trust has been greater among the working class than the middle class' and that 'the decline in trade union membership, encouraged by the governments of the 1980s, may have taken an especially hard toll on the associational life of the working class' (Hall, 1999, pp. 432, 456). Social capital, therefore, is not necessarily evenly spread or equally experienced.

What is important for the discussion here is that, unlike other forms of capital, 'social capital inheres in the structure of relations between actors and among actors' (Coleman, 1988, p. 98). In other words, it is the quality of connections and relations among people, and the positive outcomes resulting from these interactions, which produce social capital.

The term soon took on a new life when positive correlations were found between social capital and various factors such as the quality of democracy (Putnam, 1993), economic growth and prosperity (Fukuyama, 1995), and community cohesion (Blair, 1998). A correlation describes a relationship between two measures, or variable attributes. A positive correlation is suggested when the two measures increase or decrease together (so when social capital goes up, the area is more socially integrated; when it goes down, people are less integrated). A negative correlation, in contrast, is where one variable rises as the other declines. Note that correlation is only ever a description of what is observed; it does not demonstrate that one variable causes the other to change.

However, as a result of these positive correlations, social capital soon became a favourite tool for governments, policy makers and funding agencies. The problem, however, was that although there were rough and positive correlations between, for example, the amount of social capital and the degree of community cohesion in an area, or between social capital and the degree of affluence in an area, there was nothing to suggest that social capital was the cause of either community cohesion or prosperity. What it did suggest, to policy makers and governments at any rate, was that the responsibility for solving problems like poverty or a lack of community cohesion lay not with the state, but with those experiencing these problems. The poorest sectors of society thus become responsible for solving their own problems rather than relying on the welfare state to do so. There is an echo of the Victorian doctrine of 'self-help' in all of this.

To return to Belfast, can social capital help us to understand attempts there to make better places by integrating, rather than segregating, communities? The first point to make is that it depends on what kind of social capital one is referring to. Putnam (2000) distinguished between 'bridging' and 'bonding' social capital to try to meet criticisms that some forms of social capital can be highly damaging and exclusionary. Bonding social capital creates strong in-group loyalty, which is beneficial to those inside the group, but not necessarily to those outside. Bonding social capital may well be found in the segregated communities of Belfast where feelings of belonging and being part of a group result in high levels of social capital within the group. This kind of 'bonding' social capital, however, does nothing to build connections to those outside of the group. In order to foster wider cooperation across diverse groups rather than just within them, 'bridging' social capital is required. Various organisations throughout Belfast are trying to create precisely this kind of bridging social capital. One example is the Forthspring Inter Community Group in Belfast, which aims through various initiatives to build a 'shared neighbourhood' between the predominantly Protestant/Unionist/Loyalist Woodvale Road and the predominantly Catholic/Nationalist/Republican Springfield Road. The two communities are currently divided by a 'peace wall' (Forthspring Inter Community Group, 2014).

The second issue, however, is that it is not clear how social capital is produced and maintained. This is a chicken and egg scenario. It is not clear, for example, whether social capital produces greater social cohesion or whether it is the existence of social cohesion in the first place that leads to social capital. In short, it is not clear whether social capital is a cause or an outcome of more integrated communities. Remember that correlation is not causation. What is also not clear is the extent to which bonding social capital can create bridging social capital. Samad (2013, p. 281), however, points out that the Commission for Integration and Cohesion has argued that a simple dichotomy between good and bad capital is unhelpful, not the least because bonding capital can help to create bridging capital.

A final issue to consider is the kinds of division that social capital is intended to help overcome. The emphasis of social capital on the shared norms and values that help to connect individuals with each other ignores the inequalities within society that are often inherently conflictive. This is particularly true of class inequalities where Marx would argue that the relationship between classes is necessarily antagonistic (Marx and Engels, 1998 [1848]). Ellen Meiksins Wood also highlights the distinctiveness of class inequalities, claiming that: 'A highly democratic society can celebrate diversities of lifestyles, culture, or sexual preference; but in what sense would it be "democratic" to celebrate class differences?' (Meiksins Wood, 1995, p. 258).

Class differences are by definition unequal whereas race or gender differences are not necessarily so, even if, in practice, they often are. This might suggest that there is scope to create a more integrated community in Belfast where divisions have historically been based on religion. Yet, it is important to note the extent to which sectarian divisions have never been just a matter of religious difference: rather, religious difference intersects with a range of other differences, including those of class and gender. For example, many of the interface areas in Belfast are among the most deprived neighbourhoods in

Northern Ireland (Forthspring Inter Community Group, 2011, pp. 6–7) suggesting inequality, not just difference, needs to be overcome. This intersection of differences and inequalities suggests that overcoming such divisions will be a difficult task.

Summary

- Social capital is produced through the quality of connections and relations among people, and the positive outcomes resulting from these interactions.

- Different types of social capital exist: bonding capital results from strong in-group connections while bridging capital results from interactions across diverse communities.

- Structures of segregation in Belfast are gradually being dismantled, and there are various initiatives aimed at creating social capital through increased interaction and shared common space between communities.

- Social capital can help to understand how to make connections among different groups of people; however, it is less helpful in understanding how to make connections among groups of people who are not just different, but also unequal.

Conclusion

This chapter has focused on where and how people live, and how these can make a difference to who they are. We started by looking at the processes of urbanisation and industrialisation. By looking at nineteenth-century cities, we highlighted how 'shocking' these processes were and how disruptive they were to people's existing connections and ways of living. But, we also noted that urbanisation and industrialisation were experienced unevenly. They produced class and other inequalities that became entrenched in patterns of residential segregation, which are, to some extent at least, still visible in today's contemporary cities.

We examined a case study of a segregated city in the UK where divisions have been sectarian. In this context, we examined the consequences of segregation for people's ability to live together while often living apart. This prompted us to examine how the dynamics of segregation can shape social life in cities, including people's sense of who they are and where they belong. In particular, we explored how segregation can create both connections and feelings of belonging, and disconnections and feelings of fear and separation.

Finally, we looked at recent initiatives to help people in Belfast to live together in less segregated and more integrated ways, and examined the concept of social capital as a way of trying to understand these initiatives. Doing this highlighted both the utility of this concept as well as its limitations in understanding how to make connections among people and groups who are not just different but also unequal.

References

Allport, G.W. (1954) *The Nature of Prejudice*, Garden City, NY, Doubleday.

Anderson, B. (1983) *Imagined Communities: Reflections on the Origin and Spread of Nationalism*, London, Verso.

Atkinson, R. (2003) 'Gated communities in England: final report of the gated communities in England, *New Horizons* project', London, Department for Communities and Local Government (DCLG).

Bairner, A. and Shirlow, P. (2003) 'When leisure turns to fear: fear, mobility and ethno-sectarianism in Belfast', *Leisure Studies*, vol. 22, pp. 203–21.

Belfast Interface Project (2013) *Interfaces Maps and Database – Overview* [Online]. Available at http://www.belfastinterfaceproject.org/interfaces-map-and-database-overview (Accessed 5 February 2014).

Blair, T. (1998) *The Third Way: New Politics for the New Century*, London, Fabian Pamphlet.

Blakeley, G. (2002) 'Social capital', in Blakeley, G. and Bryson, V. (eds) *Contemporary Political Concepts: A Critical Introduction*, London, Pluto Press.

Blakeley, G. and Evans, B. (2013) *The Regeneration of East Manchester*, Manchester, Manchester University Press.

Boal, F.W. (1982) 'Segregating and mixing: space and residence in Belfast', in Boal, F.W. and Douglas, J.N.H. (eds) *Integration and Division: Geographical Perspectives on the Northern Ireland Problem*, London, Academic Press Inc Ltd.

Braddock, J.H. (1980) 'The perpetuation of segregation across levels of education: a behavioral assessment of the contact-hypothesis', *Sociology of Education*, vol. 53, pp. 178–86.

Braddock, J.H. and McPartland, J.M. (1989) 'Social psychological processes that perpetuate segregation', *Journal of Black Studies*, vol. 19, pp. 267–89.

Briggs, A. (1990) *Victorian Cities*, London, Penguin.

Byrne, J., Gormley-Heenan, C. and Robinson, G. (2012) *Attitudes to Peace Walls*, Jordanstown, University of Ulster.

Cantle, T. (2001) *Community Cohesion: A Report of the Independent Review Team*, London, Home Office.

Christopher, A.J. (1994) *The Atlas of Apartheid*, London, Routledge.

Coleman, J. (1988) 'Social capital and poverty', *Social Capital Initiative*, Working paper, no. 4, Washington, DC, The World Bank.

Davis, M. (1990) *City of Quartz: Excavating the Future in Los Angeles*, London, Verso.

Dawkins, C.J. (2005) 'Evidence on the intergenerational persistence of residential segregation by race', *Urban Studies*, vol. 42, pp. 545–55.

Dixon, J. and Durrheim, K. (2003) 'Contact and the ecology of racial division: some varieties of informal segregation', *British Journal of Social Psychology*, vol. 42, pp. 1–23.

Doherty, P. and Poole, M.A. (1997) 'Ethnic segregation in Belfast, Northern Ireland, 1971–1991', *Geographical Review*, vol. 87, pp. 520–36.

Engels, F. (1969 [1845]) *The Condition of the Working Class in England*, London, Panther Books.

Falah, G. (1996) 'Living together apart: residential segregation in mixed Arab-Jewish cities in Israel', *Urban Studies*, vol. 33, pp. 823–57.

Flint, J. (2009) 'Faith and housing in England: promoting community cohesion or contributing to urban segregation?', *Journal of Ethnic and Migration Studies*, vol. 26, no. 2, pp. 257–74.

Forthspring Inter Community Group (2011) *Towards a Shared Neighbourhood* [Online]. Available at http://www.nihe.gov.uk/forthspring.pdf (Accessed 25 January 2014).

Forthspring Inter Community Group (2014) *Forthspring Inter Community Group* [Online]. Available at www.forthspring.org (Accessed 25 January 2014).

Fukuyama, F. (1995) *Trust: The Social Values and the Creation of Prosperity*, New York, Free Press.

Geography in Action (2013) *Ethnic Diversity: Segregation in Belfast* [Online]. Available at http://www.geographyinaction.co.uk/Ethnic%20Diversity/Ethnic_PeaceLines.html (Accessed 25 January 2014).

Greenbaum, P.E. and Greenbaum, S.D. (1981) 'Territorial personalization: group identity and social interaction in a Slavic-American neighborhood', *Environment and Behavior*, vol. 13, pp. 574–89.

Hall, P. (1999) 'Social capital in Britain', *British Journal of Political Science*, vol. 29, no. 3, pp. 417–61.

Hargie, O., Dickson, D. and O'Donnell, A. (2006) *Breaking Down Barriers: Sectarianism, Unemployment and the Exclusion of Disadvantaged Young People from Northern Ireland Society*, Jordanstown, University of Ulster.

Hewstone, M., Cairns, E., Voci, A., Paolini, S., McLernon, F., Crisp, R. and Niens, U. (2005) 'Intergroup contact in a divided society: challenging segregation in Northern Ireland', in Abrams, D., Marques, J.M. and Hogg, M.A. (eds) *The Social Psychology of Inclusion and Exclusion*, pp. 265–92, Philadelphia, PA, Psychology Press.

Hill, A. and White, A. (2011) 'Painting peace? Murals and the Northern Ireland peace process', *Irish Political Studies*, vol. 27, pp. 71–88.

Jarman, N. (2012) *Belfast Interfaces: Security Barriers and Defensive Use of Space*, Belfast, Belfast Interface Project (BIP).

Leonard, L. (2007) 'Trapped in space: children's accounts of risky environments', *Children and Society*, vol. 21, pp. 432–45.

Macaulay, T. (2008) *A Discussion Paper Proposing a Five Phase Process for the Removal of 'Peace Walls' in Northern Ireland*, Portstewart, Northern Ireland, Macaulay Associates Network.

Marx, K. and Engels, F. (1998 [1848]) *The Communist Manifesto*, London, Verso.

Massey, D. and Denton, N.A. (1993) *American Apartheid: Segregation and the Making of the Underclass*, Cambridge, MA, Harvard University Press.

Meiksins Wood, E. (1995) *Democracy Against Capitalism*, Cambridge, Cambridge University Press.

Mesev, V., Shirlow, P. and Downs, J. (2009) 'The geography of conflict and death in Belfast, Northern Ireland', *Annals of the Association of American Geographers*, vol. 99, pp. 893–903.

Northern Ireland Statistics and Research Agency (NISRA) (2014) *2001 Census* [Online]. Available at http://www.nisra.gov.uk/Census/2001Census.html (Accessed 23 May 2014).

Pettigrew, T.F. and Tropp, L.R. (2011) *When Groups Meet: The Dynamics of Intergroup Contact*, Philadelphia, PA, Psychology Press.

Platt, H.L. (2005) *Shock Cities: The Environmental Transformation and Reform of Manchester and Chicago*, Chicago, IL, University of Chicago Press.

Poole, M.A. and Boal, F.W. (1973) 'Religious residential segregation in Belfast in mid-1969: a multi-level analysis', in Clark, B.D. and Gleave, M.B. (eds) *Social Patterns in Cities*, pp.1–40, London, Institute of British Geographers.

Putnam, R. (1993) *Making Democracy Work: Civic Traditions in Modern Italy*, Princeton, NJ, Princeton University Press.

Putnam, R. (2000) *Bowling Alone: The Collapse and Revival of American Community*, New York, Simon and Schuster.

Samad, Y. (2013) 'Community cohesion without parallel lives in Bradford', *Patterns of Prejudice*, vol. 47, no. 3, pp. 269–87.

Schmid, K., Tausch, N., Hewstone, M., Hughes, J. and Cairns, E. (2008) 'The effects of living in segregated vs. mixed areas in Northern Ireland: a simultaneous analysis of contact and threat effects in the context of micro-level neighbourhoods', *International Journal of Conflict and Violence*, vol. 2, pp. 56–71.

Schnell, I. and Yoav, B. (2001) 'The socio-spatial isolation of agents in everyday life spaces as an aspect of segregation', *Annals of the Association of American Geographers*, vol. 91, pp. 622–36.

Tonge, J. (2001) 'Northern Ireland', in Jones, B. (ed.) *Politics UK* (4th edn), Harlow, Pearson Education.

Weber, A.F. (1899) *The Growth of Cities in the Nineteenth Century: A Study in Statistics*, Ithaca, NY, Cornell University Press.

World Health Organization (WHO) (2013) 'Urban population growth', *Global Health Observatory* [Online]. Available at http://www.who.int/gho/urban_health/situation_trends/urban_population_growth_text/en/ (Accessed 25 January 2014).

Chapter 4
Migration: changing and connecting places

Parvati Raghuram and Umut Erel

Contents

Introduction

Parvati was driving into the centre of Birmingham on a cold, wet morning in March when she saw a temporary road sign about traffic disruption in the centre of the city. Then she remembered that the St Patrick's Day parade was being held in Birmingham that day. So she abandoned her shopping trip, parked her car, took the train into the city centre and joined the approximately 10,000 people who lined the route of this parade – the third largest St Patrick's Day parade in the world. They watched and cheered the march of the Irish Guards, the floats assembled by local Irish groups such as the Birmingham Tipperary County Association, Irish community groups from other parts of the UK and even by some people who had come over from Ireland to take part in the parade. Then there was an Indian troupe performing the bhangra dance who also participated in the parade, expanding this commemoration of the presence of Irish people in the UK to a more general celebration of the city.

Figure 4.1   St Patrick's Day parade in Birmingham, 2013

Like the Chinese New Year's Day festivities, the Notting Hill Carnival and the Diwali Mela, the St Patrick's Day parade is an event associated with a group in the UK population that has links to a different place, in this case Ireland. The street is one place where migrant identities can be displayed through parades and other festivities. Yet, the street is not always a site of celebration for migrants. Migrant women are employed as sex workers in brothels on the streets of the UK (O'Connell Davidson, 2006) and migrant workers can sometimes be seen queuing for daily contract work on streets in cities around the world. Thus, the street is one site where the contradictions of migration are displayed, through, on the one hand, the celebration of the cultural and economic contributions (especially of former generations) and, on the other, the failed hopes and exploitation of recent migrants.

The street is only one site where migrants are present: they can also be found on building sites or farms, in shops and restaurants, care homes and hospitals. You can also encounter migrants less directly, through the work they do, and the products and services that they have produced, which are on offer in the shops. Some of these migrants are highly valued but others work under exploitative conditions and their work, though important to the making of British lives, may be less recognised. This chapter discusses migration and some of the varied experiences and identities that are evoked by that term when groups of people are often described in racial or ethnic terms.

Even though 'changing places' is a part of everyday life, the presence of migrants in the UK provokes mixed feelings. For instance, at the time of writing in 2013, there was considerable debate about the opening of European Union (EU) labour markets to two new EU members – the so-called 'A2 countries', Bulgaria and Romania. Some argue that there will be a large influx of new migrants, which could drive down wages in an economy that is still faltering. Others suggest that as all EU countries will allow the citizens of the new member states to come and work, the UK will only be one of the destination countries for members of these A2 countries. Romanians and Bulgarians who wish to migrate will go to join their friends and family in other European countries, where they are already established or have historical or linguistic ties.

Migration is also an issue on which people are often asked to take up positions. Migration is a frequent topic in the news (see extract below). Perhaps it helps to sell newspapers! Newspaper articles range in content from reports on new government regulations on migration to the results of new studies on how much migrants are worth to the economy. The views expressed partly depend on the paper that you pick up, but one thing is certain – many people are interested in migration.

True toll of mass migration on UK life: Half of Britons suffer under strain placed on schools, police, NHS and housing

- Half of population lives in town/city with high immigration in past decade
- Ministers say 'uncontrolled' flow has caused problems for wider society
- There's pressure on maternity services and high infectious disease rates
- Squeeze on school places and disproportionate levels of certain crimes
- Has also resulted in inflated rents and immigrants living in 'beds in sheds'.

(Source: Slack, 2013)

Migration is also important for social scientists. Topics such as identity and consumption, which you have already encountered in this module, relate to populations and in every country mobility and migration are key aspects of who makes up a population. Who has the right to reside in a country? Who belongs to it and who does it belong to? Who is valuable to a country and who is dispensable? These are all questions raised by migration and they may be the reason that feelings about migrants often seem to run high (see Figure 4.2). This chapter cannot supply you with the final answers to these questions, but it can provide some suggestions and help you to make better sense of the debates around migration as they are currently constructed.

Section 1 of this chapter looks at various different elements that make up current debates on migration. By the end of this section, you will be able to distinguish some of the ways that arguments about migration are often structured. You will see that underlying migration stories there is a 'here' and 'there' formula, which highlights the difference between migrants' places of origin and those of their destination. Sections 2 and 3 then explore other approaches to migration, which do not hold 'here' and 'there' so far apart. Section 2 looks at how places of origin and destination are connected, and how the UK's migration story can be seen as a story of connections. It considers the role played by migrant

Figure 4.2   Home Office campaign run in August 2013 encouraging immigrants to 'go home'. The campaign attracted adverse publicity and was soon dropped after accusations that it was racist

families in making connections between different places, people and lives. Section 3 sets out how migration can involve two-way connections between places through the case of the National Health Service (NHS).

1   Migration

1.1   Who exactly is a migrant?

For many people, it will seem obvious that the Irish, the Polish and the Indian bhangra troupe who participated in the St Patrick's Day parade are all migrants. However, this may not necessarily be the case. The problem is partly one of definition. Who do we mean by 'a migrant'? If we had the task of sorting people into either 'migrant' or 'non-migrant' categories, what information would we need? The following activity explores this problem.

Activity 1

Look through the list below and decide whether you think each of the people mentioned should be classified as a migrant or not.

- Person 1 was born in the UK and currently lives there. She holds a British passport. Her ethnicity is Indian.
- Person 2 lived in the UK until she was two years old. She then moved with her parents to the USA for 20 years, only moving back to the UK three years ago.
- Person 3 is the child of parents who migrated from Trinidad to the UK in 1952 when that island was still a British colony.

There is no 'right' or 'wrong' answer for each person (and you may perhaps have noticed that these descriptions could even refer to the same person). Your answers will depend on the criteria that you used to identify a migrant. You may feel that you simply did not know enough to decide. If so, think about what other information you would have wanted about each case in order to make a decision.

According to the Office for National Statistics (ONS, 2013a), a long-term international migrant is someone who intends to migrate for a period of at least one year; with short-term migrants migrating for less than one year. However, you will find that newspaper stories, government statistics and studies that report the numbers of migrants in the country all use different criteria to define a migrant. Here are some of the criteria that might be used to define a migrant:

- *Country of birth*: In this definition, a migrant is someone who lives in a different country from that in which they were born. Studies of population stocks (that is, of people who already live in a country) such as the census, often use 'foreign born' as a criterion for identifying migrants. Of course, this means that those who were born in another country but came to the UK 40 years ago and have taken up citizenship may be considered as migrants, alongside those who only arrived in the UK one or two years ago. Children of UK citizens who were born abroad could also be seen as migrants.

- *Movement*: An international long-term migrant is defined as a person who moves to a country other than that of his or her usual residence for a period of at least a year. Studies of such movements or flows often draw on the International Passenger Survey (IPS), a survey of 10 per cent of the population who are travelling through ports of entry and exit. In 2013, this survey of departures and arrivals was the only source of data available in the UK on both emigration and immigration. It asks people about their intention for stay, but does not ascertain how long people actually stay. The IPS accordingly shows that in the second quarter of 2013, 8.9 million visits to the UK by overseas residents were recorded, while UK residents made 15.9 million visits abroad; these both followed the upwards trend observed in the year's first quarter (ONS, 2013b).

- *Citizenship*: In this definition, those who reside in the country but do not have UK citizenship are considered to be migrants. As was shown in Chapter 2, people are constructed through rules and categories. The category of citizenship, and accompanying terms like 'nationals' and 'non-nationals', do not provide a sound basis for analysing migration. Migrants who have taken up UK citizenship will not be identifiable through this category while UK citizens who live abroad also get miscounted.

If we apply these definitions to the cases in Activity 1, we can see that neither Person 1 nor 3 is a migrant in the terms of the first or second definition. By the third definition, Person 1, as a holder of a British passport, is not a migrant, and to decide about Persons 2 and 3 we would need further information about their official citizenship. Because of the problems of defining a migrant, some studies combine different definitions. For example, when studying new forms of migration, it can be useful to use 'country of birth' alongside a time frame such as 'resident in the UK for ten years'. Using 'citizenship' alongside 'country of birth' can give us information on how many migrants have taken up citizenship and how many have not. The Labour Force Survey (UK Data Service, 2014) is one dataset that brings these two variables together.

You may find that it is often not very obvious what makes someone a migrant. Yet, definitional issues are often at the heart of different accounts of migration. For example, do you remember the question raised in the Introduction about who is valuable to a country? 'Value' is itself difficult to define, but even if we narrow the issue to economic value, in terms of costs or contributions to the economy, we will find that the answer varies according to the definition of a migrant. In 2006, a group critical of current immigration levels, Migration Watch, reported that migrants 'cost' the UK economy £100 million a year, including a current annual £400 million bill for unemployed EU migrants (Migration Watch UK, 2006). Yet, just a few years earlier, a government report had made the opposite claim – that migrants contribute nearly 25 times that much, £2.5 billion a year. What can explain these very different evaluations?

The answer depends, again, on who is defined as a 'migrant'. The main difference was that the report by Migration Watch included more children in its calculations. As non-workers, these children could be seen to cost the economy money, presumably for providing schooling, health care, and so on. Of course, many people would question this way of thinking of children as costs alone – and not as assets, at present or in the future – but the special point of their definition was that Migration Watch included an additional, large group of children from 'mixed households' where one parent was UK born and one parent foreign born. According to Migration Watch, there were about 750,000 such children. Including the costs of even half of these children in the calculations would have a critical influence in challenging the government's assessment that migrants made a net positive contribution to the economy.

Table 4.1   Summary of claims made about migrants and the economy

Claim	Source of claim	Definitional differences
Migrants cost the economy £100 million a year	Migration Watch (Migration Watch UK, 2006)	Counts as migrants half of the children born of one UK-born parent and one foreign-born parent (that is, children of mixed households)
Migrants are worth £2.5 billion per year to the economy	Government report (Gott and Johnston, 2002)	Does not count children of mixed households as migrants

Source: Vargas-Silva, 2013

■   Looking at Table 4.1, which claim do you find more convincing?

Whatever your answer, you can see that definitions are important. They pop up not only in migration debates, but also in the social sciences more generally, and headline-grabbing arguments can sometimes hinge just on definitions. The definition of a migrant can be used to align people on different sides of a debate. Moreover, people can adapt their definitions to suit their own purpose and to bolster their arguments. The power of migration to evoke strong emotions means that these definitional issues are particularly important.

1.2   Arrivals: from 'there' to 'here'

You read about this process of internal migration in Chapter 3.

The Introduction to this chapter referred to 'changing places' and, of course, there are many people who move from one place to another within national borders. However, almost all of the political and media focus on migration remains on international migrants. Most of these discussions centre around three aspects:

• a concern with numbers

• a categorical approach

• a value-laden approach.

We now look at each of these issues in turn. First, the issue of *numbers* and the claim often made that there are too many migrants in the country. Underlying this notion of too many migrants is the idea that there is a 'right' number and that policymakers can find this, if only they search hard for it. These ideal figures vary. Anti-immigration lobbyists might come up with a figure of zero (that is, all migration should be stopped); others might choose a higher figure. But as social scientists, it is important to note that both sides of the argument deploy the same method: a numerical approach to migration. Both those who are in favour of migration and those who are not, draw up their evidence by recording, listing and calculating numbers. Numbers sometimes suggest a degree of precision, objectivity and trustworthiness in the arguments being presented. This use of numbers reinforces the idea that migration is a matter for scientific calculation.

Economists use **cost–benefit analysis** as a systematic method for assessing and evaluating the potential costs and benefits of an activity. By deducting the costs from the benefits, a single figure – the Net Present Value (NPV) – of the impact of migration may be calculated. That is one way of deriving the value of a migrant and hence the right number and kind of migrants. It appears to be a very straightforward and thorough method for evaluating the impact of migration. But is it? In Activity 2, we ask you to evaluate two commonly ascribed impacts of migration. These impacts include both costs and benefits.

Cost–benefit analysis
A way of evaluating the potential costs (cons) and benefits (pros) of an activity, situation, event or decision.

Activity 2

Look at the impacts and indicators in the grid below. Can you think of some issues that could influence the indicators?

Impact	Indicators	Issues that could influence these indicators
Economic impacts	• Displacement of native workers • Impact on wages • Contribution of migrant workers to the economy	
Impact on consumption of public services	• Use of schools, health and social services	

The factors influencing these indicators include:

- who is defined as a migrant
- age of migrant
- projections of migrants' health
- actual data and projections of size and stage of the family
- extent to which migrants use private provision.

Other factors to consider when analysing the costs and benefits of migration are: whether migrants are skilled workers or lesser-skilled workers; the skills of the resident population; the period over which the effect on native employment is calculated, which is affected by the age of the migrant, projections of the length of time they may work, their likely income and hence the taxes they may pay; whether and when migrants may return to the countries they have migrated from. Moreover, migrants may also generate income by setting up businesses and can encourage inflow of **foreign direct investment** that is beneficial. All of these factors are also influenced by the overall state of the economy, both now and in the future. They also have to be compared to the non-migrants' effect on the economy.

Foreign direct investment
Investment made by a corporation based in one country to acquire a long-term interest in a corporation in another country.

Evidence can be used selectively to bolster arguments and even what is often seen as hard (quantitative) data can be disputed. In the example in Table 4.1, you will note that what may appear as finite numbers also conceal complex estimates about a variety of indicators, such as how long people might live or how healthy they may be, what the state of the economy might be in years to come or how many and when migrants may return. These predictions, as you can imagine, are only that – there is no certainty to them. In short, a cost–benefit analysis that comes up with what may seem like accurate figures of NPV is dependent on a large numbers of estimates. In recognition of this, after summarising existing studies and commissioning new ones, the Borders Agency concludes that the 'calculated NPV of any change to migration policy should be treated with considerable caution and given only relatively limited weight in the final decision-making process' (Migration Advisory Committee, 2012, p. 13).

Despite this uncertainty, most people believe that there is an ideal number of migrants and that it is achievable (more or less) if migration regulations are managed properly. However, given the difficulty in calculating the impact of migration and maximising its benefits in a world where borders will always be porous and regulations imperfect,

Teresa Hayter (2000), in an influential book *Open Borders: The Case Against Immigration Controls*, suggests that instead the UK should adopt open borders. She argues that the calculations, which are made in order to try to regulate migration, are about all the wrong things – instead of calculating the costs of migration, we should be calculating the costs of controlling migration: that is, of patrolling borders, surveillance and the forced return of those who are seen to be illegal.

Calculating the costs of migration would also involve recognising the costs paid by migrants themselves for obtaining information and passports, paying for travel and sometimes paying brokers who will help them to get past border controls. Others pay with their lives, trying to enter on boats that sink or in overcrowded trucks without adequate ventilation. Hayter argues that if the current expenditure on migration control were instead spent on helping the people and places from which people migrate, migration would become less of an issue. She therefore urges governments to adopt open borders. This is an example of a different form of calculating the costs of migration and is one which is often used by those who are proponents of the 'no borders position'. In addition to the costs mentioned by Hayter, here are a few of the hidden costs that we noted (you may have thought of others):

- The emotional cost to the family of migrants in being separated from them.
- The financial costs of separation, such as phone calls and visits back.
- The lost incomes where families have been divided and possibly the cost of running two households where previously there was one.
- The cost to migrants' former communities of taxes that they would have paid if they had not moved.
- The cost to the migrants' home countries of trying to manage emigration.

A second issue relating to migrants is that they are often *categorised*. You have probably noticed that many news stories refer to illegal migrants. Rights often relate to the categories of legal or illegal migrants. But what makes a migrant legal or illegal? The rights of entry, right to work, right to stay and right to form relationships are differently apportioned to people based on their citizenship. For instance, citizens of the European Economic Area (EEA) have rights to enter, stay, work and form relationships with UK citizens, while Australian citizens have rights to enter the UK but not to stay beyond a fixed period without applying for an extension of stay. Pakistani citizens have no automatic rights of entry to the UK, work or stay – they have to apply for all of these rights.

However, this has not always been the case. It was only with the Aliens Act of 1905 that the Immigration Service gained power to refuse entry to certain groups of people. It was designed, at least in part, to reduce the immigration of Jews from Russia. Commonwealth citizens had right of entry to the UK until the passage of the Commonwealth Immigrants Act in 1962. Thus, immigration rights change over time and are modified as political relations with other parts of the world alter. One of the most significant changes in the past few years is the extension of all rights to members of eight countries in Eastern Europe in 2004, and to Romania and Bulgaria in 2014. Many people who historically have not had the right to migrate to the UK, find work and stay can now do so, while others have had those rights removed.

It is not only rules that change – people's individual situations may also alter over time. For instance, someone may come to the UK to work, then meet and marry a UK or EEA national. Or a person may come to the UK as a tourist and then decide to stay on and study. Migrants who have limited permission to work may change their jobs even though their migration status does not allow them to do so, or just before Christmas they may be pressed by their employers to work a few more hours than is legally allowed. The line between legal and illegal migration is, therefore, easily crossed. It is worth noting that in Australia, US and UK nationals are among the four largest overstayers (that is, those who stay in the Australian community beyond the time period allowed by their visas). Some of them stay a few extra days or weeks without even realising it, but in crossing that time threshold, they have moved to 'illegal' status. Rights and the categorisation of migrants as 'legal' or 'illegal' are defined by the law. When migrants are discussed in terms of fixed categories (for example, in news stories about 'illegal migrants'), this does not acknowledge how regulations might change and how people might move in and out of categories over time. Perhaps a less categorical approach to migration and migration control, and more recognition of the inevitable complexities of people's lives, might be useful (Ruhs and Anderson, 2008).

"Britannia : I can no longer offer shelter to fugitives.
England is not a free country".

The Aliens Act at work.

Figure 4.3   The Aliens Act 1905 at work: a 1906 cartoon showing Britannia refusing entry to immigrants on the basis of new immigration laws

A third issue, which is closely linked to the second, is that the categories of migrants are *value-laden* – in other words, they suggest that some types of migrants are more desirable than others. However, it is not easy to define 'value'. Activity 3 shows some of the difficulties in valuing migrants.

Activity 3

Imagine that you are deciding on the value of prospective migrants to the UK (that is, people who want to migrate here). Rank the following people in order, according to the contributions they could make. Would it be possible to measure those (prospective) contributions in monetary terms or using another quantitative measure?

- ballet dancer
- cook
- nurse
- investment banker

- scientist
- student
- business woman
- footballer.

You probably found that it is not easy to rank the different occupations. Placing a figure on their value would be even harder. For instance, you might have noted that a ballet dancer has a 'cultural' value, which is difficult to count in economic terms.

The right to migrate to the UK often seems to be a kind of reward given to those who are young, have high earnings and are highly educated. The situation is similar in some other countries, including Australia, New Zealand and Canada. The argument may be that young people are desirable migrants because they have a longer working life ahead of them in which to contribute to economic growth and pay taxes, before they draw pensions or make other demands on the state. Similarly, people who can earn more will usually be seen as desirable residents because they pay higher taxes, are less likely to depend on state benefits and also contribute to the general economy through their higher spending levels.

Human capital
The economic value of the education, experience and skills of an individual.

The value placed on the education and qualifications of prospective migrants may be less obvious. One way of understanding this is through theories of **human capital**. The economist Adam Smith suggested in his book *The Wealth of Nations*, first published in 1776, that the four inputs that produce wealth are: land; buildings; machinery; and human beings. Human capital theory focuses on that fourth input and suggests that the economic performance of a person increases with their education, experience and skills. It is very difficult to count knowledge, so in effect, most countries have taken educational qualifications or skills as a measure of knowledge. They then use that measure as a central criterion in managing migration, filtering out those with less relevant or valuable skills and encouraging those with skills that (they hope) will drive economic growth. The emphasis on education has also increased in recent years, as many social scientists believe that we now live in a 'knowledge economy' in which economic advantage lies in more advanced knowledge rather than in physical labour, which may therefore be devalued.

Remember the mind and body separation discussed in Chapter 2.

Looking at the regularly updated list of shortage occupations for which immigration is permitted suggests that over the years the kinds of skill that have been valued in prospective migrants are medical, engineering, information technology, actuarial and management skills (UK Border Agency, 2013). Cleaning, caring and cooking are seen as less important to a knowledge economy. (Feminists argue that these kinds of work are not recognised as having economic value because they have conventionally been done by women within domestic environments.) However, this neat categorisation can be challenged.

Activity 4

Imagine once again that you are evaluating prospective migrants, but this time you are deciding between the following pairs of migrant workers. For each pair, which migrant do you think has skills that are more useful to the economy and why? Are any of their jobs unnecessary?

- A well-paid corporate employee from the USA who will work in the city of London *or* a cook who will be employed in the well-paid corporate employee's office restaurant.
- A nurse who will work in the NHS *or* a nurse who will work as a carer in a residential home for the elderly.
- A cook who will work in a restaurant *or* a person who will cook in his/ her employer's house as a domestic worker.
- A nanny *or* a carer who looks after old people.

You may have decided that the first person in each choice is more likely to get a visa. The well-paid corporate employee seems to be generating money; there are always shortages of nurses in the NHS; restaurants need staffing and good childcare is always in demand. However, if you think about these further, you may think that office restaurants are a necessary part of the infrastructure of working places and they too require staffing. With the second pair of migrants, the formal accreditation of skills, the place where the work is done and the extent to which nurses can take part in curative activities will all influence how we think about the skills that each migrant possesses. With the third pair of migrants, we find that when the same work is done in the public sphere, it is more valued than when it is done within people's homes. Women are also more likely to find employment as domestic workers while the cook in the restaurant is more likely to be a man. Young people are often considered to be more valuable to society than older people, so with the fourth pair of migrants, you may find that nannies and *au pairs* are considered more valuable than carers who look after older people. Based on these four examples, we can see that the value of skills seems to depend on the tasks that are done, where they are done, who does them and who they are done for. It is therefore not easy to decide whether one migrant is more necessary than another or what jobs and skills matter.

1.3   Different directions: departure and circulation

Did you notice that up to now we have concentrated almost exclusively on migrants coming into the country? It is commonplace to think that stories of migration are always stories of arrival, from 'there' to 'here', yet the UK is also the site of departure and circulation. The following activity looks more closely at some of the patterns of emigration (people moving out of the UK). Social scientists who study population (known as demographers) are interested in both the arrival of migrants and in emigration (Sriskandarajah and Drew, 2006). Some of these patterns are shown in the graph in Figure 4.4.

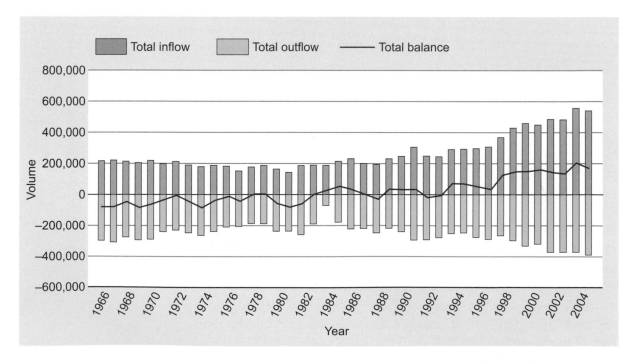

Figure 4.4   Bar chart and line graph showing annual international migration flows to the UK of all nationalities, 1966–2005 (Source: Sriskandarajah and Drew, 2006, p. 13, Table 3.1)

Activity 5

Look at Figure 4.4, showing UK immigration and emigration, and see if you can work out answers to the following questions:

* In which year did the inflow of migrants first exceed outflow?
* In which year was the outflow highest?
* To what extent do the inflow and outflow patterns mirror each other?
* Can you suggest what categories of people these flows might refer to?

Broadly, the inflow and outflow do mirror each other. There were higher flows in the late 1960s and early 1970s. Inflows exceeded outflows for the first time in 1983. The lowest flows were around 1980 but after that both emigration and immigration increased, especially after 1991. The outflow was highest in 2005.

As Sriskandarajah and Drew point out:

> Between 1996 and 2005, the UK experienced a total loss of around 2.7 million British nationals. In other words, every year for the past 40 years, around 67,500 more British nationals left the UK than came back to it. In 2005, some 198,000 British nationals are estimated to have left the UK, while some 91,000 are estimated to have returned, resulting in a net outflow of 107,000.

(Sriskandarajah and Drew, 2006, p. 13)

Figure 4.5 provides updated estimates on migration flows. It shows the long-term migration flows to and from the UK from 2003–12, including immigration (that is, people coming to the UK), emigration (that is, people leaving the UK) and net migration (the balance between arrivals and departures). As well as providing data for the whole year, government migration figures are provided in four quarters. These are based on January to March (q1), April to June (q2), July to September (q3) and October to December (q4). When you look at Figure 4.5, you will note that the data for 2003 to 2009 is only shown for quarters 2 and 4, while for 2010–12 the data for all four quarters is shown.

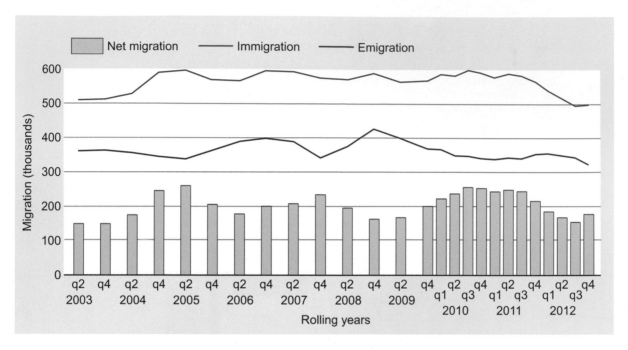

Figure 4.5   Bar chart showing long-term international migration estimates to the UK for the period of 2003–12 (Source: ONS, 2013c)

Figure 4.5 shows that in 2012, the provisional estimate of total long-term international immigration to the UK was 497,000; whereas the total long-term emigration from the UK in the same year was 321,000. Net long-term migration to the UK in 2012 therefore stood at 176,000. This contrasts with the situation in 2008, when total emigration from the UK peaked at 427,000. Similarly, the highest recorded figure for net migration was in the year 2005, when it reached 260,000 (ONS, 2013c).

The UK has the eighth largest stock of people living overseas, making it the highest among the Organisation for Economic Co-Operation and Development (OECD) countries (World Bank, 2011). Eight per cent of its citizens live abroad. Home Office figures show that emigration is also a significant dimension of migration and mobility (Home Office, 2012).

The map in Figure 4.6 shows the expatriate population and its location around the world. The size of each country has been redrawn in proportion to the size of the UK expatriate population resident there. (This type of map is called a cartogram.)

■   Can you see which countries have the highest UK expatriate population?

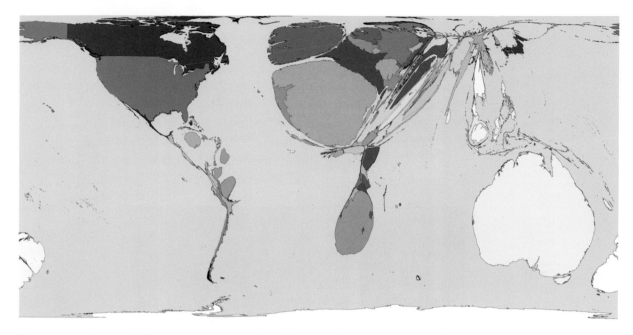

Figure 4.6   Map of UK expatriate population (Source: Worldmapper, 2006)

The five countries with the highest population of formerly British residents (counting those who have lived there for a year or more) are the ones that are largest on the map: Australia, Spain, USA, Canada and Ireland.

Although there is a popular perception that the emigration of British citizens is largely for lifestyle reasons as part of retirement migration, IPS data from 2010 (cited in Murray et al., 2012, pp. 11–12) showed that only about 3 per cent of these emigrants were above the pension age of 65 years for men and 60 years for women, while 55 per cent were in the 25–44 age group, an age when people are likely to move for employment-related reasons (Murray et al., 2012). This was also confirmed in an IPS study in 2011 (cited in Murray et al., 2012, p. 28), which showed that 72 per cent of those passengers leaving the UK were going to work abroad or look for work.

However, the IPS data is based on a sample and so is subject to the errors of any study that uses samples to estimate the behaviour of a population. One way of strengthening the accuracy of data in order to provide better evidence is to corroborate data from multiple sources. For emigration data, some of the sources are: matching of immigration data with emigration data; passport data; UK pensions data on where people draw their pensions; information on people giving up their driving licence or deregistering from their doctor before they leave.

You came across the term 'sample' in Chapter 6 of *Understanding Social Lives, Part 1.*

However, even these data sources may not always be accurate or complete, so data is extrapolated and estimated in order to come up with the figures you see above. Another aspect of migration that receives little attention is the circulation of migrants as people travel to another country for a few days, perhaps to attend a meeting or close a business deal, visit friends and family or see a few tourist spots, and then return to their base country. (The transit lounges of airports deal with an even faster circulation: the people who land for a few hours between flights, without officially entering the country at all.)

Figure 4.7   British pensioners in Spain

A large number of migrants also come to the UK for one or two years, typically moving into London offices of accountancy, management and consultancy firms before they return to offices in their home countries. They provide a layer of border-straddling managerial knowledge for companies with offices in multiple countries. Such inter-company transfers account for a large number of migrants from countries such as India, Japan and the USA (SOPEMI, 2012). In sectors of the labour market such as information and communications technology (ICT) (92 per cent), professional services (73 per cent), and financial and insurance services (63 per cent), they account for large proportions of migrants. They provide specialised on-site knowledge and expertise for specific projects for some months and may then return to their home countries and continue working on the project from a distance.

Another system that is based on circulation is the Youth Mobility Scheme. This allows young people from selected countries such as Australia, Canada, Japan and New Zealand to come and work in the UK for up to two years. They are usually employed in low-paid, lesser skilled jobs such as those in the hospitality or tourism sectors. This regulatory framework facilitates movements that in many ways are equivalent to the gap year that some UK students take when they travel abroad.

Processes of transit and circulation are not just an effect of the speeding up and ease of contemporary travel. Even in earlier times, when most travel was by ship and train, the UK was a place of transit and circulation. The ports of London, Hull and Liverpool were not only places where migrants disembarked from ships as they came to settle in the UK but also places through which migrants moved to other parts of the world. For example, between 1836 and 1914, up to 30 million Europeans moved to the USA, of whom 20 per cent travelled through

Figure 4.8   British emigrants on board the steamship *Herald Liverpool* leaving Liverpool, bound for Australia, in the early 1900s

the UK (Evans, 2001). Although large numbers arrived in the UK at this time, it was still largely a country of emigration. For example, between 1876 and 1900, about two million adult males left the UK for North America alone (Green et al., 2003).

This information about immigration and emigration might lead you to think that the whole UK population is constantly moving. However, a final point to note is that only 12.4 per cent of the population of the UK are foreign born and 7.8 per cent are registered as foreign citizens (ONS, 2013d). Although these proportions have gone up, on the whole, few people move internationally. Yet migration is an important and ongoing event that is continually making and remaking the contemporary UK through different connections, disconnections and reconnections.

Summary

- Although migration is widely discussed, the exact definition of 'a migrant' is often not specified, and different definitions are possible and in use.

- Different definitions of 'migrant' produce different quantitative evidence.

- Migration is not just about arrival, but also about departure and circulation – all of which are important features of past and present UK migration.

2   Connecting places

When people migrate, they change the places where they live. However, whether migrants come for a short or long time, they do not cut off their ties with the countries from which they came. Migrants not only make new connections in and to the places in which they stay but they also retain connections to other places, especially those from which they migrated.

2.1   Travelling goods

In the late 1990s, Umut was chatting with a friend of Turkish origin in Germany who told her that his mother was preparing for her holiday in Turkey by packing her luggage with all kinds of foodstuff. Umut wondered what kind of foodstuff he might be talking about:

Umut:	Really, what kind of things? Is she into German bread? Or Muesli?
Friend:	No, she fills her suitcase with Turkish sausages, Sucuk!
Umut *(surprised)*:	Sucuk?! But there's plenty of that in Turkey!
Friend:	Yes, but it doesn't taste as good as the ones produced in Germany – that's what she says!

They both burst out laughing.

This conversation reminded us of the 1970s and 1980s, when many migrants living in Germany used to travel 'home' to Turkey during the summer holidays. Often large families or at times several families would squeeze into one car together with their baggage fixed to roof racks. They would take presents and consumer articles such as hairdryers and television sets from Germany to Turkey. Yet, on the return journey, the roof racks would still be full. Many people took foodstuffs back 'home' to Germany: perhaps home-made cheese or pickles but also foodstuff that was readily available in Germany, such as crates of tomatoes or aubergines.

Why do you think these migrants went to all the trouble of transporting a crate of tomatoes in the summer heat on the roof rack on a journey lasting up to a week in the 1970s and 1980s? What made Umut's friend's mother pack Turkish sausages (made in Germany), when going for her holiday in Turkey in the 1990s? Both examples of carrying food from one place to another can be understood as migrant families connecting two places and, in doing so, making both of these places 'home'.

Mothers can play an important role in keeping up traditions, values and cultural practices from the home country, such as speaking the language, cooking specific food and celebrating religious, cultural or family festivals. They keep in touch with family and friends and hence play an important role in connecting people in different places. They maintain ties with the country of origin while making a home in the new place, so that their families can feel settled and safe despite the disruption of migration. By doing the housework, preparing familiar food, finding schools and making new friends, migrant mothers help their families to cope with everyday life. They create and maintain conditions that encourage their families to connect to and make a home in new surroundings (Gedalof, 2009).

Migrant mothers' work of bringing up children and creating for themselves and their families a sense of belonging is often not valued very highly. Indeed, it is often seen as simply repeating what they have learnt from their own mothers. Sometimes, these activities are seen as engaging only in the reproduction of the culture of the country of origin, rather than engaging in the production of new identities. Yet, this is a problematic distinction. Migrant women are mostly made responsible for creating a stable home in migration. These efforts require them to cope with changes both in the home and in the public sphere, so that change and repetition are intertwined. Activities such as preparing the food of 'home' in a different place, perhaps with slightly different ingredients, is an example of the ways in which repetition can produce something new.

Returning to the story about Turkish migrants carrying food from Germany to Turkey and back: for the migrants of the 1970s and 1980s, bringing tomatoes and aubergines all the way from the 'home' in Kurdistan meant re-creating the smells and tastes from there in their new 'home'. Yet, as Umut's friend's mother who filled her suitcase with German-produced 'Turkish sausage' shows, this attempt to recreate home had become a two-way process in the 1990s. What made Umut and her friend laugh in that instance was the recognition that this mother's homemaking practices had become mobile. This mother was creating a home not in one place anymore, but in the movement between the two places.

2.2 Diaspora

One way to describe the connections that the migrant families make between their old and new homes is through the term '**diaspora**', which is derived from Greek and means a dispersed population who share some common cultural elements or heritage arising from their linkages to a home – real or imagined. The term diaspora was originally used to describe the experience of Jews who were expelled from their homeland after the Babylonians' conquest of Judea in the sixth century BC. As such, diasporic populations were generally defined as forcibly displaced peoples who long to return to their homeland. However, the scope of the term diaspora has been expanded to include the experiences of a variety of migrants whose moves have been sparked by more recent processes such as slavery, colonialism and decolonisation, trade as well as refugee movements. Social scientists now discuss different categories of diaspora. For example, the Jewish diaspora is often seen as a 'victim diaspora' because of its history of expulsion. The Chinese diaspora is described as 'entrepreneurial', as many Chinese have travelled out to other countries in order to set up businesses while using links with China to help build their enterprises. What is common to these categorisations is the emphasis on a diaspora as a social group that is geographically dispersed but has some collective memory or identity in relation to the place that it left.

Diaspora
A geographically dispersed population who share some links to a common home – real or imagined.

There are several reasons for the increasing use of the term 'diaspora' and the expansion of its meaning. One is that, with **globalisation**, people, ideas, money and goods flow into and out of nations, linking and connecting places so that the role of nation states in social processes is changing. National boundaries appear to be more porous and dynamic. The term 'diaspora' is useful because it helps us to understand how people can have continuing attachments to place, which cannot be explained if we think of populations as static and territorially bound in nations. Another reason why the term 'diaspora' is useful is that it refers not only to the social consequences of migration such as diasporic networks, but also, at a more personal level, to a form of consciousness and an awareness of home. These personal feelings, identities and relationships are often deeply meaningful to migrants.

Globalisation
Refers to the process of increasing integration and interaction between different countries.

Yet, some social scientists are critical of the use of the term 'diaspora' to describe any mobile group of people because migration is such a dominant feature of the contemporary world that almost any group of people can be described as diasporic.

Activity 6

Write down your own 'migration' history. As you have read, there are different definitions of migration. Make a record of your own history of changes of residence. For example, you may have moved up the road with your parents, then moved into some shared accommodation with your friends for two years, then into a flat of your own, perhaps moving to another town when you got that good job.

Now look in your clothes cupboard and your food cupboard. Can you find any items that you think have been influenced by your history of migration?

It is likely that even if you have lived in the same place all your life, you will have experienced some mobility, and migration will have impacted on your life in different ways. Clothes might be part of your own story and part of a wider narrative about where they were made, as well as where they were bought. Similarly, food in your cupboard might reflect the places where you have lived or visited, as well as reflecting different places of origin.

2.3   Diasporic relations: making new connections and new identities

Diasporic cultural identity is often invested with a search for origins, yet it undergoes constant transformation. One example of this can be found when we consider that the idea of a homeland itself is not always straightforward. Indeed, for many migrants, the idea of a homeland is contested, particularly for refugees. Many groups become refugees because the place they see as their homeland is also claimed by other ethnic groups and they flee ethnic conflicts, such as the Tamils in Sri Lanka or Kurds in the many nations in which their homeland is located (that is, Iraq, Turkey, Iran and Syria). Kurdish people share not only language and culture but a sense of belonging to a contested homeland, including the territory known as Kurdistan, which was recognised by the Iranian government in 1970 but is not a self-governed independent state. Kurdish people are also the dominant ethnic group in parts of eastern Turkey, northern Iraq and north-western Syria. In Turkey, Kurds and Kurdish identity have not been officially recognised since the foundation of the Republic in 1923, and those publicly identifying as Kurds have been marginalised or persecuted. The most violent expression of the conflict is the Turkish state's war against Kurdish guerrillas, which has been ongoing, though intermittently, since the mid 1980s. It has cost an estimated 40,000 lives and forced internal displacement of approximately one million Kurdish villagers (ECRI, 2011).

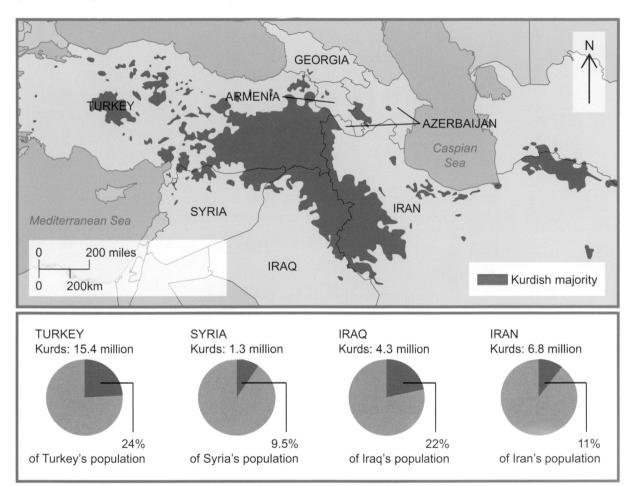

Figure 4.9   Location of Kurdish population

In the UK, the largest group of Kurds are Turkish refugees who moved to the UK since the late 1980s (Erel, 2009). Kurds from Iraq arrived as students and business people, and as refugees fleeing political persecution or the Gulf wars and their consequences. Kurds have also fled the conflict in Syria. Depending on the time and circumstances of their arrival, Kurds in the UK have different legal and residence statuses – some have arrived as asylum seekers, others as family migrants, some on business visas and some have taken on British citizenship – though the majority are refugees.

Against this backdrop, it is not surprising that some mothers explicitly state that they wanted to instil in their children a clear sense of Kurdish identity. A series of in-depth interviews (Erel, 2013) with skilled and educated migrant women from Turkey, in Germany and Britain, explored the experiences of immigrant mothers, which have hitherto received little attention. The interviews centred on the mothers' own experience and issues of how they tried to maintain Kurdish identities for their children and themselves. The research found that regularly visiting ethnically defined community centres, learning Kurdish or Turkish (that is the language with which to communicate with their relatives back home) and attending religious, political and other social events were seen as important strategies to enable such a clear Kurdish identification in their children. One of the interviewees emphasised:

> I have not changed. My ideas have not changed. I live my own culture here which I learned back home.
>
> (Evin, 39, Kurdish from Turkey, in Erel, 2013)

Evin emphasises that she has not changed herself. She also feels that she has successfully defended her children from 'anyone else's culture'. Evin is proud that she has managed to create a Kurdish identity through shared intergenerational activities, despite the disruption of migration. It is one way of connecting their place of origin with their new home in London.

Evin points out that before migration she could not publicly express her Kurdish identity:

> [In London] I am closer to my ethnic community and identity than compared to the past. This is because I am with my family [of origin]. I used to have just Turkish neighbours in Turkey and as I said, they do not like Alevis and Kurds. You have to conceal your identity in Turkey.
>
> (Evin, 39, Kurdish from Turkey, in Erel, 2013)

Coming to London has allowed Evin to openly express her Kurdish ethnic identity, not only in the private space of the home, but also in public. In Turkey, speaking Kurdish in public was illegal until the early 2000s and continues to be stigmatised in many places. Migration has allowed her to reconnect the family with their Kurdish identity.

Yet, these Kurdish mothers do not just transmit an existing cultural identity from the home country – they create a new, Kurdish cultural identification through which they connect London with their 'homes' back in Turkey. For instance, because of **assimilationist policies** in Turkey, Evin did not have a good command of the Kurdish language. However, attending Kurdish community centres, claiming a publicly visible identity as Kurdish in Britain and connecting this with particular traditions and values, are ways in which she makes new identities of Kurdishness both in London and the homelands. These Kurdish mothers make new identities for themselves and their children as British Kurds or Kurdish British.

> **Assimilationist policies**
> Policies or practices aimed at encouraging the process by which a group's language and cultural practices come to resemble those of another group.

2.4 Translocalism

In addition to the concept of diaspora, which was considered in Section 2.2, another way of understanding people's simultaneous links to more than one locality is through the concept of **translocalism**. This refers to migrants' simultaneous attachment to the places that they have left and the places they move to, as the case study on Kurdish migrants has shown. Translocalism focuses on how the links between these two places are maintained. It emphasises the many activities that migrants engage in to maintain these relations across space.

> **Translocalism**
> A way of understanding people's simultaneous links to more than one locality.

Translocal practices have become more and more common, as it has become easier to travel and keep in touch with people on the phone and internet. However, even when communication was more difficult and distances seemed larger, people kept in touch through letters and networks of friends and relatives who travelled between destination countries and countries of origin. These communication routes also encouraged and assisted newer migrants who would decide where to go, where to stay and what jobs to get.

Migration clearly connects people, places, things and cultural practices in creative ways, producing new ways of life in the process. Yet, not all people are in a position to move around freely, so disconnection is an equally important part of migration. A study of Zimbabwean asylum-seeking mothers who had left behind their children when fleeing to the

UK found that those whose claims to refugee status had not been recognised were unable to have their children join them (Madziva and Zontini, 2012). In light of the threat to violence that these migrants may face if forced to return to Zimbabwe, they are not deported but left in limbo. Because of their status, they were also unable to work for long periods so that they could not send money home to their children. Thus, they felt that they had failed in both their roles as mothers – providers of financial and emotional sustenance. Transnational mothering had become unsustainable and migration had disconnected people from their country of origin, family and an important aspect of their social identity – that of mothering. The concept of translocalism might be less helpful in understanding this context of families who 'severely struggle to operate transnationally or are broken by the migration experience' (Madziva and Zontini, 2012, p. 429).

Summary

- People who migrate to different parts of the world from the same place form a diasporic population who can maintain some connections with each other and establish new ones.

- Migration gives rise to complex global flows of goods, ideas and cultural practices, from both destination countries and countries of origin.

- Migrants can have 'translocal' connections to more than one place, but there are also disconnections.

3   Uneven connections

Migration can also establish two-way connections that make institutions and the societies in which they are located in particular ways. The NHS illustrates this two-way process. Since it was established in 1948, the NHS has provided a comprehensive service to people in the UK, 'from cradle to grave', as Aneurin Bevan, one of its chief architects, said. Most British people think that the NHS is a positive symbol of the real Britain (Jolley and Katwala, 2012) and one of the institutions that makes the contemporary UK distinctive. The NHS is a very British institution. Or is it?

Activity 7

What does Table 4.2 tell you about the importance of migrants within the NHS? Do you notice any limits to the quantitative data, such as the associated information that is *not* provided by these percentages?

Table 4.2   Percentage of NHS staff born outside of the UK in 1975

Selected medical grades	% born outside the British Isles
Consultant	14.2
Senior Registrar	27.7
Registrar	57.4
Senior House Officer	60.0
All staff	35.2

Source: Kyriakides and Virdee, 2003, p. 292

Two points of information that the figures in Table 4.2 do not provide are:

1   How many of the staff are recent migrants: Table 4.2 might include people who were born elsewhere and came to the UK a number of years ago, even as children.

2   The race and ethnicity of staff: the important point to note here is that 'migrant' status does not indicate race and ethnicity. For example, Table 4.2 will include people who were white British nationals born in countries that were former British colonies.

You read about race and ethnicity in Chapter 1.

These figures raise the question of why doctors migrate. You probably have some ideas of your own but some possible reasons are:

- There are no jobs available for them in their own countries.
- They can receive better pay in the UK.
- UK hospitals are better to work in than the hospitals in their own countries (for example because there is better equipment or more staff).
- They prefer to live in the UK (for example because it is safer than their own countries).

These factors fit with a push–pull approach to explaining migration. Migration is caused by both the factors that 'push' people away from where they currently live, such as low wages and poorly equipped workplaces, and the factors that 'pull' people to other destinations, such as better hospitals to work in and more opportunities for training.

This approach assumes that migration occurs as a result of the rational economic decisions made by individuals. In other words, people decide to migrate by weighing up the economic costs and benefits of making a move or staying, and they decide as individuals rather than larger social units (such as, say, people belonging to the Kurdish diaspora or larger population groups like the rural people who moved to British cities during the nineteenth century).

A second and rather different way of explaining medical migration would be to think of migrants as social actors (rather than isolated individuals) who are part of various social groups or networks. For example, some doctors move because other family members have moved – often their spouses, many of whom are also doctors. Existing connections between places can also shape migrations and professional networks can play an important role.

A third way of approaching migration is to look at movements of people in a longer-term historical context. A historical approach to migration shows us that if we go back far enough in time, most people have moved in some way. We can see how the Normans, Danes and Vikings, Anglo-Saxons, Romans, and before that, the Celts, were all migrants into the islands that make up the UK. Moreover, the UK as an entity only emerges well after, and in many ways because of, these migrations; it has been made up through political settlements, and by people and territory coming together over time. In sum, migration is not a one-off or spectacular event but one that, over time, may be considered quite commonplace.

A historical approach can therefore show how migrations produce the connections and disconnections that actually make places and institutions. In the case of medical migration, we know that, since its inception, the NHS has been highly dependent on migrant labour. It employs a large number of staff, including doctors and nurses. Between 1992 and 2003, 42 per cent of doctors entering the NHS obtained their primary medical qualification outside of the UK (Hann et al., 2008). They have not only staffed hospitals but also led in the development of disciplines, such as geriatric medicine and general practice. The labour of migrant staff is therefore an essential part of this national institution.

Yet, this is not just a one-way connection. The historical links of Commonwealth countries and their education systems to the UK health system meant that migrants from the UK also helped to produce the health services in other countries. For instance, the teachers in the first medical college in India were all from the UK. Migration to India also provided special opportunities for female health professionals from the UK. In 1885, Queen Victoria established the Dufferin Fund to enable women in the UK to train in medicine and then go to India to provide medical care for upper-caste Indian women who supposedly would not accept care from men during childbirth. Medical training for women had only been available in the UK since 1867. The Fund supported British women's demands for the expansion of this training. Travelling to India also enabled women medical workers to gain experience in surgery, which remained a male preserve in the UK, and to run and manage small hospitals by themselves. As a result of the opportunities that India provided, at the turn of the twentieth century as many as a third of the graduates of the Royal Free Hospital in London wanted to work there (Guha, 1998). Hence, the UK's medical history also depended on the access and experience that India gave to at least some UK-trained doctors.

But although medical migration might be a two-way connection, this is not an even or equal process and there are also disconnections. Cometto et al. (2013, p. 1) claim that together the UK, USA, Australia and Canada employ 72 per cent of all foreign-born nurses and 69 per cent of doctors working in the OECD countries. This represents a significant 'brain drain' from the countries supplying medical professionals to these more affluent countries. Some countries, for example the Philippines, export their trained health workers in order to gain economic benefit from the foreign remittances sent back (Cometto et al., 2013, p. 1). For example, the Philippine economy can benefit if its citizens who work abroad send back money to their families, particularly if it is sent back in a stable currency like the US dollar or the Euro, as this money is then spent in the Philippine economy and contributes to its growth. In many countries, however, the migration of health workers threatens their ability to meet the health care needs of their own populations and can exacerbate global health inequalities. A World Health Organization (WHO) report in 2006 claimed that 37 per cent of the world's health care professionals were living in the Americas, particularly in the USA and Canada, yet these countries suffered comparably fewer health problems than Africa, which had only 3 per cent of the world's health care workers (cited in Zubaran, 2012, p. 513).

Figure 4.10   An Asian doctor working in the NHS in the 1960s or early 1970s; and Dr Suri and his young daughter Sandhya, along with other hospital staff, in a hospital in the late 1960s. Sandhya Suri is the director of the film *I for India*, which records the experiences of both her family in the UK and of the family they left behind in India

Yet, any picture of medical migration is a moving one and different factors affect migration over time. The various European countries that joined the EU in 2004 experienced concerns about losing their doctors to the more affluent countries in the EU (British Medical Journal, 2004, p. 310) and this might yet be a concern for the A2 countries mentioned at the beginning of this chapter, Bulgaria and Romania.

Table 4.3 summarises the different approaches to understanding migration that have been discussed in this chapter.

Table 4.3 Strengths and weaknesses of the three theories of migration

Theory of migration	Strengths	Weaknesses
Push–pull	• Easy to understand • Gives due importance to economic factors	• Doesn't account for the role of social networks such as family or friends • Doesn't really take account of regulatory factors such as immigration control, which limit people's ability to move • People's decisions are sometimes made in less rational, more spontaneous or emotional ways than the theory suggests
Social networks	• Shifts the analysis away from the focus on individual choices • Explains why a group may move at the same time	• Doesn't acknowledge the influence of other factors such as better wages, better environment, and so on. (These may affect the movement of the whole social group, although individuals within it will be differently affected.) • Doesn't show the larger picture, over time
Historical –structural	• Looks at the unequal distribution of economic and political power on a worldwide basis • Takes account of established inequalities, which may take a long time to overcome	• Leads to an overemphasis on inequalities • Leaves out the people whose movements don't follow these larger patterns

Summary

- Migration can often be a two-way process that connects places and professions.

- Migrants can help to make institutions and the societies in which they are located in particular ways.

- The effects of migration are not experienced evenly, and there can be both connections and disconnections.

- There are different approaches to understanding migration and each has strengths and weaknesses, as shown in Table 4.3.

Conclusion

In this chapter, we began by looking at the importance of migration and talk about migration in everyday life, public representations and political discussions. A lot of this talk is 'polarised', presenting migration in extreme for/against, good/bad terms, so it is important for us to get behind the scenes and try to understand the issues better.

This chapter has used different theories and sorts of evidence to support the claims that are made about migration and its effects. It has included personal accounts of the experience of migration, quantitative evidence of the numbers of people who migrate, and maps that offer pictorial representations of patterns of migration.

Migration clearly matters but current discussions are somewhat limited. Migrants' contributions can be counted, categorised and valued differently, and even the definition of a migrant is unclear. Furthermore, although migration is usually talked of in terms of arrival, departure and circulation also have a role to play in making the UK. Migration does not simply tell us about movement from 'here' to 'there', but is a way of connecting people to each other and to places in various ways.

References

British Medical Journal (2004) 'Could joining EU club spell disaster for new members?', *British Medical Journal*, 7 February, vol. 328, p. 310.

Cometto, G., Tulenko, K., Muula, A.S. and Krech, R. (2013) 'Health workforce brain drain: from denouncing the challenge to solving the problem', *PLOS Medicine*, vol. 10, no. 9, pp. 1–3.

Erel, U. (2009) *Migrant Women Transforming Citizenship*, Aldershot, Ashgate.

Erel, U. (2013) 'Kurdish migrant mothers in London enacting citizenship', *Citizenship Studies*, vol. 17, no. 8, special issue *Citizenship and Reproduction/ Reproducing Citizens*, pp. 970–84.

European Commission Against Racism and Intolerance (ECRI) (2011) *ECRI Report on Turkey* [Online]. Available at http://www.coe.int/t/dghl/monitoring/ ecri/Country-by-country/Turkey/TUR-CBC-IV-2011-005-ENG.pdf (Accessed 4 March 2014).

Evans, N. (2001) 'Work in progress: indirect passage from Europe transmigration via the UK, 1836–1914', *Journal for Maritime Research*, vol. 3, no. 1, pp. 70–84.

Gedalof, I. (2009) 'Belonging and migrant mothers: narratives of reproduction in feminist migration studies', *Feminist Review*, vol. 93, pp. 81–100.

Gott, C. and Johnston, K. (2002) *The Migrant Population in the UK: Fiscal Effects*, RDS Occasional Paper 77, London, Home Office.

Green, A., MacKinnon, C. and Minns, C. (2003) 'Dominion or republic? Migrants to North America from the United Kingdom, 1870–1910', *Economic History Review*, vol. 55, no. 4, pp. 666–96.

Guha, S. (1998) 'From dais to doctors: the medicalisation of childbirth in colonial India', in Lingam, L. (ed.) *Understanding Women's Health Issues: A Reader*, New Delhi, Kali.

Hann, M., Sibbald, B. and Young, R. (2008) *Workforce Participation Among International Medical Graduates in the National Health Service of England: A Retrospective Longitudinal Study* [Online], Human Resources for Health. Available at http://www.human-resources-health.com/content/6/1/9 (Accessed 26 January 2014).

Hayter, T. (2000) *Open Borders: The Case Against Immigration Controls*, London, Pluto Press.

Home Office (2012) *Emigration from the UK*, Research Report 68 [Online]. Available at https://www.gov.uk/government/uploads/system/uploads/ attachment_data/file/116025/horr68-report.pdf (Accessed 15 November 2013).

Jolley, R. and Katwala, S. (2012) *Hopes and Fears: The British Future, State of the Nation Report*, London, British Futures.

Kyriakides, C. and Virdee, S. (2003) 'Migrant labour, racism and the British National Health Service', *Ethnicity and Health*, vol. 8, no. 4, pp. 283–305.

Madziva, R. and Zontini, E. (2012) 'Transnational mothering and forced migration: understanding the experiences of Zimbabwean mothers in the UK', *European Journal of Women's Studies*, November, vol. 19, pp. 428–43.

Migration Advisory Committee (2012) *Analysis of the Impacts of Migration*, London, UK Borders Agency.

Migration Watch UK (2006) *The Fiscal Contribution of Migrants*, briefing paper [Online]. Available at http://www.migrationwatchuk.co.uk/briefingPaper/document/12 (Accessed 4 March 2014).

Migration Watch UK (2013) *UK Taxpayer Picks Up Annual £400 Million Bill for Unemployed EU Migrants*, 17 October [Online]. Available at http://www.migrationwatchuk.org/press-release/371 (Accessed 26 January 2014).

Murray, R., Harding, D., Angus, T., Gillespie, R. and Arora, H. (2012) *Emigration from the UK*, Research Report 68, London, Home Office.

O'Connell Davidson, J. (2006) 'Will the real sex slave please stand up?', *Feminist Review*, vol. 83, pp. 4–22.

Office for National Statistics (ONS) (2013a) *Topic Guide to: International Migration* [Online]. Available at http://www.statistics.gov.uk/hub/population/migration/international-migration (Accessed 23 October 2013).

Office for National Statistics (ONS) (2013b) *Overseas Travel and Tourism, Q2 2013* [Online]. Available at http://www.ons.gov.uk/ons/dcp171776_327243.pdf (Accessed 22 October 2013).

Office for National Statistics (ONS) (2013c) *Migration Statistics Quarterly Report, August 2013* [Online]. Available at http://www.ons.gov.uk/ons/dcp171778_324444.pdf (Accessed 23 October 2013).

Office for National Statistics (ONS) (2013d) *Population by Country of Birth and Nationality Report, August 2013* [Online]. Available at http://www.ons.gov.uk/ons/dcp171776_324663.pdf (Accessed 23 October 2013).

Ruhs, M. and Anderson, B. (2008) *The Origins and Functions of Illegality in Migrant Labour Markets: An Analysis of Migrants, Employers and the State in the UK*, COMPAS Working Paper 30a, Oxford, University of Oxford.

Slack, J. (2013) 'True toll of mass migration on UK life: half of Britons suffer under strain placed on schools, police, NHS and housing' [Online], 4 July, *Mail Online*. Available at http://www.dailymail.co.uk/news/article-2355208/Toll-mass-migration-UK-life-Half-Britons-suffer-strain-places-schools-police-NHS-housing.html (Accessed 26 January 2014).

Smith, A. (1776) *An Inquiry into the Nature and Causes of the Wealth of Nations*, 2 vols, London, W. Strahan and T. Cadell.

SOPEMI (2012) *International Migration and the United Kingdom, SOPEMI Correspondent to the OECD 2012*, University College London, London; also available at http://www.geog.ucl.ac.uk/research/transnational-spaces/migration-research-unit/pdfs/sopemi-report-2012 (Accessed 15 November 2013).

Sriskandarajah, D. and Drew, C. (2006) *Brits Abroad: Mapping the Scale and Nature of British Emigration*, London, Institute for Public Policy Research.

UK Border Agency (2013) *Tier 2 Shortage Occupation List* [Online]. Available at http://www.ukba.homeoffice.gov.uk/sitecontent/documents/workingintheuk/shortageoccupationlistnov11.pdf (Accessed 26 January 2014).

UK Data Service (2014) *Catalogue: Quarterly Labour Force Survey, January–March 2013* [Online]. Available at http://discover.ukdataservice.ac.uk/Catalogue/?sn=7277&type=Data%20catalogue (Accessed 16 February 2014).

Vargas-Silva, C. (2013) *The Fiscal Impact of Immigration in the UK*, Oxford, Migration Observatory.

World Bank (2011) *Migration and Remittances Factbook 2011*, Washington, DC, The World Bank.

Worldmapper (2006) *Worldmapper: The World as You've Never Seen It* [Online]. Available at http://www.worldmapper.org (Accessed 22 July 2009).

Zubaran, C. (2012) 'The international migration of health care professionals', *Australasian Psychiatry*, vol. 20, no. 6, pp. 512–17.

Chapter 5
Reflections on 'Connecting lives'

Kath Woodward

Contents

Introduction

In this second strand, 'Connecting lives', you have encountered another set of ways of thinking about the core social science questions:

- How is society made and remade?
- How are differences and inequalities produced?
- How do social scientists know?

The focus of 'Connecting lives' has been on the wide array of relationships, attachments and associations that represents the different ways in which people's lives are connected. This ranges from intimate connections in daily life, where our sense of self is bound up with our relationships to others, to the broad span of connections that brings the rest of the world into people's lives, whether through the latest in travel and communications technologies or simply by coming across an old family photograph. Being connected has become something of a real concern to social scientists because the contemporary world is so marked by mobility and new connections, for example through the migration of people across borders and within states, and by the speed and accessibility of communication systems. Mobile phones, laptops and tablets mean that there are no boundaries around when and where communications can take place in people's 'mobile lives' (Elliott and Urry, 2010). Social scientists therefore try to understand the impact of this on people's lives, and what it means when relationships and attachments between people who are far apart can sometimes be stronger than those living next to one another on the same street. Of equal concern, however, has been the recognition that connections can be broken, ties can be dissolved and much of what is taken for granted about people's connected lives can begin to unravel.

Social scientists have come to recognise that they cannot understand one side without the other; that connections and disconnections have to be grasped both separately and together. This was the case in each of the preceding chapters, and in what follows I want to reflect on the significance of this relationship between connections and disconnections, and what it means for understanding social lives. First, though, it may be helpful to take stock of your studies thus far.

1   The story so far ... making and connecting

In the 'Making lives' strand, much was made of the fact that individuals and groups make society, yet people's lives in turn are made by society. The emphasis was on the ways in which people actively make something of themselves and, in so doing, add, no matter in how small a way, to the making of society. From one generation to the next, people live out their lives, even as the forces of history shape much of what it is possible for them to contribute to the ongoing sequence. Importantly, though, as you are no doubt aware, people do not make something of themselves or society on their own, they do so *with others*. That message, no matter how seemingly trivial, is what puts the *social* into social science. It highlights the social relationships between people, the attachments and ties that connect people to one another, which, when multiplied a thousand fold or more, start to build up a web-like image of what a society looks like if you were to look down on it from above. Connections, in that sense, take in the personal and the social, the private and the public, and the local in the global. They are the very stuff that make up the social world.

That last sentence also suggests a certain slippage in vocabulary, one that is easily glossed over. 'Society' and 'social world' are terms that are often used interchangeably, so that one can substitute for the other with no loss of meaning. When social scientists talk of a connected world or a world of connectivity, however, it is often the relationships, attachment and ties that *criss-cross* society that they have in mind. The social world, according to this view, can stretch beyond the UK and capture relationships between people and places across the globe. Equally, it can cut across communities within the UK, which previously may have been held apart, such as those divided historically by ethnicity, class or religion. Or it can cut across the boundary that marks off the self from society.

Social worlds, then, are made up of any number of cross-cutting connections. As with the 'Making lives' strand, there is an active side to the process of connecting – relationships and ties are not given; they are forged between people, although not in circumstances of their own choosing. It is therefore useful to consider the work that goes into making connections.

Activity 1

Think back across the 'Connecting lives' strand and identify some
examples of the ways in which connections are made.

There are many examples to choose from but here are a few that
sprang to my mind:

- Chapter 1 talked about the ways in which families display
  photographs to highlight which connections are important to them.

- In Chapter 2, sport was shown to make connections in numerous
  ways – whether that was connecting participants and spectators,
  connecting people through the identities they assume as fans or
  followers of particular sports, or through connecting people and
  places across the globe through mega-sporting events like the
  Olympic and Paralympic Games.

- Chapter 3 discussed initiatives in Belfast such as the Forthspring
  Inter Community Group, which helps forge connections across
  previously divided communities.

- Chapter 4 talked about the various practices of migrants to maintain
  connections to people and places left behind, while making new
  connections to the people and places where they have settled.

Together, these different examples highlight two ways in which the work
that goes into making connections happens:

1 One is the direct way in which people connect *to* others, *to* places
   and *to* their history.

2 Another, less direct, way is the number of ways in which people
   connect *through* such things as travel and communications
   technologies, of which the internet is probably the most obvious
   example.

It's worth dwelling on each of these ways of connecting in turn.

Perhaps the clearest example of the work that goes into connecting to
others is that of Goffman's (1959) dramaturgical approach (set out in
Chapter 1). This is where people perform certain roles to provide clues
about who they are and claim a particular identity, be it the 'best friend'
sharing intimate details or the more detached role of the 'neighbour'.
The stress on drama and role playing is intentional, as it conveys to

others an impression of how one would like to be seen. Equally, however, the connection only works if the performance is convincing and adheres more or less to an agreed social script about how a friend or neighbour should act in the specific social setting. Such scripted roles are the basis of social interaction, which on an everyday level involve people reflecting on what kind of impression they are making, even down to how they hold themselves, the types of gesture they make and the way that they talk. The idea that much of social life can be understood as a kind of drama, a play in which we all have scripts and roles, may seem odd at first glance but you might want to think about other social instances in the 'Connecting lives' strand where 'theatrical' props and roles also seem to apply.

The one that I have in mind are the accounts of segregation given in Chapter 3, where the dramatisation of difference and distance is played out for all to see on both sides of a divide – be it a barrier that exists in people's perceptions or one made of bricks and mortar. The significance of the wall murals in Belfast is a case in point, where the different kinds of scene depicted speak to a sense of group identity about who belongs on either side of the wall. A connection to a particular piece of territory, a specific place, is reinforced by wall murals as props, theatrical backdrops, against which people on both sides of the wall act out their respective roles, which highlight their religious differences at the expense of a whole host of other characteristics that they may possess. To find yourself on the other side of the wall is to be 'out of place', yet with an identity and role that can only be understood *in relation* to the group or groups on the opposite side. It is in that sense that the separation and differences felt by those on either side of a segregated geography are, somewhat paradoxically, also a form of connection: divided social groups can come to rely on their perceived differences from one another to reinforce a collective identity.

Connections to place, however, do not have to be based on segregation and opposition. The example of migration set out in Chapter 4 provides a quite different account of group identities formed through attachments to both the places migrated to and those left behind. The notion of diaspora captured the sense in which migrants can make connections between their old and new homes, which owe as much to continuing attachments to the family and friends left behind, as they do to the new relationships forged in their place of destination. Such connections may cut across the borders of UK society, stretching across the globe, yet the distances involved may be more social than physical, based on personal feeling and an intimate sense of culture that connects people to their place of origin. This can be thought about as a form of simultaneous attachment, a connection from one local place to another, defined in Chapter 4 by the concept of translocalism. Such connections have to be worked at – by people keeping in contact, travelling back and forth where possible, and maintaining a sense of belonging to more than one place.

This takes us closer to the ways in which people connect *through*, rather than *to*, some things. The connections involved are less direct, mediated through the likes of travel and technology. By 'mediated' here, I mean that something makes the connection for us, it brings us into contact, often collapsing the barriers of physical distance, of which the most obvious are the communications technologies that offer near instantaneous contact. The flash of email, text messages, telephone conversations, Skyped communications, and so on, brings a different meaning to the notion of simultaneous attachment. They offer the possibility for some people, not all, to communicate in something approaching 'real time', where the immediacy and speed of the connection draws people together at the same time, yet at a distance from one another. Such technological developments can help migrants to maintain a sense of connection to more than one place, but if social scientists like Manuel Castells (1996; 2009) are to be believed, they also herald a new age of connectivity, a social world of networks that brings people and places closer together. Being connected, according to this view, gives a new twist to the relationships and attachments of people who were previously far apart in terms of physical distance.

Such interactions and connections can have their own personal drama, as much as those that involve eye-to-eye contact, but they have also led some social scientists to question what is really at stake here: namely, to what extent do people actually live such connected lives? Is the degree of connectedness overblown?

1.1 Over-connected lives?

There are at least two ways to approach the question, do people in the contemporary UK live over-connected lives?

- The first is to draw attention to the number of ways in which people experience disconnection in their lives. Each of the chapters in this strand has pointed to instances of separation and division or exclusion of one kind or another, which point to the dangers of exaggerating the significance of connectedness in contemporary life.

- The second is a rather different angle and that is to flag up over-connectivity as an issue in itself, one with the potential for the rapid spread of threats and crises across the globe, as well as opportunities. The sense in which things can go 'viral' hints at the types of contagion involved, where connections can feed upon themselves.

It may be helpful to consider each approach in turn.

The first approach, which concerns the undue stress placed on connections, is countered by the simple fact that for many people connectedness is not the only thing going on in their lives, if at all. Disconnection through exclusion or the severing of ties is just as much a hallmark of the contemporary age as is connection and inclusion. The two often go hand in hand, with some groups benefiting through their connections and others experiencing harm through the disconnected nature of their lives. As stated earlier, connections and disconnections have to be grasped both separately and together, and they are not experienced evenly across society.

Activity 2

Think back across Chapters 1–4 and note down some examples of disconnections.

There are at least four examples of disconnection in Chapters 1–4 that come to mind:

- The exclusion of the Street People in New York who find themselves disconnected from the mainstream by the imposition of a negative collective identity (Chapter 1).

- There can be disconnections between what politicians promise and what is achieved, for example in the case of the Olympics and the legacy of the Games (Chapter 2).

- Living apart together in Belfast, where a sectarian geography produces segregation and separation for both communities (Chapter 3).

- The severing of ties between mother and children experienced by Zimbabwean asylum seekers who are no longer able to travel freely in their home country (Chapter 4).

Each of the above instances draws attention to the dangers of highlighting connectedness at the expense of exclusions and divisions. Moreover, as society changes, some connections may start to unravel, and ties, which were once strongly held, can loosen and dissolve, as we shall consider shortly. So some social scientists are cautious about the claims that are made over the degree to which connections are the focal point of today's world. The evidence points just as much to borders and boundaries, walls and exclusions, as it does to relationships and attachments that connect people to one another.

The second approach to the question of over-connectivity is more concerned with the information and communications technologies (ICT) that seem to affect people's lives today. The issue here, perhaps surprisingly, does not revolve around there being too much technology in people's lives. Rather, it revolves around the possible spread and proliferation of threats, as well as opportunities, that an age of over-connectedness can bring. Spurred on by the speed and rapidity of technological networks, which can reach far and wide, the potential for threats to go viral, spreading from one institution to the next, one country to another, is looked upon with a degree of trepidation. The spread of financial crises from one capitalist economy to the next is a frequently cited example (Davidow, 2011; Sampson, 2012). On the plus side, though, networked communications can hold out the possibility for social movements to mobilise people who were previously scattered far and wide to effect social change. The very same rapidity and virality that some fear can make connections between like-minded political groups to mobilise for environmental or democratic change across national borders and continents (Castells, 2012).

Social scientists make different claims about such things, pointing to different kinds of evidence to back up their views. In this respect, they are all, to varying degrees, engaging with the first of the module questions – how is society made and remade? – although now in the context of the span of connections that brings the rest of the world into the equation, as well as past historical events and disconnections.

2   Making and remaking society

The sense in which connections may cut across UK society, drawing in influences from elsewhere and being shaped by events and forces far beyond it, points to the porosity of its borders. What happens elsewhere in the world, life-changing events like wars and economic crises, can have a profound impact on the fabric of UK society. How a society changes, how its economy and culture get remade, should not in that sense be divorced from what it is connected to in terms of global markets, technological networks and patterns of migration. As noted in the 'Making lives' strand, however, such currents of change are not simply the products of the brute force of history, where their effects can be written in advance. There is always a degree of agency involved, as individuals and groups, sometimes in an attempt to avoid being crushed by life-changing events, make something of the consequences.

This struck me forcibly from some of the accounts of migration set out in Chapter 4, where wars and ethnic conflicts drove people to migrate to the UK and forced them to make something of their lives in a new country. Whether it be Kurds fleeing political persecution in Iraq, Tamils escaping from ethnic conflict in Sri Lanka or Somalis fleeing violence in their homeland, different groups of migrants have arrived in the UK in recent years and have contributed to making what had already become a multicultural UK society. The diversity of ethnic groups in the UK cannot be grasped outside of the wide-ranging connections, historical and contemporary, which connect the UK to elsewhere. Often these connections are shaped by the history of colonial relationships that were formed when a large part of the world was ruled from Britain as the imperial centre, yet new relationships are formed through contemporary processes of globalisation. The dissolution of past ties, the renegotiation of existing relationships and the making of new connections are all part of the way that lives have been remade in new settings and contexts.

Life-changing events, of course, come in many different forms, as do the consequences that flow from them. The spread of financial crises across capitalist economies mentioned above is another instance of events elsewhere having a direct impact on the lives of many in contemporary UK society. The interconnected, not necessarily over-connected, nature of markets across the globe has shaped the life chances of people in the UK, especially the young, in terms of job opportunities and local disinvestment. It may have seemed somewhat inevitable that the labour market would contract in the wake of economic recession, but there was nothing historically determined about the fact that a generation of young people would bear the brunt of such events, nor that the use of zero-hours contracts would proliferate among the most vulnerable in society. None of that was written into the script of economic crisis – such consequences involve political choices and the use of power to influence who benefits and who loses in such situations.

Not all change, however, is simply triggered by events outside of the UK. UK society may be part of an interconnected world but it would be misleading to think that significant events always take place elsewhere. Connections and ties, as mentioned earlier, criss-cross society, taking in parts of the UK while bypassing others. The 2012 London Olympics and Paralympics, events of global significance (outlined in Chapter 2), have also had local repercussions in terms of an urban remake of East London.

Activity 3

Look back at Chapter 2 and jot down some of the ways in which the 2012 Olympic Games attempted to remake parts of East London.

In some respects, it is arguably too early to say how parts of East London have been remade as a result of the Olympic Games because the legacy of this event was deemed to require a 20-year period to bear fruit. Nevertheless, the intention was to remake East London through the creation of employment, the provision of housing and the improvement of the population's health and well-being so that it would 'converge' with the more affluent west of the city within 20 years.

As a sporting event, the 2012 Olympic Games may have brought the rest of the world to London, but it was not only sporting connections that were driving it – so too were those of global investment and regeneration. 'Regeneration', for want of a better way of expressing it, is a form of an urban makeover. It holds out the promise of developing what are often run-down areas of cities to bring them into productive use, as well as benefit local residents. There were examples of urban regeneration in Chapter 2 in the context of the Olympic and Paralympic Games, and in Chapter 3 in the account of Manchester's urban development over time. Regeneration was also part of the process of bringing together divided communities in Belfast, as these sectarian communities were often also deprived communities.

In the case of London and the 2012 Olympic Games, from the very outset the bid for the Olympic Games was explicitly justified in terms of its regeneration legacy for areas of industrial wasteland with high levels of social deprivation (Poynter, 2009). The post-Games legacy, however, was always embedded within a wider network of connected developers and investors acting within and beyond London. A significant proportion of the housing in the Athletes Village, for example, was bought by Qatari Diar, the real estate arm of Qatari Investment Authority, Qatar's sovereign wealth fund and a powerful coalition of actors, involving international developers and engaging international financial interests in the negotiation of future deals. Such connections are, in many respects, characteristic of the wider influences that cut across the contemporary urban terrain, responsible for the remaking of places long considered to be disconnected from the wealthier west of the city.

Past connections and breaks are in that sense just as significant as those of the present. Social scientists are as much interested in how society and its relationships have changed over time, as they are in the make-up of today's cross-cutting arrangements. History as much as geography has a part to play in the way society gets remade through processes of connection and disconnection.

Perhaps the best example of what this involves can be seen from the example of urbanisation discussed in Chapter 3. The mass movement of people from the countryside to the towns in the nineteenth century represented a significant break from the way that people had previously lived. A process of largely internal migration, internal that is to UK society, wrought its own pattern of broken connections as well as the formation of new ties and attachments. You may recall the list of disruptions, ranging from people having to negotiate new ways of living together in greater densities as well as moving among strangers in public places, to the encounter with differences in culture, accent and religion. The shift from agricultural to factory work, and the break that represented the familiar rhythms of the working day and the tempo of the seasons, also had a profound impact on lifestyles and relationships. The concept of 'dislocation' is often used by social scientists to grasp the unsettling experience that characterises all of these broken relationships, severed connections and new attachments. It's a characteristic that can be found among many groups of people, including today's global migrants, who experience the wrench from a known past to an unknown future.

Urbanisation and industrialisation in the nineteenth-century UK developed in tandem. Today, the process of urbanisation continues to be a dislocating force, this time on a global scale, as old connections are lost or weakened and new ones forged. In the process, new patterns of inequality and difference have been thrown up to challenge the increasing mass of present-day city-dwellers.

3   How are differences and inequalities produced?

How, then, do connections and disconnections play a part in making differences and inequalities? Perhaps the answer is simple: well-connected people accumulate wealth and power (reflecting the popular sociological observation that 'it's not what you know, but who you know that counts'). In parallel, disconnected people (like the 'Street People' discussed in Chapter 1) are likely to experience marginality and exclusion, and may be treated as different from the norm. Indeed, as I was writing this chapter in 2013, there was a debate going on about the dominance of public school educated people in the UK, started by the last non-public school educated Prime Minister, John Major, who said: 'In every single sphere of British influence, the upper echelons of power in 2013 are held overwhelmingly by the privately educated or the affluent middle class' (BBC News, 2013).

You came across this dominance in Chapter 2, which showed how medal winners at the 2012 London Olympics, especially in some sports, were predominantly privately educated. The same research by the Sutton Trust (2012) also indicated that privately-educated people were over-represented in other professions, including journalism (54 per cent), and among judges (70 per cent) and Members of Parliament (MPs) (35 per cent). This view of inequality is linked to the idea of social class, which you encountered in Chapter 1.

Activity 4

What sorts of connection do you think might be involved in this class-based view of inequality?

There are several possible answers to this question because social scientists will want to distinguish between the following:

- *Family connections*: for example in terms of inherited wealth or networks of connection with similar types of people.

- *Schooling connections*: in the sense that being at public schools (Eton and Harrow, for instance) enables connections that might make career choices easier or more profitable (such connections are sometimes known as 'old boys' clubs', which also highlights the gendered nature of these inequalities).

- *Cultural connections*: sharing a common identity or attitudes and expectations (of how the world works and one's place within it).

- *Economic connections*: in the sense of shared enterprises or economic activities (as company directors, investors, and so on).

- *Political connections*: both to political parties and other groups or movements that try to shape the political direction of the country, the region and even the world.

In such ways, patterns of connection might shape this sort of inequality through which economic, social and political power becomes concentrated (and is maintained in the same way). These connections might also be associated with patterns of difference: of experience, education, culture, and even of identity. These are, after all, people who might identify with one another, recognising 'people like us'. Not all identities and patterns of difference are so directly connected to inequality. There are many types of difference that are not translated into such patterns, and which differences 'matter' in these terms vary between societies and across time.

The debate about this dominance of a public school elite in the UK also points to the implications of possible *disconnections*, not least in the claim that such shared backgrounds make it difficult for this elite to know how 'ordinary people' live and the struggles they face in everyday life. For example, in 2012 the (Conservative) MP Nadine Dorries criticised the Prime Minister David Cameron and Chancellor of the Exchequer George Osborne:

> Earlier this year, Mid-Bedfordshire MP Ms Dorries told the Financial Times that government policy was 'being run by two public school boys who don't know what it's like to go to the supermarket and have to put things back on the shelves because they can't afford it for their children's lunch boxes'.
>
> … 'Unfortunately, I think that not only are Cameron and Osborne two posh boys who don't know the price of milk, but they are two

arrogant posh boys who show no remorse, no contrition, and no passion to want to understand the lives of others – and that is their real crime.'

(BBC News, 2012)

This is one popularly expressed account of how connections and disconnections might be in play in making – and maintaining – social, economic and political inequalities. Such connections and disconnections appear as profoundly social – embedded in sets of economic, social and political relationships. Other inequalities, however, which are part of people's bodies, such as those illustrated in Chapter 2, might appear to be fixed. There is an inevitability about some of the aspects of bodies and embodiment: for example everyone ages, even if the process is experienced differently according to social and economic circumstances. Yet, the chapter demonstrated that even what appears to be fixed can be subject to all sorts of intervention by which the body can be enhanced, improved and changed. Even ageing can be changed by a variety of technical or medical interventions, from changing body parts to drug regimes.

Another aspect of the *flexibility* of bodies involves the classification processes through which people, for example athletes with disabilities, are categorised. Categories change – and indeed many social conflicts take place over such body categorisations: from types of citizenship to census identifications, or to the ways in which people have been classified as disabled (there is a long history of challenges to such terms as 'invalid' (in-valid) or 'handicapped'). Chapter 2 showed that gender categories are also subject to change. Such contestations around the terms and categories of disability demonstrate how differences (and some of the related inequalities) are constructed, even in situations where, for example, it seems as if the disability is all in the body of the person rather than shaped by social forces.

As noted at the start of this section, disconnections may lead to inequality but they are not the same as inequalities. For example, the 'Street People' discussed in Chapter 1 experience forms of disconnection – from work, from home, from networks of family or friends. Such disconnections also produce inequalities: loss of income and residence, for example, are usually conditions of poverty, or lead to people becoming poor in societies where income from work and a home are assumed to be the norm. So, Street People are likely to be poor and socially excluded – that is, treated as abnormal, deviant or 'failures'. Yet, people may connect to others who experience the same inequalities, for example through connections of social class, ethnicity, disability, race and gender. Such connections may lead to people organising to challenge the way their shared identity is linked to inequality. In such cases – from the US civil rights movement to women's movements and grassroots groups in Belfast – the object is not to change the shared identity, but to break the link that has been constructed between the identity (for example being black) and forms of inequality and exclusion (that being black should not mean being poor or excluded from social and political rights). Think about the list of inequalities that we have suggested here: class, ethnicity, race, disability and gender. They are all social categories and each of these differences may lead to unequal treatment.

What makes these differences between groups of people inequalities? At what point does a difference become an inequality? One recurring puzzle relates to pay and how reward is allocated sometimes by gender rather than according to the value of the work. Even though the Equal Pay Act was passed in 1970, there is still a 15 per cent gender pay gap. Each year, the Fawcett Society (2013), which campaigns for women's rights, identifies the day at which women stop being paid. In 2013, 7 November marked Equal Pay Day – the point in the year when women in effect 'stop earning' because of the 15 per cent gender pay gap.

In many instances of such disconnections, embodied differences are assumed, especially in sport. Chapter 2 suggested that these embodied differences were often the result of classificatory systems. Bodies are categorised and classified by social and political organisations, often using largely social criteria even though they are justified by reference to 'natural' or 'biological' characteristics. As the chapters in this strand have shown, however, there is no simple or absolute division between the 'natural' and the 'social'. Understandings of what is solely natural or biological (and therefore beyond the reach of social and political challenge or change) have been changed in many ways. For example, professions are no longer restricted to just one sex; nor is it generally assumed that boys or girls are 'naturally' better at certain subjects. Nevertheless, arguments about the superiority of one gender over another (or of one race over another or of one class over another) are still often underpinned by biological arguments.

At the time of writing, Boris Johnson, the mayor of London, gave the annual Margaret Thatcher lecture in which he 'mocked the 16 per cent "of our species" with an IQ below 85 as he called for more to be done to help the 2 per cent of the population who have an IQ above 130' (*The Guardian*, 2013). Although his comments were severely criticised by others in the coalition government, it is telling that such arguments can still be articulated publicly.

3.1   Talking about class

Differences among people can become issues of inequality and the subject of social science inquiry when the unequal treatment is justified by the difference to which it may be completely unconnected (think about whether genital differences explain the pay gap between men and women, for example).

Social class makes no such appeals to embodied differences, but it is concerned with inequalities and with connections and disconnections. How much choice do we have in determining our class? Can we change our class? Is class dependent on social and economic circumstances, and how do they influence our class position and life experiences? The concept of social class has been an important part of social science inquiry and has re-emerged in recent years as a means of explaining inequalities. What do we mean by class? Which sorts of connection are included? Is it about the work you do – or do not have? Or your pay? Or where you live? Some sociologists have tried to incorporate a whole range of factors, including the things people consume, and spend time and money on. This includes the sorts of cultural activities they enjoy, such as the sort of music they like and the sports they play or watch.

A group of sociologists (Savage et al., 2013) worked with the BBC Lab UK in 2011 to develop a class survey based on Bourdieu's (1984) approach to social and cultural capital (social – as in the connections or networks in which a person was located; cultural – questions of taste and habits, such as dressing or speaking 'well'), which looked at a person's cultural and social life as well as their economic standing. In this, Bourdieu famously extended the idea of 'capital' from its usual economic meaning (the resources of economic wealth) to other resources that people could acquire and could invest or mobilise in social life to advance or maintain their social position. Like economic capital, Bourdieu treated these other capitals as unequally distributed in society, and thereby providing forms of advantage and distinction to some groups over others. In the study by Savage et al., respondents were asked about their income, the value of their home and savings ('economic capital'), their cultural interests and activities ('cultural capital'), and the number and status of people they know ('social capital').

This survey identified seven classes based on consumption as well as economic factors (combining economic, social and cultural capital). The seven classes are:

- *Elite*: this is the most privileged class, which has high levels of all three capitals. Economic capital sets this class apart from everyone else.
- *Established middle class*: members of this class have high levels of all three capitals, although not as high as the Elite. They are a sociable and culturally engaged class.

- *Technical middle class*: this is a new, small class with high economic capital, but which seems less culturally engaged. Members have relatively few social contacts and so are less socially engaged.

- *New affluent workers*: this class has medium levels of economic capital, and higher levels of cultural and social capital. Members are a young and active group.

- *Emergent service workers*: this new class has low economic capital but has high levels of 'emerging' cultural capital and high social capital. This group is young and often found in urban areas.

- *Traditional working class*: this class has little investment in the three capitals, although they are not the poorest group. The average age of this class is older than the others.

- *Precariat*: this is the most deprived class with low levels of economic, cultural and social capital. The everyday lives of members of this class are precarious.

(BBC Science, 2013)

This classification system is strongly based on people's consumption of goods, services and cultural products. For example, liking opera can mean that you possess high cultural capital. In that respect, it reflects the interest in a 'consumer society' that you encountered in the 'Making lives' strand. Consumption has become a more important way of differentiating between people and these differences – in taste and culture – can be mapped. The study offers a careful and detailed description of life in the UK in the first part of the twenty-first century. However, for some social scientists, the theory on which it is based seems to give less weight to economic factors. As a result, it offers little analysis of how the classes relate to each other, as in the Marxist model (in which capitalists and workers are separated but linked by the process of production). It does not account for how society and the position of different groups have changed over time nor for the operation of power that shapes these classes and which separates the *precariat* at the bottom of this hierarchy. In this respect, the study gives a richly detailed mapping of one society at a particular moment in time, but is less directed at explaining this pattern or the changes that have brought it into being.

This is a characteristic tension in the social sciences: is it preferable to achieve as richly complicated an account of some aspect of social life as possible – or is it better to simplify in order to establish the main causes of the dynamics of social change? There is, of course, no simple answer, because it depends in part on the originating question or puzzle being examined. If the question is 'what sorts of classes are there in Britain today?', the approach taken will be different from the starting point of a question like 'how does class work in Britain today?'. When thinking about approaches, it can be important to see whether they are pursuing the same question – or different ones.

4   How do social scientists know?

Surveys like the one constructed by Savage and his colleagues present one way of understanding the social world by undertaking a form of social science inquiry. These sociologists started with questions about how important social class is in the contemporary UK and some tentative claims: first, about its continued relevance and importance in the twenty-first century; second, about class involving a more complex picture than the two-class Marxist model of bourgeoisie and proletariat. Savage et al. (2013) then worked out ways of trying to gather evidence that would indicate some of the complexity of what they saw as social class today in the UK. Surveys like this one are largely quantitative in their approach, although this study used focus groups and more detailed interviews to help design the questions that were used in the survey. The data generated from the survey was then used to develop the account of class today, including the process of distinguishing the different types of class (categorisation).

More often, quantitative approaches begin with already existing categories. This enables them to trace change over time – remember the study of migration in Chapter 4: are there more or fewer migrants than ten years ago? Do they come from the same points of origin as migrants of a decade ago? Studies like the population statistics collected regularly by the Office for National Statistics (ONS) and the recurring census are valuable sources of 'big data' evidence for social scientists. They often work on a scale that academic researchers typically lack the financial resources to undertake themselves, but such researchers are able to access these large studies and re-analyse the data. In doing so, they can pursue questions that were absent from the governmental concerns and objectives that shape these large-scale exercises. You may remember encountering studies that used the government's 'household expenditure survey' in your work on the 'Making lives' strand or the Active People Surveys in Chapter 2 of the 'Connecting lives' strand.

Quantitative approaches are one of the main ways of knowing in the social sciences, in part because governments – and other organisations such as the European Union (EU) and the Organisation for Economic Co-operation and Development (OECD) – regularly collect and publish large-scale data on valuable topics. But sometimes, governmental data is not collected with the questions in mind that concern social scientists. So, as in the Savage et al. study, some social scientists will find ways of collecting their own evidence. While some of this is quantitative, other studies produce and use qualitative evidence. Again, this choice of method is in part driven by the character of the question being explored. While Savage et al. were interested in the patterns of class in the UK today, there are other questions – about the experience of life in a class society or what class means to individuals – that are harder to explore in large-scale surveys. As a result, many social scientists use qualitative methods, such as open-ended questionnaires, interviews and focus groups, to explore questions of meaning and experience. In Chapter 4, you saw both sorts of evidence – quantitative data about migration (and its economic value) alongside interviews with Kurdish migrant mothers. Chapter 1 used a different sort of qualitative data – the family photograph – as a way of exploring how documents might tell researchers something about relationships, and how they are represented and remembered. Other documents (from newspaper articles to treasured household objects) provide sources through which social scientists try to understand how particular social worlds are organised and understood by those who live in them.

The 'Connecting lives' strand also made use of another particular research approach to data collection and analysis: case studies. Chapter 2 used case studies of two athletes to show the complex intersection of different social factors, such as disability, gender and class. In Chapter 3, there was a case study on urbanisation in Manchester and another on segregation in Belfast. A case study involves social scientists focusing their attention and looking in detail at a particular issue, place or event. It may involve tracing something over a period of time; it may involve looking at how an issue, place or event is connected to other issues, places and events. We can talk generally about two kinds of case study.

First, some social scientists use case studies in order to trace broader processes. So, for example, Engels looked at the detail of Manchester's urbanisation in order to say something about urbanisation more generally, and to produce a more general argument on how and why nineteenth-century urbanisation happens, and what its common characteristics or effects are. In this way, he pioneered a form of social science that uses a case study to develop arguments about broader, historical processes.

Second, case studies can be used to draw attention to the irregularities rather than the general themes of social life. They focus on social complexity, the unfinished qualities of social life. They suggest that social life is made of things that don't quite fit together. They are less happy with the notion that there are bigger forces that can be used to explain a case. Urbanisation in Manchester, in this view, involves much more than changing relationships between employers and employees. For Engels, the working-class populations of towns and cities were something of a mass. Engels had little to say about religious divisions, seemed to accede to a derogatory view of Irish immigrants and had nothing to say about gender. Later, feminist and post-colonial social scientists would go on to focus on the inconsistencies within the broad category of class.

While the emphases certainly vary, in practice most social scientists do both of these things – they look for general themes, irregularities and multiple connections. They look for patterns in their data but are aware that things may not fit, so they need to be alert to what they might miss if they become too general or too focused.

4.1 Putting evidence to work

During this strand, you have seen social scientists using a variety of evidence as they explore specific questions. Gathering and using evidence is a critical part of the process of social science inquiry – and this is reflected in the way that 'how do social scientists know?' is one of the module's recurring questions. But what is it that evidence does? Or what do social scientists do with the evidence?

These are quite difficult questions, not least because social scientists do not always signpost what they are doing. So you may not have seen many sentences that go: 'Here is my evidence … This is what it does for me and my argument'. But in all of the chapters here, you have encountered social scientists identifying issues, topics or questions – about identities, bodies, people, places, processes and experiences of migration. For each of those topics, you have seen social scientists advancing arguments or making claims about how social lives are connected – and disconnected – in particular ways. In each of those arguments, social scientists have presented evidence – evidence that advances the argument; evidence that contradicts other arguments; and evidence that raises further questions.

So, think about the evidence that you encountered about Street People and how they are viewed by others in Chapter 1. The evidence, taken from the observations made by Jonathan Raban (1991), is used to develop an argument about how identities are, in part, attributed by other people, rather than being our individual choice. This is part of a larger explanation of identity in which identity is treated as both personal and social. The evidence fills out, or gives weight to, this explanation. The evidence changes the presentation of the explanation. It moves it from being just a claim ('identity is social') to an explanation, in which claim and evidence combine: 'As you can see from these interactions, identity is social as well as personal'.

■   Can you think of any other examples of how evidence has been used in this way to advance or support an argument?

Evidence can also be used to counter some claims and explanations. Evidence plays this role because – for many topics in the social sciences – there is more than one claim or explanation at stake. Think, for example, about the arguments (both in the social sciences and in contemporary politics) about the costs and value of migration in Chapter 4. Evidence is used to support claims about how either the costs of migration outweigh the benefits, or alternatively, how the benefits of migration outweigh the costs. In such debates, we may also encounter different types of evidence, sometimes contradictory. For example, in the continuing public debate about migration to the UK, there are competing assessments of costs and benefits, as in the following example in 2013 about the numbers of new migrants arriving from new member states of the (EU), Romania and Bulgaria.

Bulgarian and Romanian migrant figures disputed

The number of new migrants arriving from Bulgaria and Romania could be as low as 20,000, a pro-migration group has said.

The estimate, by Migration Matters, disputes far higher estimates by anti-migration groups such as Migration Watch, which put the number closer to 300,000.

(Politics Home, 2013)

Encountering conflicting evidence demands that social scientists consider some important questions about how the evidence is produced. This might include some technical questions that underpin the module question 'how do social scientists know'? So, how were migrants defined in these two sets of figures? Who was counted according to what definition? How were these two sets of figures produced? From what sources? What is the purpose of seeking out this evidence? Who is finding out this evidence? This is not a matter of deciding what is true or false, but of assessing the relative value of the two sets of evidence and asking what their relationship is to the claims being made. Sometimes, evidence may form the basis of social scientists asking new questions.

Activity 5

Think back across the 'Connecting lives' strand and make a note of any other examples of the kinds of evidence that social scientists have used. How have social scientists used this evidence?

Another example is some of the evidence in Chapter 2 about classifying bodies in sport. The evidence – emerging from the processes of classifying (sex-typing or disability categorising) – poses new questions about how societies, and organisations within them, understand bodies and the identities that are attached to them. If someone does not look like women are expected to look, if she runs in a way that women are not supposed to run, then how do societies make decisions about her gender? What underlying assumptions might be at work in what is understood as a 'scientific' judgement? Here, social scientists have taken up the challenge posed by the evidence of social events, processes and judgements to ask new questions about bodies and identities.

5 Moving on

The 'Connected lives' strand has explored the sort of connections and disconnections that make society. Some connections – and disconnections – may be more important than others in the making and remaking of society. But what happens when these connections (and disconnections) do not work as they did before – or as members of the society expect them to work? Societies do not simply reproduce themselves over time, staying unchanged from one generation to the next or even from one day to the next.

Activity 6

Review the kind of connections that the 'Connecting lives' strand has explored. Then think about what happens when these connections break down. Who – or what organisations – intervenes when connections become broken or lives become disconnected?

You may have a list of connections ranging from friends and family to the police and courts; or from the grass-roots groups in Belfast to Citizens Advice or the government. You may have said that it depends on what sorts of disconnections or breaks are at stake. But the point is, such breaks and disconnections are a part of social lives – and not separate from them. Societies have informal and formal means for trying to repair such breaks, restore connections and ensure normal service will be resumed, even if such ambitions are not always achieved.

This activity highlights the connections that hold society together and make a society identifiable as such. Connections can make a society work because people know how they fit in and what is expected of them. Connections do not always work, however, and there are often disconnections between people and places, and among people, which suggest an *unfinished* story of social lives. If connections break down, it becomes more difficult for the society to hold together. So, how does society hold together through change that can be disruptive, especially given the disconnections and inequalities that persist?

The next strand looks in more detail at what sort of processes there are for ordering the connected lives that this strand has explored. The connections and disconnections between people at times of change and movement seem to require informal rules and processes that keep things going, and enable people to find ways of living together. But there are also moments when more formal rules come into play, perhaps when disorder threatens the way society is supposed to work. Making and connecting lives may also involve processes of ordering lives.

References

BBC News (2012) *MP Dorries Calls PM and Chancellor 'Arrogant Posh Boys'*, 23 April [Online]. Available at http://www.bbc.co.uk/news/uk-politics-17815769 (Accessed 26 November 2013).

BBC News (2013) *Private School Influence in Public Life 'Shocking' Says Major*, 11 November [Online]. Available at http://www.bbc.co.uk/news/uk-politics-24896266 (Accessed 25 November 2013).

BBC Science (2013) *The Great British Class Survey – Results* [Online]. Available at http://www.bbc.co.uk/science/0/21970879 (Accessed 18 March 2014).

Bourdieu, P. (1984) *Distinction: A Social Critique of the Judgement of Taste*, (trans. R. Nice), Cambridge, MA, Harvard University Press.

Castells, M. (1996) *The Rise of the Networked Society*, Oxford, Basil Blackwell.

Castells, M. (2009) *Communication Power*, Oxford, Oxford University Press.

Castells, M. (2012) *Networks of Outrage and Hope: Social Movements in the Internet Age*, Cambridge, Polity Press.

Davidow, W.H. (2011) *Overconnected: The Promise and the Threat of the Internet*, New York, Delphinium Books.

Elliott, A. and Urry, J. (2010) *Mobile Lives*, London, Routledge.

Fawcett Society (2013) *Equal Pay Day 2013* [Online]. Available at http://www.fawcettsociety.org.uk/equal-pay-day-2013/ (Accessed 28 November 2013).

Goffman, E. (1959) *The Presentation of Self in Everyday Life*, Harmondsworth, Penguin.

Politics Home (2013) *Bulgarian and Romanian Migrant Figures Disputed* [Online]. Available at http://www.politicshome.com/uk/story/36678 (Accessed 20 May 2014).

Poynter, G. (2009) 'London: preparing for the Olympics', in Poynter, G. and MacRury, I. (eds) *Olympic Cities: 2012 and the Remaking of London*, Farnham, Ashgate.

Raban, J. (1991) *Hunting Mister Heartbreak*, London, Pan.

Sampson, T.D. (2012) *Virality: Contagion Theory in the Age of Networks*, Minneapolis, MN, University of Minnesota Press.

Savage, M., Devine, F., Cunningham, N., Taylor, M., Li, Y., Hjellebrekke, J., Le Ropux, B., Friedman, S. and Miles, A. (2013) 'A new model of social class? Findings from the BBC's Great British Class Survey Experiment', *Sociology*, vol. 47, no. 2, pp. 219–50.

Sutton Trust (2012) *Over a Third of British Olympic Winners Were Privately Educated* [Online]. Available at http://www.suttontrust.com/news/news/over-a-third-of-british-olympic-winners-were-privately-educated/ (Accessed 28 November 2013).

The Guardian (2013) 'Boris Johnson invokes Thatcher spirit with greed is good speech' [Online], 23 November. Available at http://www.theguardian.com/politics/2013/nov/27/boris-johnson-thatcher-greed-good (Accessed 2 December 2013).

Ordering lives

Chapter 6
Living together, living apart: the social life of the neighbourhood

Jovan Byford

Contents

Introduction

The photographs of residential streets in Figure 6.1 have been taken at different locations in the UK. You cannot see any people in the photographs, but the houses look as if they are being lived in. We can therefore assume that they are inhabited by people who, to each other, are neighbours.

Figure 6.1   Some residential streets in the UK

However, the still images reveal virtually nothing about how residents of these **neighbourhoods** and local communities get on with one another. We cannot tell whether they know or visit each other, where and how

Neighbourhoods
Communities of *place* in contrast to communities of *interest* in which people are united by shared common characteristics other than place, such as religious belief or ethnic origin.

often they interact, whether they like each other, or indeed, whether they even care who else lives in their street. The photographs tell us nothing about the levels of community cohesion or neighbourhood satisfaction, about whether these streets are home to a harmonious tight-knit community in which people 'look out for one another', or whether every household lives in isolation from the rest of the neighbourhood. For all we know, these streets might be what the media and government sometimes refer to as a 'problem neighbourhood', in which some semblance of order can be maintained only with the help of antisocial behaviour orders (ASBOs), court injunctions and regular patrols by police community support officers.

What would you say is the best-known neighbourhood, street or local community in the UK? Most afternoons and evenings, millions of people in the UK settle in front of their TV sets to watch soap operas such as *Coronation Street*, *EastEnders* or *Neighbours*. One of the distinguishing features of the British and Australian soap opera, as a television genre, is that at the centre of the narrative is a 'local community' (Geraghty, 1991). The action in these dramas takes place in imaginary neighbourhoods, in London ('Albert Square' in *EastEnders*), Manchester ('Coronation Street' in the soap opera of the same name) or Melbourne ('Ramsay Street' in *Neighbours*). The neighbourhood is in fact the principal character in these programmes. As Suzi Hush, a former producer of *Coronation Street* explains, soaps are about an exemplary local network defined by the presence of 'gossip, curiosity and belonging' (quoted in Geraghty, 1991, p. 85). But such soap operas also suggest that life in the neighbourhood may not be entirely comfortable – disputes, tensions, fights and fallings out all feature as part of the dramatic landscape.

Figure 6.2   The UK's best-known street?

Because most people have neighbours somewhere nearby, the everyday practice of being a neighbour is often taken for granted. After all, human beings are believed to be intrinsically 'social animals' to whom living with and relating to others comes naturally. This implies something about the concept of social order – the idea that social life, while being unpredictable, fluid and ever-changing, is *not* disordered for most of the time. Order exists because people have shared knowledge about how everyday life and social interaction should proceed, and they use this knowledge to create and maintain order. For example, most people in this society know how to behave in a supermarket, street, cinema or library. Individuals act differently in the company of a boss, friend, neighbour or child because each of the relational identities that are taken up in those interactions ('employee', 'friend', 'neighbour', 'parent') has associated with it a distinct set of rules, habits and conventions. Life in the neighbourhood is similarly ordered and

You were introduced to relational identities in Chapter 1.

structured. It has its own norms, rules and customs; we might call these the 'grammar' of neighbouring.

As this chapter will show, living together with neighbours is not at all straightforward or easy. Take another look at the photographs in Figure 6.1. Part of any street's infrastructure are timber fences, hedges, walls, gates, doors, locks, curtains and other structural artefacts that are designed to keep residents *apart* rather than to bring them *together*. The expression 'good fences make good neighbours', which you may have heard, captures the essence of a paradox that permeates life in every neighbourhood. On the one hand, neighbourhoods are, or at least expected to be, communities of people living together, while on the other hand they are a collection of distinct spaces inhabited by individuals, families and households whose privacy is guarded from intrusion by outsiders, including neighbours.

Remember the street infrastructure in some areas of Belfast where the phrase 'good fences make good neighbours' was taken literally.

I became acutely aware of this paradox of contemporary neighbouring when my partner and I were buying our first home. As we viewed dozens of properties on the market, we noticed that sellers and estate agents, when making their sales pitch, often mentioned how great 'the neighbourhood' was. What they were selling was not just a roof over our heads, the bricks and mortar of our first home, but also a relationship with people living in the same street. What was interesting, however, was that more often than not the description of our prospective 'neighbourhood' contained within it a fundamental contradiction. On the one hand, we were told that 'the next-door neighbours are really nice and quiet – most of the time you wouldn't know that they are there', while at the same time, we were being assured that 'in this street there is a real sense of community'. Thus, neighbours were said to provide the sought-after sense of solidarity, security and proximity associated with the word 'community', but they were apparently able to do so while being virtually invisible!

Much of the social life of a neighbourhood – that is, what people *do* as neighbours and what they *expect* of neighbours – can be said to reflect this paradox. As the subsequent sections show, different aspects of neighbouring – from everyday mundane interactions (Section 1), through neighbourhood complaints (Section 2), to responses to dramatic instances of violent crime in the street (Section 3) – all revolve around the need to manage and negotiate living together and living apart.

Neighbours, in enacting the relational identity of 'a neighbour', are continuously engaged in the process of constructing, modifying, breaching and repairing boundaries, both physical and symbolic, between the 'home' and the 'street', and between 'public' and 'private' spaces. In this chapter, we explore how this is achieved, and how some semblance of social order and communal life in the street emerges from continuous negotiation and adjustment.

1   Everybody needs good neighbours?

In recent decades, sociologists, geographers, anthropologists and environmental psychologists have all been involved with the study of neighbourhoods. They have been interested in exploring neighbouring networks and practices, and assessing their meaning and significance in contemporary society. The questions in Activity 1 reflect some of the issues that have attracted interest from social scientists conducting research in this area.

A consistent finding in social science research on neighbouring in the UK relates to the question 'what makes a good neighbour?'. Studies conducted over the years in a variety of different settings found widespread agreement with regard to what residents in a neighbourhood want from those living around them. Neighbours are expected to have a 'general disposition towards friendliness' while, at the same time, respecting others' 'need for privacy and reserve' (Willmott, 1986, p. 55).

A neighbour is supposed to be 'available in times of trouble', 'friendly' and 'a bit of a giver', but they should also 'mind their own business' and not be 'intrusive' (Crow et al., 2002, p. 136). A range of studies conducted in the 1980s found that the principal neighbourly characteristics highlighted by the British public were, on the one hand, friendliness and helpfulness and, on the other hand, distance (Abrams and Brown, 1984). This finding is not unique to the UK: virtually identical conclusions were reached by researchers in the USA. In New York in the 1970s, neighbours were expected to be 'friendly', but without 'intruding on one's privacy' (McGahan, 1972, p. 402).

One conclusion that emerges from these findings is that the definition of a 'good neighbour' revolves around the division between private and public domains. Being friendly without being intrusive and distant without becoming a stranger requires neighbours to constantly negotiate the fine line between, on the one hand, their own and others' demands for privacy and, on the other hand, the need to live together and foster a sense of 'community'.

Activity 2

How do you think neighbours can achieve this balance between being a 'busybody' and a 'nobody' in the street (Crow et al., 2002)? Think back to your answers to Activity 1. Do they suggest any unwritten rules that operate in neighbouring practices?

Rules governing appropriate conduct in the neighbourhood are not contained in any special 'code of conduct' or manual that gets placed on the doorstep when a person moves into a new home. Instead, what people have is culturally specific knowledge about how to interact with those living around them. They acquire and develop this knowledge through socialisation – through the practice of being a neighbour. Most people have been neighbours and have had neighbours since birth, so they have had plenty of opportunities to pick up the necessary skills and become versed in 'being neighbourly'. Thus, when people move to a new home, even though they may not know their neighbours, they will nevertheless have some idea about how to meet, greet and interact with them, as well as about what might be expected from them as neighbours.

You came across the concept of socialisation in Chapter 4 of *Understanding Social Lives, Part 1*.

1.1 The geography of neighbouring: between public and private spaces

The unwritten rules of neighbouring – including the requirement to be friendly but without undermining the privacy of others – operate in the mundane practices of everyday life in the street, which are, for the most part, performed automatically, without conscious thought. They determine, for instance, when, where and how neighbours interact. In Activity 1, you were asked to consider where and when you talk with your neighbours. Did you mention, as I did, things like 'in front of the house', 'in the drive', 'over the garden fence', 'in the street' or 'in the local shop'? These answers indicate that my interaction with neighbours is confined mainly to public spaces (the street or a shop) or is across a physical structure (a fence or wall) that delineates the boundary between our private spaces: namely, our homes.

A 2004 study of neighbouring relations in Manchester suggests that this is quite a widespread practice. Residents reported that they communicated with neighbours primarily outside of the home. They told researchers things like, 'If I go out of the house and I see them, I'll chat with them. But we don't go in each other's houses' or 'We don't neighbour in each other's houses' (Harris and Gale, 2004, p. 34). Even those interviewees who reported visiting or being visited by their neighbours displayed an awareness of the danger of 'over-neighbouring'. The frequency and length of neighbourly visits were mediated by the need to be seen to respect the host's right to privacy.

Social anthropologist Kate Fox's (2004) light-hearted book *Watching the English: The Hidden Rules of English Behaviour* offers an interesting example of what we might call the 'geography' of everyday neighbourly interaction. Despite Fox's title, much of what she says, including the extract that follows, can be said to apply beyond England to other parts of the UK. Among the different spaces where neighbouring takes place, Fox identifies the 'front garden' as a typical venue for social interaction among residents of a street:

> A person busy in his or her front garden is regarded as socially 'available', and neighbours who would never dream of knocking on your front door may stop for a chat (almost invariably beginning with a comment on the weather or a polite remark about your garden). In fact, I know of many streets in which people who have an important matter to discuss with a neighbour (such as an application for a planning permission) or a message to convey, will wait patiently – sometimes for days or weeks – until they spot the

neighbour in question working in his front garden, rather than committing the 'intrusion' of actually ringing the door bell.

(Fox, 2004, p. 126)

Fox's somewhat caricatured account of neighbouring contains an important observation. The front of the house (even where there is no front garden as such) constitutes the interface between the public space of the street and the private domain of the home. In the UK, it is not all that common to see people sitting and relaxing in front of their house in the way that they would inside their home or in the more private back garden. This is because the front of the house – being visible from the street – is for the most part thought to be too public for what are perceived to be private activities, such as sunbathing, taking a nap or having a meal. At the same time, the front garden is not a public space in the true sense of the word. In most cases, it is closed off from the street by a boundary marker in the form of a fence or a hedge. Fox's (2004) reference to the front garden as a habitual space for social interaction reflects its status as something of a 'grey area' in terms of public/private, home/street division. It is a venue where neighbours can safely interact with each other without having to worry that intrusion or invasion of privacy will occur. While 'neighbouring in each other's houses' opens the possibility of 'over-neighbouring', doing so in front of the houses is evidently much less problematic.

1.2   The timing of neighbouring interaction: neighbouring as an occasioned activity

An ethnographic study conducted in a British suburb described neighbouring as, above all, an 'occasioned activity' (Laurier et al., 2002). Neighbours tend to exchange pleasantries with each other when they happen to meet in a public place (or the front garden, the drive, or a corridor in a block of flats), but ringing the neighbour's doorbell is usually associated with a specific reason, including misdirected post, a missing pet, an unexpected shortage of milk or sugar, or some kind of emergency.

Activity 3

Think back to an occasion when you knocked on a neighbour's door or they knocked on yours. Can you remember what was said when the door was answered? What reason did you or the neighbour give?

A neighbour recently came to my front door after a courier delivered a parcel to the wrong address and my neighbour found herself in possession of items that I had ordered from an internet bookseller. Here is how our conversation over the doorstep went:

Neighbour: Hi, Mr Byford?

Me: Yeees …

Neighbour: I'm sorry to bother you. I live over there in Cherry Avenue.

Me: Oh hello.

Neighbour: I just came over to bring you this. They accidentally delivered it to 15 Cherry Avenue, rather than Cherry Grove.

Me: Oh! Thank you very much! That's very kind of you! These things happen, I suppose, when they don't read the label properly.

Neighbour: Yes, that's right.

Me: Thanks for bringing it around.

Neighbour: No problem. Bye now.

Me: Bye … Thank you.

Let us look more closely at this brief interaction. To do this we will use a discursive psychological approach, which involves examining ordinary talk and everyday social interaction to see how identity work and self-presentation are accomplished. As people enact particular identities, they also maintain and repair order in society because they reproduce and enforce patterns of behaviour and expectations associated with that identity. Every knock on a neighbour's door and the ensuing, often brief, interaction is an enactment and a display of the relational identity of 'neighbour', inevitably reflecting the implicit 'code of conduct' of good neighbouring.

Look back to what my neighbour said. After ensuring that she is talking to the right person ('Hi, Mr Byford?'), the next thing she says is 'I'm sorry to bother you'. This is a fairly routine greeting in such encounters, even among neighbours who know each other fairly well. The regularity with which it occurs reflects its underlying social function. It constitutes a subtle way of acknowledging that the unexpected arrival of a neighbour on the doorstep might be seen as an 'intrusion', an invasion of private space, both in a physical and symbolic sense. My neighbour's apologetic and polite greeting implicitly acknowledges my right to privacy, and recognises that a knock on the door might be interpreted as an infringement of that right.

The next sentence is similarly revealing: 'I live over there in Cherry Avenue'. This establishes the caller's identity as a neighbour. The category 'neighbour' carries with it certain entitlements. In contrast to a representative of the gas company eager for me to change supplier, or a door-to-door salesperson offering cleaning products, a neighbour, when they knock on someone's door, can expect to be listened to courteously. After all, the norm that neighbours should be friendly and helpful to each other is one of the principal rules of neighbouring. By identifying herself as a neighbour, the caller invokes my response of 'Oh hello' rather than the much less courteous 'Thanks, but no thanks!' with which I usually greet door-to-door salespeople. This sentence is therefore not just a piece of factual information about where the caller lives; it is a way of invoking a particular relational identity and initiating a mode of conduct associated with 'friendliness', or at least civility.

My neighbour's third utterance in our brief conversation reveals the actual reason why she knocked on my door, saying 'I just came over to bring you this' effectively pre-empts a possible question such as 'how can I help you?' or 'what can I do for you?'. In other words, both of us, as skilled neighbours, were aware that knocking on someone's door is usually an 'occasioned activity' for which there ought to be a logical reason, usually a minor favour. I was expecting a reason and the neighbour provided one without me having to prompt her.

So, in a few fairly routine sentences, probably uttered automatically, without careful consideration, the basic principles of neighbouring were played out – my right to privacy was acknowledged, the assumption that neighbours are to be treated in a friendly and helpful manner was invoked, and the expectation that interaction between neighbours is purposeful and occasioned was met. Note that I did not invite the neighbour to come inside the house. I am quite sure that she did not expect to be invited in either. The place of our interaction, over the doorstep and across the boundary between the outside and inside of my home, reinforced the required standards for friendliness and distance that are enshrined in neighbouring relations and which govern even such mundane, routine interactions.

1.3   Different forms of neighbouring

You encountered the various ways in which people live together, yet apart, in Chapter 3.

Nevertheless, different societies have developed different styles and habits of neighbouring. For example, gated communities try to create a type of neighbourhood from which 'bad influences' and people who are 'not like us' can be excluded by fences, gates and security staff. In an ethnographic study of gated communities in the USA, Setha Low (2003) has argued that they are:

> Redefining the meaning of 'community' to include protective physical boundaries that determine who is inside and who is outside. … Gated community residents are interested in 'community', but a specific kind of community that includes protecting children and keeping out crime and others while at the same time controlling the environment and the quality of services. The 'community' they are searching for is one imagined from childhood or some idealized past. In a variety of ways, these residents are all searching for their version of the perfect community, one where there is no fear, no crime, no kidnapping, no 'other' people, where there is a reassuringly consistent architectural and physical landscape, amenities and services that work, and great neighbours who want exactly the same things.

> Gated community residents use gates to create the community they are searching for. But their personal housing decisions have had unintended social consequences. Most important, they are disruptive of other people's ability to experience 'community': community in the sense of an integration of the suburb and the city, community in terms of access to open public space, and community within the American tradition of racial and ethnic integration and social justice.

> Architecture and the layout of towns and suburbs provide anchoring points of people's everyday life. These anchoring points reinforce our ideas about society at large. Gated communities and the social segregation and exclusion they materially represent make

sense of and even rationalize problems Americans have with race, class and gender inequality and social discrimination. The gated community contributes to a geography of social relations that produces fear and anxiety simply by locating a person's home and place identity in a secured enclave, gated, guarded and locked.

(Low, 2003, pp. 229–31)

Here is a distinctive form of neighbourhood and a set of neighbourly relations that seeks a particular type of social order. Low's ethnographic study is interesting because she points to a paradox: that the search for order and security might itself create, or deepen, anxieties and fears among the residents.

Other types of neighbouring have also been associated with anxiety and fear. In the Soviet bloc after the Second World War, people were often fearful about their neighbours, suspecting that they might be reporting on their behaviours and beliefs to 'the authorities'. Such suspicions conditioned the relationships and interactions between neighbours, putting a certain sort of social and political distance into the spaces of proximity (see, for example, Funder, 2003). In a different study of housing in East Germany (the former German Democratic Republic), Völker and Flap (1997) suggest that what they describe as 'shallow and homogeneous neighbourhood networks' were an 'unintended effect of the party's political control of private life' (1997, p. 241). They argue that 'one would be unlikely to invest in relations that posed a threat and with individuals one did not trust, such as neighbours, who were dissimilar to oneself and who, because they lived next-door, knew about one's private life as well' (1997, p. 241). In such examples, we can see that neighbourhoods – and the relationships between neighbours – can take different forms, with different combinations of proximity and distance, and different attempts to manage the relationships between private and public.

Summary

- Neighbouring – the practices of being a 'good neighbour' – involves a paradox: good neighbours are expected to be friendly but not intrusive, requiring a balance of proximity and distance.

- Neighbouring works across public and private spaces, linking or bridging them in particular ways.

- Neighbouring is an 'occasioned activity', with unwritten rules governing its timing and conduct.

- The expectations, unwritten rules and practices of neighbouring vary considerably between societies.

2   When neighbouring goes wrong: disorders in the neighbourhood

The previous section noted that the rules that guide life in the neighbourhood are not set in stone. The boundaries between helpfulness and distance, friendliness and intrusiveness, are often fuzzy and subject to interpretation. When neighbours cannot agree on a particular interpretation of neighbouring rules, disputes arise. Because disputes between neighbours are invariably about an alleged violation of some rule of neighbouring etiquette, they provide a useful insight into the way in which social order in the neighbourhood is made and remade. In this section, we will look at a discursive psychological study that examined mediation sessions aimed at resolving neighbourhood disputes.

2.1   Dealing with 'noisy neighbours': studying neighbourhood complaints

■   What do you think are the main causes of disputes between neighbours?

According to the Citizens Advice service, the most common sources of breakdown in neighbouring relations in the UK are disputes over space (boundaries, high hedges, parking space, and so on) and 'noise'. News reports and TV shows often show 'neighbours from hell' who listen to loud heavy metal music, or own dogs that bark in the night. However, the noisy neighbour problem is more complex than that because noise is not a value-neutral phenomenon definable solely through the measurement of volume. It is sometimes about *what* neighbours can hear.

Social psychologist Elizabeth Stokoe (2006) examined neighbourhood complaints about a very specific noise: namely, the sounds of sexual intercourse emanating from 'next door'. What makes this type of noise the subject of neighbourhood complaint is often not the volume, but the fact that the sound itself – because of its normatively private nature – seems to violate the neighbours' private space. The widely held expectation that neighbours should maintain distance includes keeping private activities private.

In her study, Stokoe looked at transcripts from recordings of mediation sessions involving complaints about intimate noises. (A transcript is a written record of talk, of the kind discussed in Section 1.2 of this chapter.) She found that making a complaint of this nature is rarely straightforward. Taking up the government advice and simply talking about the problem can be difficult. This is at least partly because the complaint itself could be interpreted as infringing the neighbour's right to privacy, like a meddling attempt to interfere in someone's freedom to behave as they wish in their own home. What is more, any display of knowledge about what goes on in next door's bedroom leaves the person making the complaint open to accusations that they acquired that knowledge through excessive curiosity and nosiness.

Stokoe examined how neighbours in dispute managed and negotiated the various problems and difficulties associated with making and responding to complaints about intimate noises. Consider the following extract from a mediation session in which a neighbour is discussing with two mediators the conduct of a couple next door that gave rise to their complaint:

> We still talk to next door don't get us wrong, we're not uh, you know, we're not sort of walking by or whatever else, but that was basically the final straw wasn't it, but we put up with very bad language hadn't we, effing and blinding and on three occasions we've had to come in from the garden because, how shall we – well in a delicate way of saying the young lady's love making next door with all the windows open, you know, you wouldn't have known more of what was going on if you'd have been actually in the room.
>
> (Stokoe, 2006, Paragraph 1.1)

The extract is interesting for several reasons. First, before describing the behaviour about which he complained, the speaker presents himself and his cohabitants as good, reasonable and tolerant neighbours. They are doing everything that neighbours are expected to do: they 'talk to next door', they are not 'walking by', they even tolerate 'bad language'. The speaker emphasises the issue of tolerance by stating that he did not complain straight away: his family retreated ('had to come in from the garden') three times before finally going to the authorities. Thus, in giving an account of the activities of the inconsiderate 'young lady' and her partner, the speaker also describes his actions as those of the good neighbour.

Second, note that in making the complaint, the emphasis is placed not so much on the activity itself (love making), but on the neighbours' failure to take the necessary steps to minimise the intrusion on others. The focus of the complaint is making love with 'all the windows open'. By suggesting that 'you wouldn't have known more of what was going on if you'd have been actually in the room', the neighbour making the complaint implies that he and his family were not being 'nosy neighbours', eavesdropping on the young couple. Rather, they could not help hearing what they heard. The complaint is that their privacy had been invaded and their routine (sitting in the garden) disturbed by the insensitive and inconsiderate neighbours.

What this extract shows is that the very act of making a complaint about neighbours involves a negotiation of what constitutes appropriate conduct. There is a description of what neighbouring *should* be like: neighbours should speak to each other on the street, they should be friendly and courteous, they should be tolerant and put up with occasional transgression, but also considerate to others and take every step to ensure that their private activities do not encroach on others.

Therefore, underpinning the dispute about a specific case of a 'young lady's love making' was a wider debate about what constitutes 'normal, innocuous and reasonable versus abnormal, provocative and unreasonable behaviour' in the neighbourhood (Stokoe, 2006, Paragraph 3.30). In that sense, complaints, disputes and neighbourhood mediation are all essentially about creating, reproducing and reinforcing the neighbourhood's social order.

2.2 'Distancing mechanisms': dealing with neighbourhood noise without complaining

As you might imagine, neighbourhood noise is not a new problem. In her book on the history of working-class cultures in Britain, Joanna Bourke (1994) notes that, in the late 1940s and early 1950s, in working-class estates that suffered from overcrowding and where inadequate housing resulted in poor sound insulation between adjoining homes, residents regularly heard more than they wanted from 'next door':

Neighbours complained about knowing too much about each other's intimate lives: 'you can even hear them use the [bedside] pot', blushed one woman ... Others deplored hearing neighbours talk in bed: 'You sometimes hear them say rather private things, as, for example, a man telling his wife that her feet are cold. It makes you feel that *you* must say private things in a whisper'.

(Bourke, 1994, p. 142)

There is little evidence to suggest that the residents of the estates mentioned by Bourke complained to the authorities about their noisy neighbours. They certainly did not have at their disposal a sophisticated, government-sponsored mediation process. In fact, you can see in the above quotation that residents were as concerned about the potential embarrassment of being overheard as they were about hearing what their neighbours were up to. So, in order to cope with the chronic lack of privacy, neighbours developed various 'distancing mechanisms' (Bourke, 1994, p. 142). They made minor adjustments to daily life in order to minimise intrusion. It was not uncommon, for instance, for conjugal beds to be 'turned away from the party-wall, so that "embarrassing noises" would not be heard' (p. 143). By physically moving their beds, neighbours endeavoured to create the optimal levels of 'distance' needed for good neighbourly relations to be maintained.

The various distancing mechanisms (which developed spontaneously and over time) reflect the very same neighbouring rules alluded to in the disputes examined by Elizabeth Stokoe (2006). In both instances, there is an underlying assumption that neighbours have the freedom to do what they like in their homes, provided that they take the necessary steps to minimise intrusion on those who live nearby. Furniture arrangement in the 1950s and the more formal neighbourhood complaints and mediation today are underpinned by the same underlying social function: to manage living, at the same time, both together and apart.

Summary

- Life in the neighbourhood is ordered and structured. There are rules, habits and conventions – the 'grammar' of neighbouring – which regulate how people live together and interact in the street.

- Social order in the neighbourhood is made and remade even in the most mundane neighbouring practices – it determines where and how neighbours meet and talk to each other.

- One way of studying social order in the neighbourhood, and how it is reproduced, is to look at what happens when it breaks down; that is, when disputes arise between neighbours, for instance about noise.

- Complaints, just like mundane interactions between neighbours, are about negotiating what being a 'good neighbour' is, and how a balance can be struck between the demands for 'privacy' and 'community'.

- Underpinning life in the neighbourhood is the need to manage the boundary between private and public spaces, and between home and the neighbourhood.

3   Neighbours: between bystanders and intruders

The social order of the neighbourhood is not just negotiated spontaneously in everyday social interaction, or more formally through neighbourhood mediation. Neighbourhoods are a popular topic of wider public discussion and a favourite target for policy makers. There is currently a government department in charge of 'communities and local government' whose remit includes 'helping communities and neighbourhoods to solve their own problems so neighbourhoods are strong, attractive and thriving' (Department for Communities and Local Government, 2013). Also, the UK media write and broadcast about 'problem neighbourhoods', helping to perpetuate the culturally available assumptions about how neighbours should conduct themselves. Neighbourhoods are typically presented as places that ought to offer a sense of belonging, solidarity, proximity (psychological as well as physical), equality and security, but also tolerance, acceptance and a respect for autonomy, privacy and independence.

One of the most basic assumptions about the function of the neighbourhood is that it should offer a sense of security to its residents. A 2001 government survey found that 84 per cent of respondents defined the 'neighbourhood' as a place where people 'look out for each other' (Attwood et al., 2003, p. 58). Authors of the Manchester neighbourliness study (who published their findings under the title *Looking Out for Each Other*) also found that respondents spoke of their neighbourhood as a 'safety zone' and as providing a 'sense of protection' (Harris and Gale, 2004, p. 16). All this suggests that, within the culturally available assumptions about neighbouring, looking out for one another is regarded as an intrinsic part of what it means to live together.

Because of the importance of security in popular understandings of neighbourliness, instances where specific neighbourhoods apparently fail to fulfil the prescribed protective role attract considerable attention and controversy. This is the case, for instance, when the inattention of neighbours seems to have allowed violent crimes to be committed. In this section we examine two specific examples, one from the USA and one from the UK, and explore what they can tell us about how people live together in contemporary society.

3.1   Victims of dysfunctional neighbourhoods? Catherine Genovese and James Bulger

One of the most widely reported cases of a 'neighbourhood crime' is the murder in New York, in 1964, of a young woman called Catherine 'Kitty' Genovese. She was attacked in the street where she lived late one night as she was returning home from work. During the attack, which lasted for more than half an hour, she was stabbed several times before she died, virtually on her doorstep. During the subsequent police inquiry, it emerged that the assault had been noticed by 38 residents of her street. Witnesses heard Catherine Genovese scream for help and some even observed the attack from their windows. And yet, apart from a single person who yelled at the attacker to 'leave the girl alone', none intervened to help the young woman. Eventually, one of the neighbours called the police, but by then Genovese was already dead. The coroner later stated that she would have survived had the ambulance arrived only minutes earlier (Rosenthal, 2008 [1964]).

Figure 6.3   The scene of Catherine Genovese's murder

In the 1960s, murders in New York's suburbs were so common that they were not widely reported, but the Catherine Genovese story made the front page of the *New York Times*. As well as receiving huge press attention, her tragic death was later turned into a play, a feature film and a book. Many saw in the event not just a tragic end to a young life, but also the failure of a modern neighbourhood and local community to fulfil the duty of care expected of neighbours. Commentators, journalists and professionals blamed the actions of 'indifferent' bystanders on a broader social problem, a 'Cold Society' populated by a new breed of selfish city-dweller, alienated from the community and oblivious to responsibilities towards fellow citizens (see Rosenthal, 2008 [1964]).

Periodic anxiety about the failure of the neighbourhood is not unique to the American press. Almost 30 years after the Genovese case, similar debates occurred in the British media following the abduction and murder of the three-year-old James Bulger. In February 1993, he was taken from the Strand shopping mall in Merseyside by two ten-year-olds, Jon Thompson and Robert Venables. After leaving the shopping centre, the two boys walked with James through the suburbs of Bootle and Walton for over two hours, before taking him to an isolated section of railway track where they killed him.

The murder of James Bulger and the subsequent trial of the killers attracted unprecedented media attention both in the UK and abroad. Much of the astonishment and public outrage associated with the case was provoked by its most unusual and shocking feature: namely, the fact that the killers were only ten years old. However, this was not the only aspect of the case that attracted press attention. During the trial of Venables and Thompson in November 1993, 38 members of the public appeared in court and testified that they saw the three boys as they walked through the streets of Merseyside. (It is a curious coincidence that the same number of bystanders – 38 – were present in both the Bulger and the Genovese cases.) Most of the eye-witnesses reported that they were aware that James Bulger was in distress. Some stated that they were concerned at the time that the older boys were too young to be left in charge of a toddler without adult supervision. Others remembered observing inappropriate behaviour towards James: the older boys were said to have been 'rough'; the three-year-old was seen being 'dragged' and even 'kicked' by one of the accused. And yet only a couple of witnesses reported challenging Venables and Thompson, urging them to take the injured child to his mother. None of the 38 'bystanders' intervened in a manner that might have prevented the tragic outcome of the abduction.

Figure 6.4 CCTV footage of James Bulger being taken away by his abductors from the Strand shopping centre

The apparent indifference of the 38 witnesses was instantly pounced on by the media. The newspapers branded the witnesses the 'Liverpool 38', 'the ones who saw but didn't act' (Morrison, 1996, p. 68), who 'passed by on the other side and who allowed it to happen' (Horan, 1993, p. 25). An editorial in *The Guardian* ('Lessons of an avoidable tragedy', 1993, p. 25) wondered 'Does no one "have a go" any more?', implying that the 38 bystanders should have intervened to protect the young child from harm. Although the witnesses were not James Bulger's immediate neighbours, their failure to intervene was interpreted as the violation of the norm that all of us, as good neighbours, responsible citizens and members of the community, sharing a common space, walking the same streets and living together, ought to look out for each other and especially for the most vulnerable members of society: children. Just as in the Genovese case, the conduct of the 'Liverpool 38' was interpreted as a breach of a social norm governing life in and on the street.

Activity 4

- Why do you think bystanders did not intervene to help Catherine Genovese or James Bulger?
- Do you think the same reasons applied in each case?

The murders of James Bulger and Catherine Genovese both prompted social psychological research on 'bystander intervention' to investigate the factors that determine whether onlookers (including neighbours) will or will not assist someone in an emergency situation. In the rest of this section, we will explore two specific psychological studies: one from the

1960s, which followed the murder of Catherine Genovese, and the other from the 1990s, which deals directly with the James Bulger case. We will look at the insight they provide into bystander responses to real-life crimes and at two possible explanations for the 'malfunction' of neighbourhood norms that the murders were said to have exposed. The two studies used very different methods to investigate the topic of bystander behaviour, so you will be introduced to two different approaches to social psychological research.

3.2   Experimenting with emergencies: from the neighbourhood to the laboratory and back

In the aftermath of the murder of Catherine Genovese, two American psychologists, Bibb Latané and John Darley, sought to explain the failure of the 38 bystanders to intervene and stop the attack. They argued against the dominant media accounts, which focused on the alleged 'apathy' of the neighbours (Latané and Darley, 1970). Latané and Darley pointed out that Genovese's neighbours were, in fact, not at all 'apathetic' or 'indifferent'. Contrary to what was reported in the media, they were disturbed by what they witnessed, and at the time of the attack they were sincerely concerned for the welfare of the young woman. The problem was that none of them did anything about it, at least not until it was too late. Therefore, the whole issue was not about what the bystanders thought or felt at the time of the murder (i.e. whether they were 'indifferent' or 'apathetic'), but about their failure to act (i.e. their 'unresponsiveness'). Furthermore, Latané and Darley proposed that what happened in Catherine Genovese's street had nothing to do with the supposedly alienated, self-centred and 'un-neighbourly' residents of New York's suburbs. In their view, this was a manifestation of a broader phenomenon: namely, how people respond to an emergency situation. As Latané and Darley put it, regardless of whether we are talking about a neighbourhood crime, a car accident, a fire or an instance of drowning or attempted suicide, the reality is that, when faced with an emergency, 'people sometimes help and sometimes don't'. What they were interested in was 'what determines when help will be given?' (Latané and Darley, 1970, p. 4).

You came across the concept of alienation in Chapter 3.

One specific issue about the Genovese case that Latané and Darley explored in their research was the widespread assumption that the sheer number of bystanders (38) makes their inaction more surprising and worthy of scorn, as if one passive bystander would have been excusable, but 38 could not be forgiven for their unresponsiveness. Latané and

Darley decided to test whether and in what way the presence of other bystanders in an emergency situation affects the likelihood of intervention. Are people more likely to intervene in an emergency if they are the only witness, or if there is at least one other person present?

'Lady in distress'

Latané's and Darley's research consisted of a series of cleverly designed and carefully controlled experiments. Each **experiment** consisted of a simulated 'emergency situation' (such as an epileptic seizure, an accident at work or a fire) staged in a laboratory. The pretend 'emergencies' were witnessed by people who are known in psychology as 'participants' (or 'subjects', as they were called in the 1960s). These were members of the public (mainly psychology undergraduates) who agreed to take part in the study, but who did not know what the experiment was about or that the event in question was staged. In each study, Latané and Darley systematically varied or 'manipulated' the experimental situation, including the number of other bystanders present.

Let us look in more detail at one of the experiments, which Latané, Darley and their colleague Judith Rodin called 'lady in distress'. In this study, participants were invited, either individually or in pairs, to take part in a study, which they were led to believe was about 'market research'. This was just a cover story, a minor deception used to entice prospective participants into the laboratory without having to tell them what the study was actually about. At the start of the experiment, each participant was greeted by a female 'market research representative'. The woman was a 'confederate' of the experimenters – that is, someone who acted with them in order to create the deception. She gave the participants a bogus 'market research questionnaire' to fill out, and then left the room. Shortly afterwards, the following happened:

> While they worked on their questionnaires, subjects heard the representative moving around in the next office, shuffling papers, and opening and closing drawers. After about four minutes, if they were listening carefully, they heard her climb up on a chair to get a book from the top shelf. Even if they were not listening carefully, they heard a loud crash and a woman scream as the chair fell over. 'Oh my God, my foot …' cried the representative. 'I … I … can't move … it. Oh, my ankle. I … can't … can't … get this thing off… me'. She moaned and cried for about a minute longer,

Experiment
A research method used to investigate the effect of one variable on another. It examines whether two variables (events, properties, characteristics or behaviours) are causally related.

getting gradually more subdued and controlled. Finally, she muttered something about getting outside, knocked the chair around as she pulled herself up, and limped out, closing the door behind her.

(Latané and Darley, 1970, p. 58)

The sounds from 'next door', the moans and the cries, were in fact pre-recorded and played from a tape. This ensured that each of the hundred or so participants who took part in the study had an identical experience of the 'emergency'.

The procedure was repeated over a hundred times, once for each participant, with only a very slight variation. As part of the study, the researchers varied the conditions in which those taking part heard the sounds of distress. In the original study there were four different variations, or 'conditions', but for the purposes of this chapter, we will look at three of them.

- In the first variation, 26 participants were alone in the room when they heard the 'emergency' next door. The researchers called this the 'Alone condition'.

- A further 14 participants were in the room with one other person, another confederate of the experimenter who was pretending to be a participant, but who was instructed to ignore the sound from next door and do nothing. This was labelled the 'Passive confederate condition'.

- In the third variation, participants took part in the experiment in pairs. This means that two participants who did not know each other and were both oblivious to the deception, were in the room together, filling out the bogus questionnaire when they heard the 'screams' from next door. Forty participants took part in this condition, divided into 20 pairs. The experimenters called this the 'Two strangers condition'.

During the experiment, researchers recorded the number of participants in each of the conditions who abandoned the 'market research questionnaire' and went out to assist the 'lady in distress' within the predetermined time limit of two minutes. Results from the three conditions were then compared in order to see whether there was a difference in responses. Latané, Darley and Rodin wanted to determine whether the experimental manipulation (presence of others) affected the readiness of 'bystanders' to help.

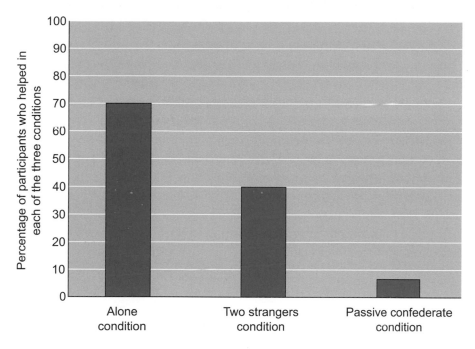

Figure 6.5   Graph representing the results of the 'lady in distress' experiment (Source: based on Latané and Darley, 1970)

Activity 5

Can you, just by looking at the graph in Figure 6.5, work out the findings of the 'lady in distress' study?

Along the horizontal axis (the x-axis) are three bars, each representing one of the conditions ('Alone', 'Two strangers' and 'Passive confederate') that were established for the experiment by Latané, Darley and Rodin. The vertical axis (the y-axis), which determines the size of the bars, indicates the percentage of participants (on a scale from 0 to 100) who responded in the emergency.

- Which condition yielded the highest rate of response?
- Which yielded the lowest?
- Try to express these findings as a sentence (or two), rather than as a graph.

This activity should take you no more than five minutes to complete.

How did you get on with Activity 5? You probably spotted that the tallest bar represents the results from the 'Alone condition'. Indeed, in this condition, where participants witnessed the emergency on their own, as many as 70 per cent (18 out of the 26 participants) intervened to help the 'victim' within two minutes of hearing the emergency. In the 'Two strangers condition', where two participants who did not know each other were together in the room, one of them intervened in only 40 per cent of the cases (8 out of 20 pairs). This is quite a dramatic finding. According to the results, being in the presence of just one other unknown 'bystander' during an emergency reduces the chances of intervention almost by half (70 per cent compared with 40 per cent). The contrast with the 'Passive confederate condition' was even more striking: in this group only one out of the 14 participants (7 per cent) helped the 'lady in distress'. Thus, seeing another bystander do nothing is enough to reduce the chances of a person intervening in a clear emergency from 70 per cent to just 7 per cent. Put differently, a person witnessing an emergency alone is ten times more likely to intervene than someone who witnesses the same event in the company of another 'unresponsive bystander'.

Bystander effect
The finding that an individual is less likely to intervene in an emergency situation when other people are present.

The finding that the mere presence of another bystander reduces the likelihood of intervention has come to be known as the '**bystander effect**'. Latané, Darley and their colleagues obtained similar results in numerous other experiments involving different types of 'emergencies' that were staged both in a laboratory and outside it. In one study, they found that even theology students going to a seminar on the Good Samaritan (the story from the Christian Bible about a person who helps a stranger in need) were susceptible to the 'bystander effect' (Darley and Batson, 1973). They were less likely to help a person in distress if there was another bystander nearby. What these findings suggest is that helping behaviour in an emergency does not depend so much on what 'sort of person' someone is, or what values they subscribe to, but rather on a variety of situational factors, most notably whether someone else is present. Going back to the Catherine Genovese case, it appears that the fact that 38 bystanders witnessed the attack actually *reduced* the chances of any individual neighbour intervening to help.

Explaining the bystander effect

How did Latané and Darley interpret these findings? Why does the presence of others inhibit intervention? First and foremost, they argued that in most cases of emergency, the appropriateness of intervention is not obvious. Most of the time, norms that regulate social life, what

Latané and Darley (1970, p. 21) call our 'mental rule book', are contradictory. For example, I have already noted the contradiction that good neighbours should be actively helpful and also distant. As Latané and Darley put it, 'the injunction to help other people' is always qualified by the requirement 'not to meddle in other people's business' (1970, p. 20). When people witness an emergency, they therefore have to make a quick decision about which of the two conflicting norms to follow.

Bystander intervention studies have found that, when alone, people are more likely than not to act in an altruistic way, in other people's interest, and offer to help the person in need. Recall that in the 'lady in distress' experiment 70 per cent of participants in the 'Alone condition' responded to the emergency. However, in situations when other bystanders are present, the dynamic is different. The presence of others means that the obligation to help, implicit in the 'mental rule book', is spread among several individuals: each bystander observing an emergency can assume that one of the others will intervene. This reduces the likelihood that any of them will do so. This is the 'diffusion of responsibility' effect: each individual bystander feels less obliged to help because the responsibility seems to be divided between all the people who are present. The effect is compounded by the fact that – in deciding about whether intervention is appropriate – people tend to look to others for clues about what course of action to take. If a bystander, faced with uncertainty, sees that others are not taking action (as was the case in the 'Passive confederate condition' in the 'lady in distress' experiment) he or she is likely to reassess the situation and conclude that intervention might in fact be inappropriate.

This diffusion of responsibility partly explains the conduct of Catherine Genovese's neighbours. During the investigation, many of the witnesses told the police that they realised that the young woman was in distress, but that they still decided not to 'get involved'. This decision was made easier by the fact that the whole neighbourhood could hear the screams. Many of the witnesses probably thought, 'Well, someone has probably called the police by now … maybe I could just stay out of it'. Also, as nobody seemed to be doing anything, bystanders interpreted this as an indication that what they were witnessing might not be all that serious. Otherwise, someone would have phoned the police already. Hence, the fact that no one acted strengthened everyone's conviction that 'doing nothing' was probably the right course of action to take.

Figure 6.6   The bystander effect?

Much of the media frenzy at the time of the Genovese murder interpreted the passivity of the bystanders as a breakdown of neighbourhood and community life. And yet, it could be argued that the 38 witnesses did not, in fact, breach any fundamental rule of 'good neighbouring'. Faced with a dramatic event in their street, they tried to work out whether they should 'look out for others' or 'mind their own business'. Latané and Darley's research on the bystander effect is valuable because it reveals a possible reason why, in this specific case, the neighbours ended up making the decision that they did. Latané and Darley's explanation suggests that many of Genovese's neighbours, had they been alone, would have acted in an altruistic way and called the police straight away. However, with so many other bystanders present, the responsibility for their neighbour's welfare became diffused: non-intervention seemed to be the most appropriate reaction.

3.3 The boundary between 'family' and 'community': a social psychological perspective on the abduction of James Bulger

Although Latané and Darley (1970) proposed the 'bystander effect' as a general principle that determines how people respond to emergencies, their findings cannot be said to be applicable to every real-life instance involving bystanders and an emergency. For instance, social psychologist Mark Levine (1999) has argued that the 'bystander effect', as postulated by Latané and Darley, cannot adequately account for the specific facts of the abduction and murder of James Bulger. In this case, there was considerable variation in the experiences of the 38 witnesses. Some were alone when they encountered James Bulger and his abductors, while others saw them in a busy street where other passers-by were present. The bystander effect would predict a difference in reaction depending on the number of people present, yet none of the 'Liverpool 38' intervened. This led Levine to conclude that something else, above and beyond the bystander effect, made the witnesses 'unresponsive'.

To explore what the decisive factor could be, Levine (1999) examined the testimonies that the 38 witnesses gave in the 1993 trial of Venables and Thompson. He analysed in detail the reasons the witnesses offered for not confronting the three boys in the street. Note the difference between the methodology used by Levine and that used by Latané and Darley. Levine did not design an experiment involving a staged emergency. Because he was interested in the details of a particular, real-life case, which took place in a specific social and historical context, like Stokoe in her work on neighbourhood mediation (2006), Levine analysed transcripts of interactions, accounts and explanations that occurred in a real-life context.

In his study, Levine (1999) found that the explanation for non-intervention given by bystanders in the Bulger case lay in the perceived relationship between Bulger, Venables and Thompson. Almost without exception, witnesses reported that they believed that at least one of the older boys was the toddler's brother. To the bystanders, the interaction between James Bulger and his abductors looked – at the time – like a situation involving a young child who had been left in the care of an older sibling. Although witnesses observed inappropriate behaviour by the older boys, they attributed it to poor or neglectful family care. None of them felt that what they saw constituted a matter of public concern or sufficient grounds for intervention by a mere passer-by.

The implication of this finding is that the inaction by the 'Liverpool 38' was not determined by some general situational factor, such as the number of bystanders present. Instead it was about the way in which witnesses, in this specific historical and social context, categorised and interpreted what they saw. They failed to act because they believed that 'strangers' do not have the responsibility (or the right) to interfere in family affairs.

The assumption that meddling in family matters is unjustified is often taken for granted in contemporary society. During the trial itself, the witnesses did not feel compelled to explain or justify either to the court or the general public why it would have been inappropriate for them as 'outsiders' to approach a group of boys whom they assumed were 'siblings'. This was accepted as part of the natural order of things. As the barrister for the prosecution noted at the time of the trial, when dealing with what is perceived as a private, family matter, non-intervention by outsiders is simply 'reasonable' (quoted in Young, 1996, p. 130). More disturbingly, this was something that the abductors, Jon Venables and Robert Thompson, were aware of. Two eye-witnesses who challenged them in the street and asked them about the injured toddler in their company backed away as soon as one of the boys misinformed them that James was his 'brother'. Thus, although just ten years old, Venables and Thompson were conscious of the fact that invoking a sibling relationship would deflect suspicion, and establish a symbolic boundary that curtails the curiosity of 'outsiders' and makes intervention less likely.

- Do you think that Levine's findings satisfactorily explain why the bystanders in the Bulger case did not intervene?

With hindsight, of course, the individual judgement of each of the 38 witnesses could be brought into question. It would have been better if at least one of them had called the police, or approached Venables and Thompson and questioned them with more determination about their actions. The bystanders themselves recognised this after learning of James Bulger's tragic fate. However, it is also apparent that the inaction of the bystanders reflected (rather than contravened) the norms that govern life in the street. As has been pointed out throughout this chapter, life in the neighbourhood is a maze of competing obligations, constraints and prohibitions. The requirement to exercise duty of care ('watchfulness') is always restricted by the boundaries that delineate 'insiders' and 'outsiders', the 'family' and the 'community', 'home' and the 'street'. The conduct of the bystanders in the Bulger case dramatically illustrates that, in contemporary society, the normal social rule is that people should not intervene in the family matters of others. As Levine (1999) points out, even though most instances of child abuse take place within the family, it is 'strangers' who are perceived as the greatest threat to children's well-being. This assumption about 'stranger danger' is so widespread that adults exhibit reluctance to approach children in the street, for fear that – as strangers – they might be viewed with suspicion. Thus, the conduct of the bystanders in this case was informed by broader cultural assumptions about what the appropriate conduct in the street is, and where the boundaries between 'privacy' and 'community' lie.

The murders of Catherine Genovese and James Bulger are more than just poignant examples of life in the neighbourhood that illustrate, in a dramatic way, an aspect of contemporary society. Because of the publicity they attracted, these cases also influenced how people interpret living together. In the aftermath of the murders, the conduct of bystanders became a topic of media scrutiny and of widespread public discussion. Mediated by the press and the electronic media, the deaths of Genovese and Bulger became embedded in popular imagination. They prompted debates, questions and re-evaluations of the norms governing conduct in the street. Like the more mundane fictional events portrayed in television soap operas, the crimes became a 'cultural resource', used by the public to make sense of the world and challenge existing assumptions about people's rights and responsibilities towards each other and the community. Even today, the conduct of Genovese's neighbours and the inaction of the 'Liverpool 38' are occasionally summoned, in both private and public debates, about what it means to be a 'responsible' neighbour or passer-by. They have become part of the contemporary discourse of neighbouring and, as such, continue to exert influence on how people perceive the world around them and how they negotiate their reaction to it.

Summary

- Social psychologists use a variety of methods to gain insight into bystander behaviour in emergencies, including experiments and detailed exploration of actual, real-life instances of bystander (non-) intervention.

- Representations of neighbourhoods in the media constitute an important tool through which people make sense of their rights and obligations as neighbours and members of the community.

- Social life in the street is dynamic. The rules that govern it evolve and are transformed in the face of experience, including dramatic instances of crime reported in the media.

Conclusion

This chapter has looked at how people live together in the neighbourhood. Section 1 examined mundane, everyday social interaction in the street – the 'where', 'when' and 'why' of neighbouring interaction. Section 2 looked at neighbourhood disputes and the different ways in which people go about resolving them, thus maintaining orderliness in the street. Section 3 looked at what dramatic instances of violent crime can tell us about how people live together, and how, by being discussed and debated in the media, they affect broader perceptions of community life and an individual's role in society.

This chapter also explored a number of social scientific methods that have been used to study neighbouring, including analysis of recorded and transcribed data, ethnographic studies and experiments.

The various aspects of life in the street that we looked at in this chapter all point to the fact that living together encompasses a complex set of social practices. The relational identity of 'neighbour' is not so much about *who* we are as *what we do*. Being a neighbour is a way of talking over the doorstep, knowing where and when it is appropriate to start a conversation, ring a doorbell, move a bed, close a window, make a complaint or, in some instances, interfere in affairs of the family or call the police. It is about knowing, following, adapting, contesting and reproducing the culturally available (but also culturally specific and continuously changing) set of informal social rules through which order in society is maintained. This is why living as a member of the community is not easy. It requires the continuous negotiation of the boundaries separating 'private' and 'public' spaces, the 'home' and 'community', as people coordinate and live connected lives.

References

Abrams, P. and Brown, R. (1984) *UK Society: Work, Urbanism and Inequality*, London, Weidenfeld and Nicolson.

Attwood, C., Singh G., Prime, D., Creasey, R. et al. (2003) *2001 Home Office Citizenship Survey: People, Families and Communities*, London, Home Office.

Bourke, J. (1994) *Working-class Cultures in Britain 1890–1960: Gender, Class and Ethnicity*, London, Routledge.

Crow, G., Allan, G. and Summers, M. (2002) 'Neither busybodies nor nobodies: managing proximity and distance in neighbourly relations', *Sociology*, vol. 36, no. 1, pp. 127–45.

Darley, J.M. and Batson, C.D. (1973) 'From Jerusalem to Jericho: a study of situational and dispositional variables in helping behavior', *Journal of Personality and Social Psychology*, vol. 27, no. 1, pp. 100–8.

Department for Communities and Local Government (2013) 'What we do: responsibilities' [Online]. Available at https://www.gov.uk/government/organisations/department-for-communities-and-local-government/about (Accessed 9 August 2013).

Fox, K. (2004) *Watching the English: The Hidden Rules of English Behaviour*, London, Hodder and Stoughton.

Funder, A. (2003) *Stasiland: Stories from Behind the Berlin Wall*, London, Granta Publications.

Geraghty, C. (1991) *Women and Soap Opera: A Study of Prime Time Soaps*, Oxford, Polity Press.

Harris, K. and Gale, T. (2004) 'Looking out for each other: Manchester neighbourliness review' [Online]. Available at http://www.local-level.org.uk/uploads/8/2/1/0/8210988/manchester_neighbourliness_review.pdf (Accessed 8 August 2013).

Horan, M.D. (1993) 'We are all guilty in the Bulger tragedy', letter to the Editor, *The Guardian*, 26 November, p. 25.

Latané, B. and Darley, J. (1970) *The Unresponsive Bystander: Why Doesn't He Help?*, Englewood Cliffs, NJ, Prentice Hall.

Laurier, E., Whyte, A. and Buckner, K. (2002) 'Neighbouring as an occasioned activity: "finding a lost cat"', *Space and Culture*, vol. 5, no. 4, pp. 346–67.

Levine, R.M. (1999) 'Rethinking bystander non-intervention: social categorisation and the evidence of witnesses at the James Bulger murder trial', *Human Relations*, vol. 52, no. 9, pp. 1133–55.

Low, S. (2003) *Behind the Gates: Life, Security and the Pursuit of Happiness in Fortress America*, New York and London, Routledge.

McGahan, P. (1972) 'The neighbour role and neighbouring in a highly urban neighbourhood', *Sociological Quarterly*, vol. 13, no. 2, pp. 397–408.

Morrison, B. (1996) *As If*, London, Granta.

Rosenthal, A.M. (2008 [1964]) *Thirty-Eight Witnesses: The Kitty Genovese Case*, New York, Melville House.

Stokoe, E. (2006) 'Public intimacy in neighbour relationships and complaints', *Sociological Research Online*, vol. 11, no. 3 [Online]. Available at www.socresonline. org.uk/11/3/stokoe.html (Accessed 17 July 2013).

The Guardian (1993) 'Lessons of an avoidable tragedy', 25 November, p. 25.

Völker, B. and Flap, H. (1997) 'The comrades' belief: intended and unintended consequences of communism for neighbourhood relations in the former GDR', *European Sociological Review*, vol. 13, no. 3, pp. 241–65.

Willmott, P. (1986) *Social Networks, Informal Care and Public Policy*, London, Policy Studies Institute.

Young, A. (1996) *Imagining Crime: Textual Outlaws and Criminal Conversations*, London, Sage.

Chapter 7

Discovering disorder: young people and delinquency

Catriona Havard and John Clarke

Contents

Introduction

The previous chapter suggested ways in which the concern with social order – and the processes of ordering lives – implies an interest in questions of disorder. You saw how the ordering of relationships in neighbourhoods can be a complex matter and produce results that appear 'un-neighbourly', lacking the sort of social order that people expect. The problems of social order and disorder appear in many forms – from rudeness to violence; from bullying to civil war. The history of the UK is full of threats and dire warnings that the social order is breaking down – from people stealing the king's firewood to internet abuse. Order appears to be haunted by the threat of disorder.

In this chapter, we are going to examine one very visible aspect of the relationship between order and disorder by exploring how social scientists have addressed disorderly behaviour by young people. Of course, social scientists' interest in youthful misbehaviour reflects anxieties and concerns of the wider society, which as the quotations in Activity 1 suggest, is a recurring concern.

You came across the term 'disorderly' in Chapter 4 of *Understanding Social Lives, Part 1*.

Activity 1

As you read the quotations below, can you tell *when* and *where* they were written?

1 *The young people of today ... have bad manners, they scoff at authority and lack respect for their elders. Children nowadays are real tyrants ... they contradict their parents ... they tyrannise their teachers.*

2 *Yobs destroy children's scarecrows in 'mindless wrecking rampage'.*

3 *For the first time since ... Robert Peel set up the Metropolitan police, areas of our cities are becoming unsafe for peaceful citizens by night, and some even by day.*

4 *A gang of roughs, who were parading along the roadway, shouting obscene language ... and pushing respectable people down.*

The first quotation is usually attributed to Socrates, the Athenian philosopher writing around 400 BC. The second quotation is contemporary, from the *Daily Post* on 29 May 2013 (Williams, 2013). The third quotation is from Sir Keith Joseph Member of Parliament (MP) in 1977 and the fourth quotation is from *The Daily Graphic*, 25 August 1898 (both are quoted in Pearson, 1983, pp. 4–5). Together they suggest that some of the same concerns about youthful behaviour are evident from the time of the Ancient Greeks to today.

Social scientists study many forms of criminal and deviant behaviour: **criminal behaviour** is behaviour that breaks the criminal laws of the country; deviant behaviour may include crimes, but refers more widely to those behaviours that break established social expectations or norms.

Criminal behaviour
An act that breaks the law and can receive punishment *or* a behaviour that has been labelled as illegal in a particular society at a particular time.

Activity 2

Can you think of any criminal behaviours that are not deviant? Can you think of any deviant behaviours that are not crimes?

We can think of a number of criminal behaviours that are not seen as deviant. For example, much white-collar crime (in businesses and offices) has long been viewed as normal, and rarely results in prosecution. Such crimes may range from stealing office stationery (often viewed as a '"perk" of the job') or 'fiddling expenses' through financial fraud to acts of organisational neglect, omission and carelessness that result in deaths or injuries to workers and/or customers (for examples, see Slapper, 2009; Tombs and Whyte, 2010).

There are also many forms of deviant behaviour that are *not* crimes (that is, offences that can be prosecuted under the current criminal law). For example, a variety of behaviours that are called 'disorders' (eating disorders, psychological disorders such as hyperactivity) are deviant without being criminal. But it is important to remember that this is not a clear-cut distinction. Laws change over time and vary between countries, so that what may be a crime in one place or at one time may not be so at another. But it is also the case that whether some behaviour gets treated as a crime or even viewed as deviant may depend on more contextual factors: *Who* did it? *Where* did they do it? We will come back to these problems later in the chapter.

For social scientists, both crime and **deviance** can be viewed as forms of social disorder. However, there is a very strong focus of attention on juvenile or youthful misbehaviour: often referred to as *juvenile delinquency*. At the core of this is criminal behaviour (behaviour that breaks the current laws of the country), but juvenile delinquency also includes what might be called *status offences* (behaviour that is illegal only for this particular age group such as under-age smoking or drinking, or truanting from school). But juvenile delinquency may involve behaviour that is judged to be deviant (breaking social norms or expectations) such as young people 'hanging about' on street corners, or congregating in loud or aggressive groups. In these ways, 'juvenile delinquency' is far from being a clear or simple concept and it is important to keep this in mind as you read further.

In this chapter, we are going to follow this focus on disorderly behaviour by young people. We will trace two main lines of approach within the study of youthful misbehaviour:

- The first of these focuses on the search for the *causes of delinquency*: what makes young people (or some young people) behave badly? This is probably where you would expect most of the effort of social scientists to be expended – isn't explaining why things happen or why people behave as they do the business of the social sciences?

- The second part of the chapter takes a different – and perhaps less expected – approach to studying delinquency. Here, the focus is on the *processes and agencies of control*, starting from rather different questions: not, why did this person do X, but why is this behaviour viewed as delinquent? Why do these people get arrested for it? Why is that group of people or that behaviour ignored or treated as normal?

Both approaches are centrally concerned with disorder, but take very different routes to understanding it. We hope that by the end of this chapter you will have a good appreciation of what each approach has to offer and why the differences between them are significant.

Deviance/deviant behaviour
Behaviour that violates (some) social norms and thus becomes labelled as deviant.

Delinquency
Failure to follow the law, often referred to in relation to a young person, for example juvenile delinquency, *or* behaviour by some groups of young people that has been labelled as deviant and delinquent.

You came across the term 'disorderly' in Chapter 4 of *Understanding Social Lives, Part 1.*

1   Studying the causes of juvenile delinquency

Social scientists have used a number of approaches to try and explain why young people misbehave. Some researchers have focused on the individual's personality, while other researchers have looked at different factors that might influence individuals to commit crime, such as their family background. The theories that focus on why some individuals may be more likely than others to commit crimes are called *micro* theories. Approaches that examine the immediate family or social context are called *meso*-level theories, while those that examine larger social or structural conditions are called *macro*-level theories. The social sciences often distinguish between these different levels of analysing things.

The following sections will focus on the work of psychologists who developed theories to try and understand why some people behave in deviant ways, and even commit crimes, as compared to those who do not. Sections 1.1 to 1.3 look at early research that focused specifically on the individual's personality, without exploring other factors that may influence a person to behave in a deviant or antisocial manner. The next section explores not only personality factors, but also other influences that may affect whether a person will become a delinquent and commit crimes, such as family circumstances and living conditions.

You came across the term 'antisocial' in Chapter 4 of *Understanding Social Lives, Part 1.*

1.1   Personality/family factors (a psychological approach)

Hans Eysenck was a psychologist who was interested in studying what made people different from one another, such as personality.

Activity 3

What is personality? Think of five words that describe you (not your appearance). For example, are you talkative, shy, and so on? Do you think you could have used those words to describe yourself ten years ago, or in ten years' time?

Now think of a family member or close friend and think of five words that describe them. Do you have any characteristics in common or are they all different?

Personality has been described as a set of fairly stable characteristics that makes a person unique, but also allows for comparison with other individuals. Social scientists have been interested in the study of personality for many years, and numerous personality theories have been developed to try and explain why people behave in a certain way. Many people frequently make judgements about other people's personalities, for example when telling a story, a person may be described as 'outgoing', 'reserved' or 'argumentative'. Sometimes a person's personality and how they react to a situation can be the driving force of an interesting tale. Therefore, maybe it is not unreasonable to suggest that some people's personality may make them more likely to behave in a deviant way, or commit crimes, as compared to other people.

Eysenck was one of the first researchers to develop a theory linking personality to deviant or criminal behaviour. In Eysenck's (1947) theory, he suggested that personality could be reduced to two dimensions, sometimes simply referred to as 'E' and 'N':

- extraversion (E)
- neuroticism (N).

These factors could be measured using a self-report questionnaire that required people to simply answer 'yes' or 'no' to a series of questions contained in the Eysenck Personality Inventory (EPI) (Eysenck and Eysenck, 1968). People who scored high on the E scale were classed as *extravert* and were lively, sociable, thrill seeking and impulsive. Whereas those who scored low on the E scale were classified as *introvert*, and were quiet, retiring and may like books more than people. On the N scale, those who score more highly may be anxious, depressed and preoccupied that things may go wrong. While those who had low scores on the N scale were relaxed, recovered quickly after an emotional upset and were generally unworried.

In a later version of his theory, Eysenck added another component, *psychoticism*, also referred to as 'P'. People who scored highly on the P scale were aggressive, lacking in feeling and antisocial, while those with a low P score were warm, caring and non-aggressive. Eysenck updated the personality scale to include the P dimension in the Eysenck Personality Questionnaire (EPQ) (Eysenck and Eysenck, 1975).

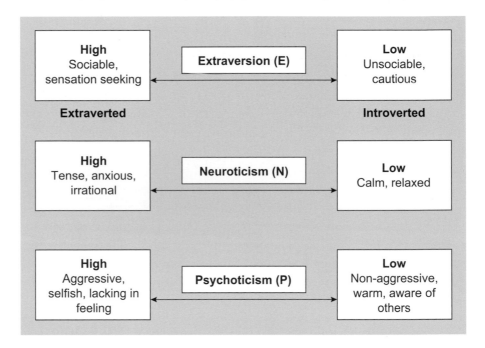

Figure 7.1 Eysenck's theory of personality

Biological approach
An approach that uses anatomical or physiological processes to try to explain behaviour, for example genetics, the nervous system or the immune system.

Eysenck thought that most people would score in the middle of the E and N scales, but at the lower end of the P scale. However, criminals would score at the higher end of each of the scales. Eysenck believed that there was a **biological** basis for personality and that extraversion and neuroticism related to arousal from the nervous system. People who scored highly on the E scale (extraverts) had low arousal levels, therefore they would seek arousal from their environment, such as socialising and thrill-seeking activities. Whereas those who had low scores on the E scale (introverts) already had an over-aroused nervous system and therefore would seek out situations that minimised or reduced their arousal, such as reading a book. People who scored highly on the N scale had a nervous system that was more easily aroused or reacted more strongly to stressful situations (Eysenck, 1964).

Eysenck suggested that the link between personality and antisocial or criminal behaviour was due to differences in learning during childhood. According to the theory, as children grow up they learn right and wrong behaviours by developing a conscience. A conscience develops through **conditioning**, where unapproved or wrong behaviours receive punishment or disapproval. Therefore, children learn to avoid behaviours that will lead to punishment or disapproval and control their impulses. Children who were higher on the E and N scales would find it more difficult to learn during childhood, as they were harder to condition. As a result, those with higher E and N scores may not develop a conscience, or correctly learn right from wrong, and may have problems with controlling their impulsive behaviour. Then in later life, those who had not developed a conscience, and had a tendency towards impulsive behaviour, may be more likely to act in antisocial ways and commit crime. Eysenck suggested that according to his theory, offenders would score more highly on each of the three scales of the EPQ, as compared to non-offenders.

Conditioning
A form of learning by association. Behaviours that are to be desirable are rewarded and those that are not desirable are punished.

Activity 4

Questionnaires are a good research method to use when you want to collect data from a large number of people. Many questionnaires can be given out for people to complete and return, or respondents can be emailed a link to an online survey.

Can you think of any problems in using a questionnaire to research an issue? What if you didn't want someone to know how you really felt about an issue, or behaved in a particular situation, because you were embarrassed or ashamed? Do you think you would answer all the questions truthfully?

One of the problems with using a questionnaire to collect data is that people may not tell the truth, as they want to be seen in a good light and favourably by others. This is the *social desirability effect*, whereby good behaviour is over-reported and bad behaviour is under-reported. This can really influence the findings from research, as it may not reflect the true frequency of behaviour. To try and determine whether respondents were telling the truth when completing the EPQ, Eysenck included a Lie (L) scale. In the L scale, there are items that try to determine whether the respondent is giving the socially desired response or telling the truth. For example, a question on the L scale could be something like 'I always try not to be rude to people'. A high score on the L scale is thought to indicate that the respondent is giving the socially desired response; a low score may indicate indifference to social expectations, as the respondent is not thinking about responses that are socially desirable. Therefore, those who have a propensity towards antisocial and criminal behaviour may have low scores on the L scale, as they do not think about what is socially desirable behaviour (Eysenck and Gudjonsson, 1989).

1.2   Evidence for Eysenck's theory

Over the years, Eysenck's theory of personality has received support from some psychologists, but has also received criticisms from others. Eysenck's theory has been praised for combining the biological (arousal from the nervous system) and social (learning throughout childhood) elements to try and understand why people's personalities differ, and why some people may commit criminal acts. However, it has also been criticised that there is little evidence that extraverts are more difficult to condition than introverts (Gross, 1996). This is an important aspect of the theory as it points to the biological basis for personality; however, if there is no research evidence to support it, then it weakens the theory that extraverts do not learn to develop a conscience through conditioning.

A number of studies have used Eysenck's personality questionnaires to determine whether there really is a difference between those who act in antisocial or deviant ways, compared to those who do not. Center and Kemp (2002) compared the results of 60 studies with children and adolescents who were grouped as exhibiting 'antisocial behaviour' or 'normal behaviour', and were asked to complete an EPQ. When all the results were compared, they found that those who were labelled as exhibiting antisocial behaviour were more likely to score highly on the P scale compared to those who were labelled as normal. Those who were labelled as exhibiting antisocial behaviour were also more likely to have a low L score, giving further support to the theory that those who exhibit antisocial behaviour do not think about whether their actions are perceived as socially desirable. However, there were few differences between groups on the E and N scales, which do not support Eysenck's theory.

There are several studies that have used adult participants to determine whether offenders in prisons differ in their personality according to

Eysenck's dimensions, as compared to non-offenders. Bourke et al. (2013) surveyed prisoners and found that those who were re-offenders (who have offended more than once) scored more highly on the P scale and were lower on the E and N scale compared to those who were first-time offenders. Boduszek et al. (2013) found that violent offenders scored more highly on the P scale. These studies seem to suggest there is some evidence that offenders can score differently to non-offenders on Eysenck's personality questionnaire; however, offenders are more likely to score highly on the P scale and either no differently or even lower than 'normal' participants on the E or N scales.

Now you have read about Eysenck's theory of personality, do you agree with his dimensions of personality, or do you think that there are characteristics not covered in his theory? Do you think there could be other factors apart from a person's personality that might influence them to behave in a deviant or antisocial manner and maybe even commit crime? The next section goes further than Eysenck's theory, and although it does accept that personality may be a factor that affects how people behave in certain situations, it also suggests that there are additional factors that may influence a person's behaviour and their propensity to commit crime.

1.3 The Cambridge Study in Delinquent Development

One method that social scientists use to investigate the causes of antisocial and criminal behaviour is to study a large group of children over a long period of time, and see if any of them commit crimes. Differences between the group can then be explored, for example personality, home life, economic circumstances and so on, to try and determine why some go on to commit crime, as compared to others who do not. This type of research is called a '**longitudinal study**', as it follows people over a long period to see if their behaviour changes or develops over time.

Longitudinal study
A study of the activities or attitudes of individuals or groups of people over long periods of time.

The Cambridge Study in Delinquent Development was a longitudinal study that began in the 1960s by the criminologist Donald West, although David Farrington, a forensic psychologist, took over the long-term running of the project. The study followed a group of 411 males from the age of 8 years (in 1961), up to the age of 48 years. All the boys were from working-class backgrounds and living in a deprived area of south London. The aim was to investigate the development of delinquent and criminal behaviour in inner-city males, and whether it was persistent over time. The study was not designed to test any one theory of delinquency, but to try and investigate:

- why delinquency began
- whether it could be predicted in advance
- if it continued into adult life.

The boys who took part in the study were interviewed and tested nine times throughout the study. The tests measured individual characteristics, such as personality and intelligence. The interviews investigated issues such as living circumstances, employment, relationships, leisure activities and offending behaviour. When the boys were at school, their teachers also filled out questionnaires about their behaviour and school attainment; and their peers were asked about issues such as popularity, risk-taking behaviour and honesty.

When the males reached 32 years of age, criminal record checks were conducted to determine how many had commited criminal offences and what type of offences they were. The study found a number of predictors at 8–10 years of age, which were thought to be related to later delinquency and offending. These fell into six categories (Farrington, 1995; Farrington et al., 2006):

1   Antisocial behaviour, including being troublesome in school, dishonesty and aggressiveness.
2   Hyperactivity, attention deficit disorder, daring, risk-taking and poor concentration.
3   Low intelligence and poor school attainment.
4   Family criminality, convicted parents, older siblings and siblings with behavioural problems.
5   Family poverty, large family size and poor housing.
6   Poor parental child-rearing behaviour, including harsh and inconsistent discipline, poor supervision, neglect and parental conflict.

The study also found that when the men were aged 32, just over a third (37 per cent) had been convicted of a criminal offence. This rose to only 41 per cent when the men were surveyed at 48 years. The most frequent number of offences were committed when the men were aged 17–20 years of age, suggesting that if males were at risk of becoming criminals, then this was the age at which they were most likely to offend. Farrington et al. (1986) found that the men in the study were more likely to commit offences while they were unemployed, as compared to being employed. When the types of offences were examined, it was found that the increase in offences when unemployed centred on offences that involved material gain, such as theft, robbery and fraud, and not offences that involved violence. This suggests that a shortage of money during unemployment may have been an increasing risk factor that led to crime.

The findings from the Cambridge study show that personality is an important factor in whether someone commits crime, for example those who are impulsive and like to take risks are more likely to commit crime. However, the findings from the study also showed that there were other factors in addition to personality that may influence young people to act in antisocial ways or commit criminal acts. The additional risk factors thought to be associated with future criminal behaviour included a family history of offending, child-rearing practices and family poverty. However, which risk factors were considered to be the most important or how they interacted with each other were not discussed in the findings from this study.

1.4   Integrated Cognitive Antisocial Potential theory

Using the findings from the Cambridge study, Farrington alone (1995; 2003; 2005) and in collaboration with colleagues (2006) was able to develop a theoretical model looking at the risk factors for crime called the Integrated Cognitive Antisocial Potential (ICAP) theory. The ICAP theory was designed to try and explain the offending behaviour of males from working-class families. The main concept is a person's antisocial potential (AP), which is their potential to commit antisocial acts and their decisions to turn that potential into the reality of committing crime. Whether the AP is turned into antisocial behaviour depends on the person's **cognitive processes** that consider opportunities and victims.

Cognitive processes
These involve the higher mental processes such as thinking, planning and decision making.

According to the ICAP theory, individuals can be placed on a continuum, from 'low' to 'high' AP, and although few people have a high AP, those who do are more likely to commit crimes. The primary factors that influence high AP are:

- desires for material gain
- status among peers
- excitement and sexual satisfaction.

However, whether these issues influence behaviour will depend on whether the individual can use legitimate means to satisfy them. For example, people from low incomes, the unemployed and those who are not successful at school may be more likely to engage in antisocial behaviour. This theory therefore suggests that males from low-income families with low school attainment and who are unemployed are more likely to commit crimes to achieve material gain (for example, the latest mobile phone), as compared to others from different backgrounds.

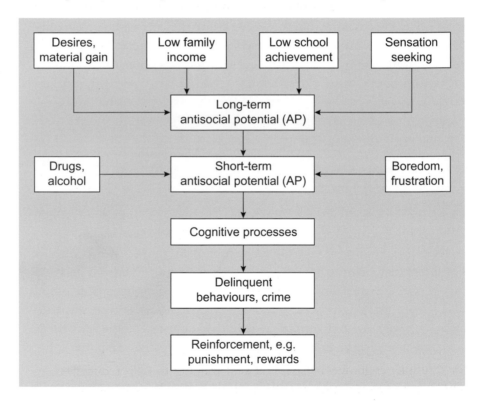

Figure 7.2   The Integrated Cognitive Antisocial Potential (ICAP) theory

The ICAP theory also suggests that there are long-term and short-term factors for AP. Individuals with long-term AP tend to come from poorer families, be poorly socialised, impulsive, sensation seeking and have a lower IQ. For example, children who are neglected or receive little warmth from their parents may care less about parental punishment and therefore do not learn to avoid behaving in antisocial ways. Individuals with short-term AP may not necessarily have been affected by these issues, but may temporarily increase their AP by situational factors, such as frustration, anger, boredom or alcohol. These situational factors may influence a person to make decisions about their behaviour that they may not make in other situations. Furthermore, short-term AP can develop into long-term AP depending on the consequences of antisocial behaviour or offending. If the consequence for offending is material gain, status and approval from peers, it is likely to be repeated. However, it may be a different matter if the behaviour leads to disapproval or imprisonment.

The ICAP theory also looks at factors that might prevent an individual from offending, and these can be social and individual reasons. For example, as a person gets older they tend to become less frustrated and impulsive. There may be important life events that reduce AP, such as marriage, steady employment or moving to a new area, which can shift interaction with peers to girlfriends, wives and children. Farrington (2003) suggests that these life events can have a number of influences to reduce AP. They can:

- decrease offending opportunities, by shifting routine activities such as drinking with male peers

- increase informal controls of family and work responsibilities – spending time with family or working may become more important than socialising with peers

- change decision making by reducing the subjective rewards of offending because the risks of being caught are higher than they previously were, for example disapproval from partner, threat of incarceration and leaving the family.

Farrington (2003) believed that as this theory established a number of risk factors for offending, it would be possible to develop some interventions to prevent those identified as most at risk from offending. For example, cognitive–behavioural skill training to help reduce impulsive behaviour, and parental education to help promote good child-rearing practices and improve parental supervision.

Strengths and weaknesses of the ICAP theory

One of the strengths of this theory is that it identifies different factors that may influence future criminal and antisocial behaviour, and how criminal behaviour may have short-term or long-term risk factors. As a result of their focus on risk factors associated with offending, the ICAP theory, along with findings from the Cambridge study, have been very influential in the development of programmes to try and reduce offending.

The ICAP theory focuses on risk factors of those who go on to commit crimes; however, there is research that has shown that many people can have these risk factors, but do *not* later go on to be offenders (Webster et al., 2006). The ICAP theory has also been criticised for only focusing on risk factors related to family, parenting and peer groups, while neglecting wider issues, such as the role of the neighbourhood (Webster et al., 2006).

Activity 5

- Now that you have read about the Cambridge study and the ICAP theory, do you think that they adequately explain why some people may be more likely to commit deviant acts, or crime, as compared to other people who do not?

- Most of Farrington's research and his theory focuses on males from working-class backgrounds – can you see any problems with focusing on this specific group?

- Do you think that this research and the ICAP theory could be used to explain why other groups in society such as females and those from middle or upper classes, or even rural areas, may commit deviant acts and go on to become offenders?

Summary

The previous sections explored the micro theories of criminal behaviour that focus on individuals, and why some people commit crimes and others do not.

- Psychological theories look at the risk factors for *individuals* to commit crime, not society more widely or why certain groups of people may commit crime.

- Eysenck's theory looked at the link between biology, personality and crime, and suggested that people who commit crimes score more highly on the three scales of extraversion (E), neuroticism (N) and psychoticism (P).

- Eysenck's theory has been praised for combining the biological and social processes to try and understand why some people commit crimes and others do not. Yet, research using Eysenck's personality measures, the EPI and the EPQ, has failed to find support for Eysenck's claim that offenders score more highly on the three scales, as compared to non-offenders.

- Farrington's ICAP theory and the Cambridge study looked at risk factors that could potentially lead to a person to commit crime. Personality is one risk factor for crime; other factors include size of family, poverty, child-rearing practices, school attainment and employment.

- The ICAP theory also examines situational factors that may influence a person to behave in a deviant way, for example alcohol, drugs, and feelings of boredom and frustration.

- The ICAP theory has been praised for its emphasis on short-term and long-term risk factors that may lead to crime, and has been influential in implementing programmes to try to reduce offending. However, the ICAP theory has been criticised for not taking into account the influence of the neighbourhood on offending.

2 Studying the control of disorder

2.1 Howard Becker and the turn to control

In 1963, the American sociologist Howard Becker published *Outsiders: Studies in the Sociology of Deviance*, which laid the foundations for a very different approach to studying deviant, criminal and delinquent behaviour. Becker's work started from a rather mundane observation: not everyone who breaks the law is caught and prosecuted. This fact falls into the 'everybody knows' category of knowledge, but Becker turned it from a rather dull observation into a different way of thinking about deviant behaviour. He drew four related arguments from it:

1 Most studies of delinquents/criminals that seek to explain the causes of crime are methodologically flawed. They tend to assume a reliable distinction between a normal group and a deviant group, and search for the factor(s) that make the difference between the two. Do deviants have the wrong chromosomes, the wrong parenting, the wrong friends, the wrong environment, and so on? But, for Becker, the only reliable difference between the two groups was that one group had been identified – *labelled* – as deviant/criminal. The others – the normals – might have done exactly the same things, but had not been detected, processed and labelled as deviant (see Table 7.1). It might also be the case that among the 'deviants' were people who had been falsely accused and labelled – people who had not committed the criminal or deviant act. So the search for the X factor (that made the difference) was fundamentally flawed.

Table 7.1 True and false negatives and positives

	Detected and labelled	Not detected or labelled
Committed the act	Positive (*Deviant*)	False negative
Did not commit the act	False positive	Negative (*Normal*)

2 Becker argued that social scientists should therefore pay much more attention to the *processes* involved in identifying some acts – and some people – as criminal or deviant. Why are some behaviours and some types of people the focus of attention? What processes of selection are involved in these processes of social control? Are they merely random (some people are just unlucky to be caught and prosecuted) or do they have social biases or logic? Becker asserted

that this meant breaking the fundamental assumption that treats deviance as the:

> ... infraction of some agreed-upon rule: such an assumption seems to me to ignore the central fact about deviance: it is created by society. I do not mean this in the way that it is ordinarily understood, in which the causes of deviance are located in the social situation of the deviant or in 'social factors' which prompt his [sic] action. I mean, rather, that *social groups create deviance by making the rules whose infraction constitutes deviance*, and by applying those rules to particular people and labelling them as outsiders. From this point of view deviance is not a quality of the act the person commits, but rather a consequence of the application by others of rules and sanctions to an 'offender'. The deviant is one to whom that label has been successfully applied; deviant behaviour is behaviour that people so label.
>
> (Becker, 1996 [1963], pp. 217–18, emphasis in original)

3   It is important to note that Becker makes a distinction between the behaviour and the person. Societies decide which behaviours are 'deviant' (and they make some of them illegal – crimes). Societies do not necessarily share the same judgements about what should be judged as deviant or criminal. For example, not all societies judge 'hate crimes' (attacks motivated by hatred of a person's ethnicity, sexual orientation, religion) as crimes or even deviant, although the UK now recognises such actions as criminal. Killing people is usually thought to be both deviant and criminal, but societies vary in the exemptions they permit (it may depend on who commits the act: agents of the government often have some immunity – think about soldiers in wartime or deaths in police custody; deaths that result from corporate action rarely result in murder charges). Indeed specific societies may change their judgements over time (for over a century, the UK treated homosexual acts between consenting male adults as crimes, but 'de-criminalised' them in 1967). Second, though, some people performing those behaviours are identified and labelled as deviant (or criminal), but perhaps not everyone who acts in these ways is identified and labelled.

4   Becker also argued that labels could have powerful consequences. Drawing on the social interactionist approach in social psychology (from the work of George Herbert Mead, 1863–1931), Becker

suggested that how others define us may well shape how we act: if we are labelled as 'bad' or 'criminal', we might start to live up to the label. Equally, the label may shape how others treat us – once labelled, people identified as criminals or deviants may face extra scrutiny, suspicion or even discrimination. A powerful label changes the situation – for the person so labelled and for others. For Becker, the arrival of a label created the conditions of people moving into a 'deviant career': the label shapes the possible future directions of both identity and action.

Activity 6

Can you think of any other examples of labels that might re-shape the conditions of a person's future possibilities?

What about medical or psychiatric diagnoses; being identified as a 'citizen' or an 'alien'; being described as a 'scrounger'; being called a 'job seeker' rather than an 'unemployed person'; becoming homeless; becoming a mother?

Becker's work has been influential in sociological approaches to the study of delinquency, deviance and social control. In fact, he put the processes of social control into a more dramatically visible position, exposing their role in 'defining the situation'. In what follows, we will trace some of the issues that emerged from Becker's focus on 'labelling'.

2.2   Labelling and deviance

One issue that emerges is the selection of what sorts of behaviour are to be defined as criminal or deviant. Remember that criminal behaviour is defined as that which breaks the criminal law; while deviant behaviour is that which breaks established social rules or norms of conduct. But this very general definition conceals a more important question for social scientists about how both the criminal law (in a particular society) and social norms change over time. If we take the criminal law in England and Wales (Scotland and Northern Ireland have different legal systems, even if many of the offences overlap), then it has changed in important ways. New offences are sometimes added: over 3500 during the Labour governments between 1997 and 2010 (see, for example, Slack (2010) or Morris (2008)). Sometimes, established offences are deleted or downgraded: it is no longer possible to be executed, imprisoned or transported for stealing timber, turf or peat from the King's Forests (see E.P. Thompson's study (1977) of the Black Act of 1723, which created 50 new criminal offences). Similarly, the content of social norms changes – reflecting shifting views of what is normal, right, proper or reasonable.

It is important to remember that neither the law nor social codes are permanent and unchanging. They change over time and are different from country to country (or from one legal jurisdiction to another).

2.3   Agencies of control: being selective

It is equally important to remember that rules may be applied selectively. In democratic societies subject to the **Rule of Law**, the principle of 'equality before the law' is an important political value. However, investigations of how the criminal law is applied suggest that forms of social difference and inequality may have a significant impact on who gets 'labelled'. There are numerous examples of distinctions being made between similar behaviour that is judged differently depending on the social identities of the actors. For instance, rowdy, noisy behaviour involving forms of criminal damage to property may be viewed as criminal or delinquent behaviour if done by young working-class men, but treated as 'high jinks' or 'youthful high spirits' if perpetrated by middle- or upper-class young men.

Rule of Law
The principle that all people and institutions, including government, are subject to and accountable to the law.

Activity 7

Read the following extract about the ideas of criminal damage in the aftermath of the English riots of 2011 and reflect on whether the comparison at stake is between types of behaviour or types of people.

'An excessive sense of entitlement' was what the mayor of London ascribed to those looting their way across our sceptred isle – but he could have been referring to himself. In the mid-to-late 80s, Alexander Boris de Pfeffel Johnson – not to mention David Cameron and his now chancellor George Osborne – were members of the notorious Bullingdon Club, the Oxford University 'dining' clique that smashed their way through restaurant crockery, car windscreens and antique violins all over the city of knowledge.

Not unlike a certain section of today's youth, the 'Bullers' have little regard for property. Prospective members often have their rooms trashed by their new-found friends, while the club has a reputation for ritualistic plate smashing at unsuspecting country pubs. It has been banned from several establishments, while contemporary Bullers are said to chant, at all hours: 'Buller, Buller, Buller! Buller, Buller, Buller! We are the famous Bullingdon Club, and we don't give a f***!'

(Kingsley, 2011)

We can see some of these differentiating social dynamics at work in the definition and control of juvenile delinquency. It is understood as a male problem: most concern about delinquency – and most arrests and prosecutions of young people – concentrate on young men. Young women have historically been the focus of rather different anxieties – fears about moral or sexual delinquency have dominated. More recently, however, are worries that young women are behaving like young men – sometimes calling them 'ladettes' or 'yobettes', as in the *Daily Mail* headline 'Yobette generation is plaguing our streets' (Wharton, 2007). John Muncie, writing about the difference between male and female juvenile offending, noted that:

Fuelled by media-driven panics about a 'new breed' of girl gangs, the numbers of girls convicted of indictable offences rose, the use of diversionary measures (cautions, reprimands and warnings) decreased and the number sentenced to immediate custody increased dramatically (by 365 percent between 1993 and 2002) (Gelsthorpe and Sharpe, 2006).

(Muncie, 2009, p. 30)

We will return to Muncie's observation about 'media-driven panics' in the following section, but here we want to consider other patterns of social difference in relation to the control of juvenile delinquency. Using two different types of evidence, sociologists have pointed to a systematic difference between who breaks the law and who is officially labelled as law-breaking. On the one hand, *official statistics* about crime – data collected by the criminal justice system that records arrests, prosecutions, sentences, and so on – identifies delinquency and criminality as a behaviour associated with young working-class men. On the other hand, *self-report studies* – in which people report their own law-breaking activities anonymously – tend to contradict this apparent distribution. Muncie summarises the situation as follows:

... the major contribution of self-report studies has been to seriously question widely held beliefs about the correlations of class position, 'race' and gender to criminality. Both Anderson et al. (1994) and Graham and Bowling (1995) found that middle-class children were just as likely to be involved in crime as working-class children. Indeed a survey by the British Household Panel in 2001 based on interviews with 1,000 13–15 year olds found that those from higher income families were more likely to commit vandalism, play truant and take illegal drugs (*Guardian*, 25 February, 2001) ... This suggests strongly that official statistics reflect not patterns of offending but patterns of policing. As a result, the relative criminality of certain groups of young people has been exaggerated. For example, inner-city working-class youths face a greater risk of arrest than middle-class youths engaged in similar activities but in areas where the police presence is lower. Ethnic minority youths are statistically more likely to be stopped and searched by the police (Burke, 1996), but self-report studies show that those of Indian, Pakistani and Bangladeshi origin have significantly lower rates of offending and that for African-Caribbeans the rate is no higher than for whites.

(Muncie, 2009, pp. 24–25)

There are two important points to draw out of this discussion. The first concerns the problem of evidence in relation to delinquency and criminality. Two types of data – official statistics and self-report studies – produce very different pictures of the social distribution of law-breaking behaviour. Each of them has problems. As Muncie suggests, official statistics tend to report police activity rather than law-breaking. Self-report studies also have potential flaws, as people may be selective about what they admit to; or may even over-dramatise their law breaking when hidden behind anonymity. Such studies tend to be conducted through questionnaires with relatively low response rates; and tend to focus on a limited set of crime behaviours (leaving out a range of possible crimes – from large-scale financial fraud to child abuse). Evidence in the social sciences is rarely perfect, but here it is the comparison between the two sorts of data that is the point of interest.

The second important point concerns the shift of attention to the processes of social control, and their critical role in defining and acting on what – and who – counts as deviant. This concern with 'defining the situation' inspired a wide range of investigations into crime, deviance and social problems more generally. For example, Bacchi's work (1999) builds this starting point into an analysis of social policies and their relationship to gender divisions, arguing that the power or capacity to define 'what the problem is' is central to the policy-making process. This issue is also central to other work on youthful disorder.

2.4   Media and moral panics

Folk devils
Individuals or groups identified as threats or dangers to social order, onto whom are projected a range of social anxieties, concerns and fears.

The sociologist Stan Cohen published a widely used study (1972) of the social reaction to fights between Mods and Rockers (two rival youth subcultures) at English seaside towns during the 1960s. Cohen analysed the media's reporting of these events and found them to be highly dramatised, turning rather banal events into sensational – and sensationalised – news. He pointed to the ways in which these groups of young people were demonised, and viewed as posing a major threat to the stability of social order in the UK. He called this process of demonisation the creation of **'folk devils'** – invented figures onto whom a whole variety of problems, dangers and anxieties could be projected.

At the heart of this process was a relationship between the mass media and figures of authority (judges and magistrates, senior police officers, politicians and others whom Cohen described as 'moral entrepreneurs' who saw an opportunity to speak out about the 'state of the nation' and the dangers posed by such young people). The mass media – print journalism, radio and television – provided the forum in which figures of authority could pass judgement, issue dire warnings and demand strong action. Cohen described this process as the creation of a **moral panic**, which he described as taking place when a 'condition, episode, person or group of persons emerges to become defined as a threat to *societal values* and interests' (1972, p. 9). The important point here is the idea of 'become defined as'. Cohen's study suggests that the fights between Mods and Rockers were treated *disproportionately* by the media and those in authority. In the process, they had other concerns and social anxieties projected onto them. The 'definition of the situation' turned the Mods and Rockers into a major threat to the future of the social order – and they were treated according to that definition (a combination of public condemnation, heavy policing and tough sentencing). Finally, Cohen suggests that the creation of folk devils and the development of moral panics – although certainly irrational and disproportionate – served some social interests. The Mods and Rockers gave a platform for 'moral entrepreneurs' to tell stories about the state of the nation and its young people; for judges and magistrates to 'defend the public' through tough sentencing; and for senior police officers to demand more resources in order to respond to this new threat to society. And, just as Becker suggested, the process of labelling had effects on those being labelled – such that Mods and Rockers tried to live up to their new public reputations: learning to perform their roles in the drama.

Cohen used the idea of a '**deviancy amplification spiral**' in which the media's dramatisation of particular events increased their visibility and the anxieties about them, such that campaigns by police, politicians, the judiciary and representatives of 'concerned citizens' increased the public focus on these actions and the 'folk devils' held responsible for them.

Moral panics
States of collective anxiety about society or social order, in which irrational or disproportionate reactions to events, acts or people are encouraged or enabled by moral entrepreneurs (politicians, journalists and others claiming to represent the public interest).

Deviancy amplification spiral
A concept that is used to describe how public anxiety and intervention may escalate around a particular problem; and how it may also increase the behaviour that was the original cause of concern.

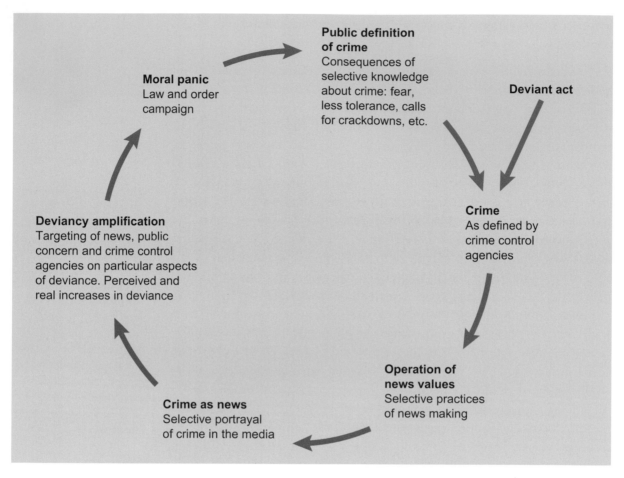

Figure 7.3   The deviancy amplification spiral

In the conclusion to the book, Cohen argued that this distinctive set of dynamics – identifying folk devils, dramatising them as other and dangerous, creating a moral panic about the threat that they pose to the social order, and amplifying the reaction to them (tougher policing, tougher sentences, and so on) – would recur:

> More moral panics will be generated and other, as yet nameless, folk devils will be created ... our society as presently structured will continue to generate problems for some of its members ... and then condemn whatever solution these groups find.
>
> (Cohen, 1972, p. 233)

Many studies have borrowed the ideas of folk devils and moral panics from Cohen, exploring the tendency of societies to enter into this cycle of discovering dangers, projecting fears and anxieties onto them, and demanding harsh responses to 'protect society' (see the discussions by Critcher, 2003 and 2008; Garland, 2001; Jewkes, 2004). Young people seem to be particularly vulnerable to being portrayed as 'folk devils' in this way. For example, Coward (1994) has reflected on the way in which 'yobs' and 'yob culture' came to be powerful images of social crisis and disorder during the 1990s:

> 'YOB', once a slang insult, is now a descriptive category used by tabloid and quality newspapers alike. Incorporating other breeds, like the lager louts, football hooligans and joyriders, yob is a species of young, white, working-class male which, if the British media is to be believed, is more common than ever before. The yob is foul-mouthed, irresponsible, probably unemployed and violent. The yob hangs around council estates where he terrorises the local inhabitants, possibly in the company of his pit-bull terrier. He fathers children rather than cares for them. He is often drunk, probably uses drugs and is likely to be involved in crime, including domestic violence. He is the ultimate expression of macho values: mad, bad, and dangerous to know.
>
> The yob is the bogey of the Nineties, hated and feared with a startling intensity by the British middle class … Individual men disappear in this language into a faceless mob, or appear only as thuggish stereotypes.
>
> (Coward, 1994, p. 32)

■   Can you identify any current 'folk devils'?

2.5   'Society must be protected': crises and control

One important study that drew on and extended Cohen's work was by Stuart Hall and his colleagues (1978), which examined the construction of a moral panic about 'mugging' (street robbery) in Britain during the early 1970s. A term that had not been used since the nineteenth century was suddenly discussed in the mass media as a 'frightening new strain of crime', possibly arriving from what the British perceived as the violent, dangerous and racially divided USA. 'Muggers' became a new type of folk devil, identified as a threat to stability and social order, and requiring tough measures to protect society. Hall et al. argued that this invention of 'mugging' needed to be understood as part of wider social and political dynamics.

They explored the different sorts of disorder that shaped British society at the beginning of the 1970s: a deepening economic crisis and a stagnant economy; growing political conflict; a variety of social divisions that were becoming more severe; and a loss of public confidence in the nation's political leaders. Describing a time in which a relatively consensual society in the 20-year period following the Second World War was becoming increasingly characterised by economic, social and political conflicts, they claimed that the figure of the 'mugger' was placed in the middle of this crisis. He (muggers were usually imagined as men – young, black men to be more precise) became the focus of social and political anxiety – the 'mugger' was seen to represent the breakdown of law and order. As a result, the mass media were full of denunciations, dire warnings and demands for tough action to be taken to save the country from this appalling threat.

For Hall et al., this invention was a way of displacing genuine social and political tensions onto a folk devil. Attention could be deflected from the deepening crises. Society would be protected – not by overcoming divisions – but by 'cracking down' on young black men on the nation's streets. Getting tough on mugging created new police powers, brought about 'exemplary' sentences for those found guilty of robbery (mugging was never a crime in a legal definition), and exposed young black men to a programme of systematic harassment by police officers (under what became known as the 'sus' law: the right of police officers to stop anyone that they suspected might have committed a crime or be intending to commit a crime). The 'suspicious person' powers derived from Section 4 of the Vagrancy Act 1824 and became a major point of conflict between the police and the black community in Britain (especially in London: see Whitfield, 2004). It was eventually abolished in the early 1980s (following the Scarman Report's recommendation of the need for more integrative 'community policing') but re-emerged in a new guise as the power to 'stop and search'. The new power continued to be deployed in an ethnically discriminatory way (what in the USA is known – and condemned – as 'racial profiling'). Whitfield indicates that:

> Ministry of Justice figures published in October 2007 reveal that black and Asian people are more likely to be stopped and searched than their white counterparts. This is especially the case in London where, in 2005/06, black people were more than seven times more

likely to be searched than whites. Outside London, they are 4.8 per cent more likely to be searched.

(Whitfield, 2009)

For Hall et al., 'mugging' helped the politically dominant groups in Britain to move attention from social divisions and political conflict onto a group of folk devils, and to argue that society needed to be protected through tougher policing and a generally stronger state. In 'cracking down' on crime and violence, particularly among young black men, the state (seen by Hall et al. to be representing the most powerful groups and interests in society) became a 'primary definer' of disorder. The media then took their cue from government, police and judges – for instance, in the use of the term 'mugging' – and extended the primary definitions further, giving them a popular ring. In this view, the deep-seated causes of social conflict, chiefly inequality, were obscured and the issue was turned into a legal and moral struggle against what was defined as 'mindless violence'. Hall and his colleagues described this as the creation of a 'law and order society' in which those defined as the enemies of the nation would be rooted out and subjected to increasingly harsh treatment. The analysis they presented has proved to be both very powerful (the book was reissued on its thirty-fifth anniversary in 2013) and very controversial. Debates about it continue that address its account of the British political situation, the relationship between institutions of social control and the mass media, and its view of the situation of young black men in Britain (see, for example, Jewkes (2004) and the special issue of the journal *Crime, Media, Culture* published in April 2008 (Clarke, 2008)).

Perhaps the most interesting question that emerges from the Hall et al. study is whether we are still 'policing the crisis': deflecting attention away from economic crises, social divisions and political conflict by focusing too much on the deviant behaviour of young people and the need to impose a 'law and order society' (Clarke, 2008). Following the English riots of August 2011, it was possible to trace very different views: between those who denounced the 'pure criminality' of the rioters; those who sought to explain rioting in terms of the social and economic conditions facing young people (young men, in particular); and those who suggested that the reaction to the riots was also a displacement of larger social, economic and political crises onto a problem of crime. For this last group, policing the crisis remained an important point of reference. The next chapter takes up the issue of rioting more fully.

Summary

This section has explored how sociologists have studied the social reactions to disorderly behaviour, beginning from Becker's view that 'deviance' is not an intrinsic property of an act, but a label applied to it. This view enables the study of how:

- some behaviours (and some types of people) come to be defined and labelled as deviant
- the media play a role in defining deviance and creating social anxiety or moral panics about some types of behaviour (and some types of people)
- agencies of social control (the police and the criminal justice system) may act in ways that concentrate on some types of people rather than others
- crime and the fear of crime may play a significant role in politics, including as a displacement of other problems and crises.

Conclusion

We have explored different approaches to the study of youthful disorder within the social sciences. In the first part of this chapter, we looked at approaches that tried to discover the causes of delinquent, criminal and antisocial behaviour; approaches that tried to explain why some people were more likely to engage in such activities. In the second part of the chapter, we looked at approaches that focused on the processes and institutions of social control (the media, the police, the courts, and so on) to see how they defined and dealt with young people's disorderly conduct. The differences between the two approaches are very significant. But the two approaches also share some important things in common.

How might you summarise the similarities?

We think it is important to begin by examining what these two approaches have in common. For example:

- They share a basic social science approach in which evidence (of different sorts) is assessed and analysed.

- They share a commitment to treating social phenomena as capable of being analysed and explained systematically.

- They both involve the use of theories (structured explanations) and concepts (key explanatory ideas) in the construction of an analysis and argument.

- They understand that presenting an analysis is also to be engaged in an argument (with other approaches and explanations).

- They share a concern with the problem of understanding contemporary social issues that are seen as being of considerable public importance. In particular, they view delinquency/deviance/disorder as posing vital questions for social science study.

- Both approaches more often focus on the behaviour of men, rather than women.

- Both approaches construct analyses using evidence (even if the evidence they use is very different).

There may well be other similarities. What do you think?

How might you summarise the differences?

Given the way the chapter is structured, it is probably easier to draw out points of difference between the two approaches. These might include:

- They start from different questions (explaining delinquency versus explaining social control).

- Psychological approaches see deviancy as originating from the individual, whereas social control theorists see deviancy as originating from social control processes and the creation of rules that classify certain behaviours (and certain people) as being deviant.

- The psychological approach investigates risk factors for delinquency, such as personality, family background and poverty. By contrast, social control theorists focus on the processes involved for those labelled as being deviant, whether they live up to the label and follow a deviant career.

- Psychologists assume there are sets of behaviour that are deviant or classified as crimes, and people may have long-term or short-term risk factors to commit crimes. However, social control theorists are interested in how the definition of deviancy may change over time, as societal norms change. Studying control provides an understanding of social order, its rules and norms.

- The psychological approach assumes that there is a group of people who are deviant or commit crimes, compared to a 'normal' group. In contrast, social control analysts suggest that it is not the people who are deviant, rather they have been labelled as deviant, and make a distinction between those labelled as committing deviant behaviour or those who are labelled as being in 'high spirits'.

- The majority of psychological research has tended to focus on white, working-class males and to develop theories from their findings. In contrast, the social control approach suggests that children from higher income families may be as likely to commit deviancy or crime (from vandalism, truancy and drug use through to corporate crime), although working-class youth and those from minority ethnic groups may be more likely to be arrested or stopped and searched.

- According to the ICAP theory, if some people are more at risk of committing crime, then programmes can be developed to try and minimise them and prevent deviancy or crime. In social control studies, we learn about social order by studying the process of making and applying rules. Such studies tell us how society works — especially in how it views and tries to control disorder.

- They tend to use different methods, and as a result, use different sorts of evidence.

- The approaches make use of and develop different theories, and perhaps have different views of the uses of social science.

Let us just return to the first point of difference here — that they start from different questions — because many of the other differences flow from this starting point. For those studying the causes of crime, the organising question is: how can delinquent/deviant behaviour be explained? This leads to a search for explanatory factors: conditions, characteristics, processes or relationships. It orients such work towards some types of evidence: questionnaire data; statistical comparisons (between a deviant group and a normal or 'control' group); longitudinal studies (following a set of individuals over a long period). It also leads to certain types of theory: theories that develop causal explanations between the critical factor(s) and the delinquent/deviant behaviour. Such theories might be pitched at different levels of analysis: the *micro-level* of individual personality and circumstance; the *meso-level* of immediate conditions and relationships: the family, the neighbourhood, the group; and the *macro-level* of the wider social, economic and political structures.

In contrast, the social control approach starts from very different questions: how does some behaviour come to be defined as deviant? How do some people come to be labelled as deviant? What do such processes tell us about social order and the way it is made and remade? This leads to a search for explanatory factors: who gets to define what is normal and deviant? What explains why some people are labelled and not others? What social purposes are at stake in the processes of social control? Why are societies prone to moments of 'moral panic'? This search orients social control studies to some types of evidence: historical studies of law making; statistical studies of legal processing (for example, stop and search processes, prosecution decisions); the social biases of social control agencies; analyses of media content; studies of the relationship between politics and social control. But here, too, social scientists work at different levels of analysis: at the micro-level they may study interactions between police officers and 'suspects'; at the meso-level, they may investigate how organisations make social order — looking at police culture, for example; and at the macro-level, they investigate why some things are turned into crimes; or why some sorts of behaviour (or people) become a problem at a specific place and time. But the starting points – the questions that begin the process of inquiry – really do make a major difference. We hope this chapter has revealed why this matters – and how both the approaches contribute something distinctive to an understanding of social order – and disorder.

References

Anderson, S., Kinsey, R., Loader, I. and Smith, C. (1994) *Cautionary Tales: Young People, Crime and Policing in Edinburgh*, Aldershot, Avebury.

Bacchi, C. (1999) *Women, Policy and Politics: The Construction of Policy Problems*, London, Sage Publications.

Becker, H. (1996 [1963]) *Outsiders: Studies in the Sociology of Deviance*, New York, The Free Press.

Boduszek, D., Shevlin, M., Hyland, P. and Adamson, G. (2013) 'Eysenck's personality model and criminal thinking style within a violent and non-violent offender sample – application of propensity score analysis', *Deviant Behavior*, vol. 34, no. 6, pp. 483–93.

Bourke, A., Boduszek, D. and Hyland, P. (2013) 'The role of criminal cognitions and personality traits in non-violent recidivism: empirical investigation within a prison sample', *Journal of Criminal Psychology*, vol. 3, no. 1, pp. 40–8.

Burke, T. (1996) *Policing and the Public: Findings from the 1994 British Crime Survey*, Research Findings, no. 28, London, Home Office.

Center, D.B. and Kemp, D.E. (2002) 'Antisocial behaviour in children and Eysenck's theory of personality: an evaluation', *International Journal of Disability, Development and Education*, vol. 49, pp. 353–66.

Clarke, J. (2008) 'Still policing the crisis?', *Crime, Media, Culture*, vol. 4, no. 1, pp. 123–9.

Cohen, S. (1972) *Folk Devils and Moral Panics*, London, MacGibbon and Kee.

Coward, R. (1994) 'Whipping boys', *The Guardian Weekend*, 3 September, p. 32 [Online]. Available at http://bxpert.co.uk/BeeDee3/MAYCD-%20Crit%20issues%20in%20Youth%2348C/ARTICLE.HTM (Accessed 20 August 2013).

Critcher, C. (2003) *Moral Panics and the Media*, Buckingham, Open University Press.

Critcher, C. (ed.) (2008) *Critical Readings: Moral Panics and the Media*, Maidenhead, Open University Press.

Eysenck, H.J. (1947) *Dimensions of Personality*, London, Routledge and Kegan Paul.

Eysenck, H.J. (1964) *Crime and Personality*, Boston, MA, Houghton Mifflin.

Eysenck, H.J. and Eysenck, S.B.G. (1968) *Manual for the Eysenck Personality Inventory*, San Diego, CA, Educational and Industrial Testing Service.

Eysenck, H.J. and Eysenck, S.B.G. (1975) *Manual for the Eysenck Personality Questionnaire*, San Diego, CA, Educational and Industrial Testing Service.

Eysenck, H.J. and Gudjonsson, G. (1989) *The Causes and Cures of Criminality*, New York, Plenum.

Farrington, D.P. (1995) 'The development of offending and antisocial behaviour from childhood: key findings from the Cambridge Study in Delinquent Development', *Journal of Child Psychology and Psychiatry*, vol. 36, pp. 929–64.

Farrington, D.P. (2003) 'Developmental and life-course criminology: key theoretical and empirical issues – the 2002 Sutherland award success', *Criminology*, vol. 41, pp. 221–5.

Farrington, D.P. (2005) 'Childhood origins for antisocial behaviour', *Clinical Psychology and Psychotherapy*, vol. 12, pp. 177–90.

Farrington, D.P., Gallagher, B., Morley, L., St Ledger, R.J. and West, D.J. (1986) 'Unemployment, school leaving and crime', *British Journal of Criminology*, vol. 26, pp. 335–56.

Farrington, D.P., Coid, J.W., Harnett, L., Joliffe, D., Soteriou, N., Turner, R. and West, D.J. (2006) 'Criminal careers and life success: new findings from the Cambridge Study in Delinquent Development', Home Office report [Online]. Available at http://webarchive.nationalarchives.gov.uk/20110220105210/rds.homeoffice.gov.uk/rds/pdfs06/r281.pdf (Accessed 14 January 2013).

Garland, D. (2001) *The Culture of Control: Crime and Social Order in Contemporary Society*, Chicago, IL, University of Chicago Press.

Gelsthorpe, L. and Sharpe, G. (2006) 'Gender, youth crime and justice', in Goldson, B. and Muncie, J. (eds) *Youth Crime and Justice*, London, Sage Publications, pp. 47–61.

Graham, J. and Bowling, B. (1995) Young People and Crime, Home Office Research Study no. 145, London, HMSO.

Gross, R. (1996) *Psychology: The Science of Mind and Behaviour*, London, Hodder and Stoughton.

Hall, S., Critcher, C., Jefferson, T., Clarke, J. and Roberts, B. (1978) *Policing the Crisis: Mugging, the State and Law and Order*, London, Macmillan.

Jewkes, Y. (2004) *Media and Crime*, London, Sage Publications.

Kingsley, P. (2011) 'UK riots: how do Boris Johnson's Bullingdon antics compare?', *The Guardian*, 10 August [Online]. Available at http://www.guardian.co.uk/politics/2011/aug/10/uk-riots-boris-johnson (Accessed 22 July 2013).

Morris, N. (2008) 'More than 3,600 new offences under Labour', *The Independent*, 4 September [Online]. Available at http://www.independent.co.uk/news/uk/home-news/more-than-3600-new-offences-under-labour-918053.html (Accessed 22 July 2013).

Muncie, J. (2009) *Youth and Crime*, 3rd edn, London, Sage Publications.

Pearson, G. (1983) *Hooligan: A History of Respectable Fears*, Basingstoke, Macmillan.

Slack, J. (2010) 'Labour is dreaming up 33 new crimes a month … including barring you from swimming into the Titanic', *Daily Mail*, 22 January [Online]. Available at http://www.dailymail.co.uk/news/article-1245189/Labour-dreaming-33-new-crimes-month-unprecedented-legislative-diarrhoea.html#axzz2KapembyW (Accessed 22 July 2013).

Slapper, G. (2009) 'Corporate crime in a global business environment', *Asia Pacific Law Review*, vol. 17, no. 2, pp. 149–66.

Thompson, E.P. (1977) *Whigs and Hunters: Origin of the Black Act*, London, Peregrine Books.

Tombs, S. and Whyte, D. (2010) *Regulatory Surrender: Death, Injury and the Non-enforcement of Law*, London, Institute of Employment Rights.

Webster, C., MacDonald, R. and Simpson, M. (2006) 'Predicting criminality? Risk factors, neighbourhood influence and desistance', *Youth Justice*, vol. 6, pp. 7–22.

Wharton, J. (2007) 'Yobette generation is plaguing our streets', *Express*, May 7 [Online]. Available at http://www.express.co.uk/news/uk/6361/Yobette-generation-is-plaguing-our-streets (Accessed 9 September 2013).

Whitfield, J. (2004) *Unhappy Dialogue: The Metropolitan Police and Black Londoners in Post-War Britain*, Collumpton, Willan Publishing.

Whitfield, J. (2009) 'Stop and search: what can we learn from history?' [Online]. Available at http://www.historyextra.com/feature/stop-and-search-what-can-we-learn-history (Accessed 22 July 2013).

Williams, K. (2013) 'Yobs destroy children's scarecrows in "mindless wrecking rampage"', *Daily Post*, 29 May [Online]. Available at http://www.dailypost.co.uk/news/north-wales-news/yobs-destory-childrens-scarecrows-mindless-4027670 (Accessed 19 July 2012).

Chapter 8
Riots and disorder on the street

Geoff Andrews

Contents

Introduction

Earlier chapters in this strand looked at the question of how social order is made and remade. This chapter will look at threats to the social order that take place in the street. In looking at 'disorderly behaviour', the chapter will take the riot as its focal point. It will explore the kind of actions and the situations that have been said to constitute a 'riot'. It will look closely and critically at the way in wich riots have been reported and represented through a range of traditional media, as well as the role that new social media has played in more recent riots. The chapter will question some of the language and underlying assumptions used, and assess the way this may shape *what social scientists know* about riots.

The chapter will look at examples of rioting drawn from quite different historical contexts and geographical locations, notably French and British riots of the eighteenth century, when rioting was a regular form of popular protest, and the 2011 urban riots that occurred in major cities in England. This will enable the identification of some common themes and points of comparison to begin to effectively analyse rioting as a form of disorderly behaviour.

Some social science explanations and arguments that have been used for understanding riots will be examined. In particular, the chapter will introduce political ideologies that offer competing approaches for understanding the causes and consequences of riots. These explanations form part of broader explanatory frameworks for understanding society, social order and social change. The two competing approaches discussed here will be *radicalism* and *conservatism*.

1 What is a riot?

'Riot' has become a widely used term encompassing a range of disorderly behaviour. This behaviour normally involves acts of violence, which might include the destruction of property, clashes with the forces of law and order, or gang fights. It is now common to hear about prison riots, race riots, religious riots and riots at football matches – all these share the general criteria described above but have some specific features.

Activity 1

You may have a clear idea of what a riot is. Jot down your definition of a riot in one sentence.

You might have come up with some of the following definitions:

*   public disorder
*   disturbance of the peace
*   rampage
*   quarrel
*   fight
*   revolt
*   lawlessness
*   violent protest
*   disturbance by three or more people.

These are broad terms with meanings that tend to overlap with other words and phrases, suggesting that the meaning of 'riot' is often held in the eyes of the beholder at any given time. For example, the terms 'disorder' and 'riots' may be used alongside 'violent protests' and 'violent demonstrations' depending on whether they are linked to political conflicts.

Perhaps something more ought to be said here. In most accounts there is an overwhelmingly negative dimension to the meaning of 'riots'; something against the norm, regressive, destructive, violent, even 'irrational', actions.

■ Read the two following extracts and jot down what you think are the key phrases. The first extract concerns anti-austerity demonstrations in Greece in 2008. The second extract reports from the protests in Tahrir Square in Egypt during the Arab Spring protests of 2011.

Those Greek riots

Greece has been torn apart by the worst riots in decades, now entering their third week. Bands of self-declared anarchist youths have rampaged through the streets of Athens and other major cities causing hundreds of millions of dollars in property damage, setting off a spiral of unrest in which the nation's unions, among other groups, have taken part. Both shops and hotel lobbies have been ransacked, and hospitals, airports, and transport have been brought to a standstill. What sparked the riots was the accidental police shooting of a 15-year-old boy, Alexandros Grigoropoulos. But as usual in such cases, there was much more in the way of causes lying beneath the surface.

Youth unemployment is high throughout the European Union, but it is particularly high in Greece, hovering between 25 and 30 percent. With few job prospects, rampant poverty in the face of nouveau riche prosperity, a public university system in shambles, a bloated government sector in desperate need of an overhaul, and a weak, defensive Conservative government with only a one-seat majority in parliament, it is a ripe period for protests, which have had as their aim the fall of Prime Minister Costas Karamanlis.

(Source: Kaplan, 2008)

Mubarak regime in crisis as biggest anti-government demonstrations in a generation sweep across Egypt

'This is the first day of the Egyptian revolution,' said Karim Rizk, at one of the Cairo rallies. The protests against decades of poverty, oppression and police torture had been declared illegal by the authorities and were met with a fierce response. Teargas and water cannons were fired into the crowd and rocks were thrown into the air by demonstrators and security forces.

'We have taken back our streets today from the regime and they won't recover from the blow,' said Rizk.

Protests also broke out in the Mediterranean port city of Alexandria, where posters of Mubarak and his son Gamal were destroyed. Roads were also blocked in the Sinai peninsula, and large rallies were reported across the Nile delta and the Suez canal region.

The protests were called by a coalition of online activists, who promised 25 January would be a 'day of revolt'. Apparently taken by surprise at the size of the crowds, police initially stood back and allowed demonstrators to occupy public squares and march through the streets, unprecedented in a country where political gatherings are outlawed and demonstrations normally shut down quickly.

But as the marches grew, the government moved to isolate them. Access to internet, phone and social media networks was shut down, spreading confusion among protesters and temporarily sealing the largest Arab country off from the rest of the world. Access was later restored, although services remained intermittent.

(Source: Shenker, 2011)

The first extract describes a 'riot', in which the participants are 'self-declared anarchist youths have rampaged through the streets of Athens …'. In the first paragraph, the focus is on *destruction* and *anarchy*. Yet in the second paragraph, social factors such as unemployment and poverty are mentioned and the author even suggests it was 'a ripe period for protests'. Greece at the time was in a severe state of economic debt, at the centre of the Eurozone crisis, and had to be bailed out by the European Union (EU) and the International Monetary Fund (IMF). The Greek Prime Minister resigned the following year as a result of the crisis. This article seems to confirm that there is sometimes a fine line between seeing riots as merely destructive and seeing them as protests for political change.

The second extract describes an even more violent situation where people have been killed, but the word 'riot' does not appear. Those participating are 'protesters', who are said to be taking part in a 'revolution'. This report describes the 'day of revolt' in Egypt, which was crucial in bringing down the Mubarak regime. Riots in this case appear as a 'last resort', a form of protest taken up when all other channels or processes have proved unsuccessful. Note also the significance of online protests and clampdowns – non-violent activity that contributed in a key way to the protests. Various forms of media, as you will see, have often had crucial roles in protests and disturbances.

The articles emphasise how easily meaning and language can influence how events are understood. In this case, the term 'riot' appears to be confined to situations that are threatening, irrational and destructive; that is, 'disorderly' behaviour, disruptive of the existing social order. Yet, events depicted as 'riots' in the case of the Arab Spring are often linked to revolutions, important social reforms and even the introduction of democracy. This suggests that the language that underpins 'riot' carries particular social meanings, which can change over time. As will be explored later, these different interpretations often form part of wider ideological positions on what is wrong with society and what needs to change (or what needs defending). For now, the key point to bear in mind is that riots have been viewed both as symbols of discontent, which can drive social and political change, as well as destructive threat, which reflects a weakened or 'broken' social order.

Summary

- The term 'riot' is usually applied to perceived acts of disorderly behaviour, which often includes destruction of property or other acts of violence.

- Riots, protests and demonstrations are often used interchangeably to describe the same set of circumstances, and underpinned by assumptions about the purpose of the participants.

- The Greek riots of 2008 and Egyptian riots of 2011 were also protests against governments or regimes as 'last resort' symbols of discontent.

2 The modern origins of rioting

We can now turn to earlier examples of 'riot'. During the eighteenth century, riots formed a recurrent feature of the social and political life of France and Britain. The following sections will explore some of the questions that such events raise for thinking about rioting.

2.1 Orderly disorder

Historically, riots have had a central role in social and political change in Britain. They were a common form of protest from the mid eighteenth century until the growth of organised trade unions and political organisations from the mid nineteenth century onwards. These riots included the Wilkes agitations of 1760s–70s, the Gordon riots (1780), the 'Church and King' riots that recurred throughout the eighteenth century, the Bristol Riots (1831) and the Birmingham Bull-Ring riots (1839). Then there are riots that took on a more violent, 'insurrectionary' nature, such as the 'Luddite' machine-breaking riots (1811–13), the Rebecca Riots in South Wales (1839 and 1842) and the Plug Riots among the Staffordshire miners (1842). According to the historian E.P. Thompson:

> The British people were noted throughout Europe for their turbulence. The eighteenth and early nineteenth century are punctuated by riots, occasioned by bread prices, turnpikes and tolls, excise, 'rescue', strikes, new machinery, enclosures, press-gangs and a score of other grievances.
>
> (Thompson, 1991a, p. 66)

Riots took place in both urban and rural communities, and were often composed of a mix of social groups, including many skilled artisans. While there was often emotive language used to describe the rioters at their most threatening, with very harsh penalties for those who were convicted of the more serious offences, they were also seen as a regular component of community protest and politics. Food riots were particularly frequent and were often sparked by a combination of hunger, rising prices, and the perceived fraudulent activity of traders and dealers, who were widely thought to have made unfair profits and put essential foodstuffs beyond the reach of ordinary people.

However, food riots were more than spontaneous outbreaks of rebellion. They were often recognised as legitimate forms of protest. For example, in Devon, 'one of the most riotous counties in England' (Bohstedt, 1983, p. 27), by the late eighteenth century the actions of food rioters were perceived by many as 'rational' and 'coherent' responses to rising food prices. A common tactic used by the rioters was to steal food and leave in its place a fee decided by *themselves* as fair and just. This elicited sympathy among many, including magistrates and others in authority who felt that the harsh economic measures needed regulating if social harmony was to be restored. The rioters included people often viewed as 'pillars' of the community; that is, they were respectable citizens of some social standing, whose actions had a bearing on public opinion and who were at the forefront of practical social changes. In this respect, the riots have been described as acts of 'orderly disorder' (Bohstedt, 1983, p. 27) because they had the pragmatic function of modifying prices and restraining the excesses of farmers and food dealers.

Activity 2

Jot down a couple of lines on what you think is meant by the term 'orderly disorder'.

You might well have pointed to the apparent contradiction in that phrase. Perhaps you were also struck by the possibility that riots could even have a constructive and not merely destructive effect. The term suggests that the actions of rioters could in some way even *strengthen* or restore the social order rather than weaken it. Thompson (1971) argued that the eighteenth-century crowds who took to the streets to riot over food prices did so under the impression that they had the support of the wider community. He found that when rioters protested against the price of bread, or demanded that farmers sell openly at the market (rather than fixing the price beforehand), or stopped exporting corn from the parish at times of scarcity, those in authority were forced to listen. At times, they were even said to be 'prisoners of the people', while at other moments, they mediated between the rioters and those they targeted. This effect of rioting in exercising constraint and extracting concessions was given wider legitimacy by what Thompson (1991b) called 'the moral economy' of the poor, by which he meant a constraint imposed by a sense of fairness among the people arising from what was regarded as acceptable levels of economic hardship. It was therefore perceived as *immoral* to increase the price of essential provisions as a way of making profit out of people's needs. The food riots reflected a collective feeling that the free market undermined a consensus around fair social conditions.

The role of the press was another factor in influencing attitudes towards the rioters. Although there were frequent calls for harsh penalties and the demonisation of the culprits, there were exceptions. Newspapers like the *Manchester Herald* provided alternative sources of information and sympathy. Sympathetic representations of rioters also appeared in the work of popular artists, and in the prints made by the eighteenth-century political and social critic William Hogarth. This meant that the representations of the rioters' living conditions and motives were contested and even helped generate support for their actions.

The social backgrounds of the rioters were also significant in eliciting wider sympathy. They were often skilled craftsmen or artisans who had influence in the community. Many women were also among the rioters. In Nottingham, regarded as the 'most riotous town in the kingdom' in 1794, 'crowds made up mostly of women, stole bread, scattered adulterated flour and plundered barges and warehouses. But they also observed traditional rituals, forcing food dealers to reduce their prices in some instances' (Bohstedt, 1983, p. 206).

2.2 The crowd in the French Revolution

Riots were common forms of protest during the same period in France. In a study of the riots and social upheavals that took place during the French Revolution of 1789, the historian George Rudé also discovered that the majority of the rioters were 'respectable' citizens. They were 'drawn in their overwhelming majority from the Parisian sans-culottes – from the workshop masters, craftsmen, wage-earners, shopkeepers and petty traders ...' (Rudé, 1959, p. 178).

Sans culotte Parisien.

Figure 8.1   The 'sans-culottes' were mainly urban labourers and politically left-wing members of the working class who were distinguished from the wealthier, more moderate middle-class radicals who wore culottes (knee-breeches)

Rudé was able to study the social origins and motives of the rioters from first-hand police reports, as distinct from official press or government accounts. He rejected the view that the rioters were a homogeneous mass of people responding instinctively to the speeches of radical political leaders. The pre-revolutionary riots at the *Palais de Justice* (law courts) during 1787 and 1788, for example, were led initially by lawyers' clerks and ushers. At the Reveillon riots of April 1789, the houses of two manufacturers were destroyed by 'angry crowds' of workshop journeymen and labourers. The records also show that some of the rioters present in Reveillon were 'prosperous merchants' (Rudé, 1959, p. 179).

At its peak between 11–14 July 1789, the revolutionary crowd included an estimated quarter of a million armed demonstrators. Among those who set alight customs posts were the 'aristocratic adventurer' Musquinet de Sain Felix. The police records indicate that other 'well dressed' as well as 'roughly dressed' men and women involved in the demonstrations included wine merchants and professional smugglers (Rudé, 1959, pp. 180–1). In fact, wine shops, along with workshops, were a 'potent channel of communication' (Rudé, 1959, p. 214).

'Looting' at Saint Lazare Monastery, Rudé discovered from the police records, was 'carried out by small tradesmen, employed and unemployed labourers and the local poor' (Rudé, 1959, p. 181). The march on Versailles in October 1789, one of the defining moments of the revolution, was 'led by the women of the markets, including not only fish-wives, stall holders but also, "*des femmes à chapeau*" [the well-dressed women of the bourgeoisie]'. Many women, notably laundresses, cooks and domestic servants, played a central part in the ensuing food riots.

Figure 8.2 A typical rioter?

Like the 'respectable' rioters of mid-eighteenth-century Britain, Rudé found that while many of the rioters in the French Revolution were depicted by the authorities as 'criminal', or professing a 'desire to loot', there was limited evidence to support widespread looting. Rather, the records demonstrated that the crowds involved in the upheavals, both during and after the revolution, embraced the slogans of liberty and the 'rights of man' advocated by Jacobin leaders and clubs. It was clear that they had strong political allegiances, evident from the slogans and chants on the streets. However, the underlying reasons for the riots, according to Rudé, were social and economic. Perhaps it was another moment that could be described as 'a period ripe for protest'.

This led Rudé to reject the notion of rioters as a 'mob', 'ruffians' or 'assassins', 'vagabonds', 'bandits' and 'brigands'. These derogatory terms were used in some official accounts as well as some authoritative works on the impact of the French Revolution, including Edmund Burke's (2003 [1790]) *Reflections on the Revolution in France* (which will be discussed shortly). Rudé found that the crowds and rioters were motivated by social needs rather than self-interest or financial gain. While the sans-culottes were most typical, it was misleading to describe them as constituting a 'mob' intent on irrational and destructive actions.

Summary

- 'Orderly disorder' explains the way in which eighteenth-century riots, although disruptive and violent, often strengthened the social order by regulating prices and redressing the excesses of the economy.

- By 'the moral economy of the poor', Thompson implied that the riotous actions of food rioters to obtain a fair price against injustices imposed by large farmers and merchants had the support of a wide consensus.

- The economic circumstances and social backgrounds of the eighteenth-century rioters were a key factor in creating sympathy for their causes.

- Women were involved in the eighteenth-century riots, and played a significant role in the riots during the French Revolution.

- Rudé drew on police records, which provided a rich source of evidence on the composition of the 'crowd' in the French Revolution. He found that the language of the 'mob' reflected assumptions of the political opponents of the crowd and was an inaccurate description of them and their motives.

- The underlying motives of the riots during the French Revolution were social, economic and political, and primarily over the price of food.
- The unofficial media helped to disseminate ideas and mobilise opinion among the crowd.

3 A 'crowd' or a 'mob'? Explaining eighteenth-century riots

Rudé (1959) used the term 'revolutionary crowd' to distinguish the political role from that of the 'mob'. However, this amounted to more than different terminology. It suggests a movement from below, emerging from subordinate social groups (sometimes called the 'popular classes' in France), which had radical political ideas and the objectives of challenging injustices. As we found with the extracts on the Greek and Arab Spring cases, the riots, sometimes referred to as 'protests', were the prelude to a challenge to the social order. In the case of the French Revolution, this was clear in the wider critique of France's regime of monarchical government that was initially made by the Jacobins and subsequently adopted by a wider movement from below.

3.1 Political ideology

The Jacobins drew on a set of ideas, cultural symbols and language – notably 'the rights of man' – that were widely held and which helped mobilise opinion and political action. These are functions of all political ideologies, which combine critiques and prescribe solutions or alternatives. Ideologies can also help to resist change and preserve the existing order of things, for example by promoting particular moral beliefs or making a call to national unity. It follows that ideologies have a broader function, as explanatory frameworks, in helping to make sense of society. It does not necessarily mean that people will be motivated to get up and take action on the streets. Nor does it mean that individuals must have read great works of philosophy to become 'ideological'. Ideologies are much messier than theories and can incorporate slogans, cultural symbols and forms of propaganda, and 'being ideological' may include a discussion in a bar, an argument in a newspaper column or a piece of artwork. They do, however, provide the link between individuals, parties and movements, and public opinion. Ideologies often draw on intellectuals, writers and artists, and others who 'produce' ideas and help disseminate them.

Ideologies often contain a critique of the world as it is, but can also perform the role of legitimising the existing order. The next two subsections explore two contrasting ideologies that play such roles in the case of riots:

- *radicalism*, which argues that many riots have played an important part in delivering social change *from below*, and

- *conservatism*, which believes that gradual change and modification *from above* is the key to social cohesion and maintaining social order.

3.2 Radicalism

Following the criteria set out above, eighteenth-century radicalism can be defined as an ideology. According to Rudé (1959), the French riots were essentially social and political protests from below against tyranny, including the 'legitimate' actions of impoverished classes against social and economic injustice. There are strong similarities with the riots in Britain in the same era. Description of people taking to the streets as a 'mob' detracted from their political agenda and implied irrational actions of disorganised looters. These radical ideas attracted a large following and helped to mobilise the actions of many, aided by the medium of political pamphlets that were privately printed in order to escape censorship by the monarchy. Their ideas were driven by a wide set of political arguments, notably the 'rights of man', and reflected in the slogan *liberté, egalité et fraternité* (liberty, equality and brotherhood). In fact, the intellectual origins of the French Revolution are normally traced to the French Enlightenment ideas of *reason, progress* and *reform*. The role of intellectuals such as Voltaire, Rousseau and Diderot was crucial in setting out and disseminating many of the ideas that were subsequently adopted by the revolutionaries. The leading role of the Jacobins, a name derived from the political club and composed initially of Deputies (MPs), was also important in organising the ideas into a more coherent political agenda for change. This was evident, following the fall of the Bastille and the removal of the monarchy, in the Declaration of the Rights of Man and of the Citizen.

Figure 8.3   The storming of the Bastille on the morning of 14 July 1789 was a key moment in the French Revolution

The impact of the French Revolution's early years of protest was also felt in Britain. Tom Paine's influential *Rights of Man*, Mary Wollstonecraft's *A Vindication of the Rights of Woman* and William Godwin's *An Enquiry Concerning Political Justice* were all published between 1791 and 1795. The same radical ideas inspired the London Corresponding Society and similar societies in Manchester, Sheffield and Derby, which set out demands for universal (male) suffrage and parliamentary reform. The response of the authorities to such agitation was severe: Paine's book was banned; Mary Wollstonecraft was derided as a 'hyena in petticoats'; and the London Corresponding Society was made illegal, with its leading members arrested.

This ideology of radicalism was underpinned by three main themes or organising concepts. First was the idea of popular sovereignty, which in its simplest terms can be defined as 'government by the people'. For radicals, **popular sovereignty** embodied the political aims of the French Revolution. It was behind the riots on the streets of Paris, where the institutions of justice were targeted, the Bastille attacked and the monarch arrested. Radicals maintain that the social and economic inequalities were perpetuated by political despotism and the lack of democratic freedoms; therefore, the demonstrations and protests were

Popular sovereignty
The principle that government is based on, and sustained by, the consent of the people.

legitimate in representing the views of the disenfranchised. This view was set out in Paine's critique of hereditary or monarchical government in *Rights of Man*. For Paine, who personally experienced both the French and American revolutions, forms of hereditary government lacked any legitimacy because they were not based on the consent of the people. He argued that it would be as absurd to allow for hereditary mathematicians or poet laureates as hereditary rulers, and that such a system would inevitably lead to abuses of power:

> All hereditary government is in its nature tyranny … To inherit a government is to inherit the people, as if they were flocks and herds.
>
> (Paine, 1971 [1791], p. 194)

His argument that sovereignty should rest with the people put him on the side of the French and American revolutionaries who took to the streets to demand their rights and oppose tyranny. This radical view of popular sovereignty also rested on what might be called a 'broad' view of politics. The rioters were seen as 'political' because their actions had the higher goals of changing the political system and incorporating the voices of the people from below.

The second organising concept, which underpinned popular sovereignty, was the idea of ***universal rights***. Paine's view was that the 'rights of man' were natural and 'inalienable', a view taken from John Locke, and which had been incorporated in both the American and French constitutions. Universal rights were the basis of citizenship to be decided at citizen conventions and incorporated within constitutional declarations of citizenship. The first article of the revolutionary Declaration of the Rights of Man and of the Citizen of 1789 declared that 'men are born free and equal in rights'. The 'rights of man' (and they did mean 'man'), by asserting equal status for all, required the accountability of those in power to the people and mechanisms – which later became the basis of **representative democracy** – for ensuring that individual freedoms were guaranteed. The actions of the rioters on the streets of Paris and elsewhere were those of the people asserting their demands for political rights.

Universal rights
A set of rights that people acquire by virtue of their humanity.

Representative democracy
A form of 'indirect' democracy in which adult citizens elect representatives to rule on their behalf.

The third organising concept of radical ideology is the idea of progress (sometimes called 'meliorism'), whereby social change, including human emancipation, and the extension of rights and freedoms, is seen to be progressive and the outcome of developments in science, technology and the spreading of knowledge. It has its modern roots in the French Enlightenment and the growing belief that society could be explained and organised on the basis of reason, rather than, say, religion, superstition or through traditional forms of knowledge like folklore and allegiance to long-standing customs. According to this view, the eighteenth-century radicals who took to the streets of Paris and London and elsewhere, were making 'new worlds' (a term associated in particular with the American Revolution). This was marked by new constitutions or, in the case of the French Revolution, demands for the dismantling of the *ancien regime*, and new legal system, new calendar and weights and measures. The actions of the protesters, therefore, were seen as progressive and rational responses towards the development of a more enlightened social order; in fact, the rioters could be seen as remaking the social order along rational lines.

3.3 Conservatism

Edmund Burke, in *Reflections on the Revolution in France*, written very soon after the events and published in 1790, had a very different interpretation from the radicals (Burke, 2003 [1790]). His book has become known as one of the classical works of modern conservatism. Fearful of the impact of the French Revolution on British society, he set out his defence of traditional British political institutions and values. He argued that the French Revolution was not driven by genuine desire for reform, but was motivated by self-interested and disruptive elements. France was not in need of major social change or transformation from below, but could have been reformed gradually from above. In particular, Burke took issue with the idea of the 'rights of man', which was at the centre of the radicals' argument. For Burke, the 'rights of man' was an abstract concept, the result of utopian and dogmatic thinking driven by the belief that society could be constructed anew on the basis of ideas and theories. In place of the 'rights of man', Burke maintained that social inequalities and hierarchies were indicative of an 'imperfect' system, which had evolved over time and could not be

Constitutional monarchy
A system of government in which the hereditary head of state is constrained by the constitution.

remedied by a constitution embodying universal rights. Burke was a supporter of the 1688 'Glorious Revolution' in Britain – in effect, a modification of the existing political system that resulted in a **constitutional monarchy**. He therefore believed that stability and social order were best maintained by a natural hierarchy. This idea of natural hierarchy can be seen as one of conservative ideology's organising concepts.

Its second organising concept is the focus on a narrower or more limited view of politics than the one held by radicals. Conservatives are pessimistic over human nature and what can be achieved by plans, blueprints or radical programmes and reforms, preferring piecemeal changes and checks and balances guided from above. The actions of the French revolutionaries and other eighteenth-century radicals amounted to a crusade and an imposition of untested ideas. This led Burke to reject the idea of popular sovereignty as the basis of a new political system. The values of political leadership needed to be learnt, and social and political change needed to be gradual and consistent with existing structures. Burke therefore rejected the idea that a new kind of society could be delivered by popular protest from below without ending in violence, destruction and instability.

The third organising concept was a preference for wisdom, rather than reason, as the basis of political change. It was dangerous, according to Burke, to believe that reason and enlightenment could direct the actions of individuals in the creation of a new civilisation. He, and later conservatives, believed that it was wisdom, not reason, which held the key to the social order. Wisdom was based on experience and knowledge that had been transferred across generations, and consolidated in the institutions and customs of the society. Ideas of progress were 'abstract' theories, contemptuous of long-standing customs and traditions. The stability of the social order, according to Burke, depended on 'a partnership not only between those who are living, but between those who are living, those who are dead and those who are to be born' (2003 [1790], p. 82) This meant that he saw the French Revolution as entirely disorderly, influenced by elites and driven by the actions of a 'mob' that were motivated by greed and violence, and incapable of exercising political judgement. They were demands for rights and freedoms, which could not be obtained without undermining the natural hierarchy on which all political systems depended. Those that had taken part in the riots promised a 'revolution in sentiments, manners and moral opinions' (2003 [1790], p. 69); in other words, a rejection of dominant values accumulated over many years and around which social order was organised. If the events in France were repeated elsewhere, then all the wisdom and experience of governing that had been 'learned' by successive generations of 'natural protectors and guardians ... will be cast into the mire, and trodden down under the hoofs of a swinish multitude' (Burke, 2003 [1790], p. 68).

Summary

- Ideologies are explanatory frameworks that help to make sense of society.

- Radicalism as a political ideology viewed the riots in France as the legitimate grievances of those who had suffered social and economic inequality, and political repression.

- The main organising concepts of radicalism include the idea of progress, universal rights and popular sovereignty.

- Conservatism as a political ideology put the riots in France down to: the destructive and disorderly actions of a mob; the undermining of long-standing institutions, conventions and hierarchies; moral decline; and the influence of liberal or radical elites.

- The organising concepts of conservatism include natural hierarchy, limited politics and wisdom.

4 A broken society? The 'Blackberry riots' of 2011

A series of riots took place over four days in England in August 2011, following the shooting of Mark Duggan, a 29-year-old black man from the Broadwater Farm Estate in Tottenham, north London. These have been regarded as the worst acts of disorder in the UK since the 1980s and affected several English cities, including London, Birmingham, Manchester and Nottingham, as well as Salford, Huddersfield and Croydon. The use of social media, notably Blackberry Messenger, was a central feature of the riots, with many commentators and critics citing their role in mobilising support, spreading news and keeping people ahead of the police as events unfolded. In a very different way to the pamphlets, prints and newspapers of the eighteenth century, the media were once again a key player in generating ideas, images and news.

After initially seeming to take the government by surprise during a busy holiday period, the riots were met with a swift series of punitive measures. A large number of arrests followed and there was a rapid prosecution of offenders who were given seemingly harsh sentences. There was a strong consensus among those in government that the riots were symptomatic of a 'broken society', reflected a breakdown in moral values and constituted a threat to the British way of life.

4.1 Conservatism and disorder

Prime Minister David Cameron, in a speech in his Witney constituency shortly after the riots, set out his view on the causes of the riots.

■ Read the extracts from Cameron's speech below.

David Cameron's speech

It is time for our country to take stock.

Last week we saw some of the most sickening acts on our streets.

I'll never forget talking to Maurice Reeves, whose family had run the Reeves furniture store in Croydon for generations.

This was an 80-year-old man who had seen the business he had loved, that his family had built up for generations, simply destroyed.

A hundred years of hard work, burned to the ground in a few hours …

Everywhere I've been this past week, in Salford, Manchester, Birmingham, Croydon, people of every background, colour and religion have shared the same moral outrage and hurt for our country.

Because this is Britain

This is a great country of good people.

Those thugs we saw last week do not represent us, nor do they represent our young people – and they will not drag us down.

Why this happened

… what we know for sure is that in large parts of the country this was just pure criminality.

So as we begin the necessary processes of inquiry, investigation, listening and learning: let's be clear.

These riots were not about race: the perpetrators and the victims were white, black and Asian.

These riots were not about government cuts: they were directed at high street stores, not Parliament.

And these riots were not about poverty: that insults the millions of people who, whatever the hardship, would never dream of making others suffer like this.

No, this was about behaviour …

… people showing indifference to right and wrong …

… people with a twisted moral code …

… people with a complete absence of self-restraint.

Politicians and behaviour

Now I know as soon as I use words like 'behaviour' and 'moral' people will say – what gives politicians the right to lecture us?

Of course we're not perfect.

But politicians shying away from speaking the truth about behaviour, about morality …

… this has actually helped to cause the social problems we see around us.

We have been too unwilling for too long to talk about what is right and what is wrong.

In this risk-free ground of moral neutrality there are no bad choices, just different lifestyles.

People aren't the architects of their own problems, they are victims of circumstance.

'Live and let live' becomes 'do what you please.'

Well actually, what last week has shown is that this moral neutrality, this relativism – it's not going to cut it any more.

One of the biggest lessons of these riots is that we've got to talk honestly about behaviour and then act – because bad behaviour has literally arrived on people's doorsteps.

And we can't shy away from the truth anymore.

Broken society agenda

Do we have the determination to confront the slow-motion moral collapse that has taken place in parts of our country these past few generations?

Irresponsibility. Selfishness. Behaving as if your choices have no consequences.

Children without fathers. Schools without discipline. Reward without effort.

Crime without punishment. Rights without responsibilities. Communities without control.

… In my very first act as leader of this party I signalled my personal priority: to mend our broken society.

That passion is stronger today than ever.

Yes, we have had an economic crisis to deal with, clearing up the terrible mess we inherited, and we are not out of those woods yet – not by a long way.

But I repeat today, as I have on many occasions these last few years, that the reason I am in politics is to build a bigger, stronger society.

Stronger families. Stronger communities. A stronger society.

This is what I came into politics to do – and the shocking events of last week have renewed in me that drive.

So I can announce today that over the next few weeks, I and ministers from across the Coalition government will review every aspect of our work to mend our broken society ...

... on schools, welfare, families, parenting, addiction, communities.

... on the cultural, legal, bureaucratic problems in our society too:

... from the twisting and misrepresenting of human rights that has undermined personal responsibility ...

... to the obsession with health and safety that has eroded people's willingness to act according to common sense.

We will review our work and consider whether our plans and programmes are big enough and bold enough to deliver the change that I feel this country now wants to see ...

So yes, the broken society is back at the top of my agenda.

(Cameron, 2011)

Activity 3

You might like to read Cameron's speech again before thinking about the following questions. You might find it useful to jot down key words or phrases that you think help sum up Cameron's message.

- In general, how would you describe the general tone of Cameron's speech?

- Note the short sentences, partly written in note form, and short paragraphs. Why do you think the speech appears in this form? (You will probably find that your tutor may have something to say if you presented an essay in this format!)

4.2 An ideological agenda: Cameron, Burke and conservatism

Cameron is making a speech, not setting out a philosophical argument like Burke, but he insists that the riots drove him to a sense of 'moral outrage'. At many points he uses emotive language, with the decline in moral standards and values at its core. He describes the 'slow-motion moral collapse' which had engulfed British society, and a 'twisted moral code' among those who rioted. He also implied that 'moral neutrality' and moral 'relativism' have led to 'do what you please' behaviour.

Think back to Burke's emphasis on 'manners and moral opinions'. The march on Versailles in October 1789, a defining moment of the French Revolution, had started with angry groups of women protesting over the price of bread, which then became merged with demands for political reforms and a new constitution. Burke argued that this amounted to a 'revolution in sentiments, manners and moral opinions' because it threatened the existing social order, undermined the existing moral values and challenged social hierarchies and distinctions; ones which had endured through long 'tried and tested' experience over generations.

Cameron also attributes the behaviour of rioters to a clash of values, and what might also be called a challenge to conventional 'sentiments, manners and moral opinions'. He makes a powerful contrast, for example between people like Maurice Reeves who work hard and live in 'strong families' and 'strong communities' (and who cleaned up the mess left by the rioters) and others, apparently 'without fathers' or discipline, who 'get reward without effort'.

In the end, the 'broken society' needed mending – and this was a political task at the top of his priorities.

4.3 The conservative critique

We have to remember that Cameron, like the leader of all political parties, is a politician with a political agenda. He makes it clear in his speech that he has a major commitment to 'mend our broken society' – a theme he took up soon after he was elected leader of his party. What we see here are Cameron's underlying political ideas, his ideological assumptions, about what is wrong and what needs to change.

In order to get their ideological message across, politicians often speak in 'sound bites' – short, catchy phrases – which often reduce complex questions to more simple equations. The riots, Cameron said, were:

- 'not about race'
- 'not about government cuts'
- 'not about poverty'.

They were, he argued, acts of *'pure criminality'* (Cameron, 2011, emphasis added).

It seems here that Cameron is clear to distinguish between different *causes* that have been suggested for the riots. This is an important part of his ideological approach, where his own position emerges from a critique of rival explanations. He says the riots are not about 'race', 'cuts' or 'poverty' and seems to put the blame on certain families, schoolteachers and the welfare system. Is this a similar dismissal of elites to that made by Burke in his critique of the Enlightenment philosophers and 'literary elites' for their 'abstract' claims to human rights? Cameron himself blames the riots partly on the 'twisting and misrepresenting of human rights' that has undermined personal responsibility.

In other words, the buck stops with the individual rather than underlying social causes. Nor were the causes political: the riots were 'directed at high streets not Parliament'. They had nothing to do with the economic crisis and were certainly not the outcome of a ripe period for protests. They were not social protests but acts of vandalism and thuggery, symptomatic of a society that is bereft of moral leadership. This seems to reflect the conservative idea of a narrow or limited concept of politics.

4.4 The virtues of private property

The violent destruction of private property was foremost in Cameron's mind. He starts his speech by referring to Mr Reeves, the Croydon furniture shop owner whose family firm had lasted for generations: 'A hundred years of hard work, burned to the ground in a few hours' (Cameron, 2011). Here, the implication seemed to be that private property was something that seemed to have a wider significance. It was a core part of society's values and had helped bring stability. British society had been organised in a way that allowed private property to flourish, and the inequality that resulted from it was an inevitable and natural consequence. Private property was also crucial to Burke:

> The power of perpetuating our property is one of the most valuable and interesting circumstances belonging to it, and that which tends the most to the perpetuation of society itself. It makes our weakness subservient to our virtue; it grafts benevolence even upon avarice.
>
> (Burke, 2003 [1790], p. 44)

Much of Cameron's focus was on acts of looting, with, as he perceived it, rioters acting out of self-interest and greed, with no respect for property.

4.5 Reporting the riots

As we have seen, Cameron's speech on the riots was part of a wider critique of the 'broken society'. The 'broken society' was a theme he had developed in opposition and made it a key part of his election campaign in 2010. It resonated with the use of 'broken Britain' by *The Sun* newspaper and a similar language used by Cameron's predecessor, Iain Duncan Smith. The phrase has reached wide currency and has been taken up both by critics (for example *The Guardian* newspaper) and supporters. Following the riots, it took on a new urgency and received further coverage. This is an illustration of the way the media can also assume an ideological function in setting out political agendas, putting forward opinions, drawing on stereotypes (in the case of tabloids in particular) and appealing directly to the public. Newspapers covering the riots also mirrored some of the ideas in Cameron's speech, albeit with even more emotive language.

The role of the media in creating 'folk devils' was discussed in Chapter 7.

The Daily Telegraph: 'Rule of the mob'

The Sun: 'Anarchy'

The Daily Mail: 'The anarchy spreads'

Daily Star: 'Anarchy in the UK'

Daily Express: 'Flaming morons'

The Scotsman: 'London under siege as mobs roam streets'

(Greenslade, 2011)

What did you make of these headlines? It is noticeable that the language used to describe rioters has changed little in more than two centuries! Note the focus on riots leading to 'anarchy', a term that is now commonly used for 'disorder', where the state has lost control. The view in all this newspaper coverage is that riots, anarchy and disorder are inextricably linked. The tendency to include all the rioters under the same 'mob' label and other references to 'gangs' seemed to imply that it was solely an inner-city phenomenon. However, there were riots in suburban areas, notably Croydon, which was described as a 'war zone' in some reports and was referred to by Cameron at the start of his speech. According to the social theorist Rupa Huq (2013), this reflected the end of the 'suburban dream' based on an affluent, isolated existence. In fact, many suburban areas now shared similar characteristics to the inner city, including multiculturalism, family diversity, inequality and street violence.

A recurring theme in many of the reports was the role played by Twitter and Blackberry (*The Sun* in its 9 August edition called on the authorities to 'Nail the Twitter rioters' (France and Flynn, 2011)). The press reports claimed that social media were used extensively to organise the rioting, naming meeting points and galvanising supporters, as well as coordinating attacks on police and property. They also pointed to examples of rioters putting up images of the products they had looted and called for 'a Twitter clampdown' to prevent further disturbances, though critics would argue that this focus on the instruments of the media can obscure the broader social *causes* of the riots.

Activity 4

Jot down your own impressions of the role that social media played in the riots.

There is no doubt that social media played an important role in the 2011 riots – as they did to a greater extent during the Arab Spring of the same year – providing more spontaneous dialogue and unedited material beyond forms of censorship and monitoring. They allowed activists to share information in reporting events as well as helping to mobilise support.

Summary

- In his speech on the riots, Cameron discounted social conditions such as poverty and unemployment as reasons for the 2011 riots, and focused instead on criminality and morality.

- Cameron emphasised the 'selfish' motives of rioters involved in the widespread looting as part of a wider ideological attack on the 'broken society'.

- Cameron and Burke both place emphasis on the importance of 'manners and moral opinions' in the creation of disorder.

- Politicians and other prominent public figures and institutions, including the media, have important roles in influencing how we think about riots and disorderly behaviour.

- The majority of the press used similar language to describe the rioters in 2011, implying an ideological consensus on the disorder.

- As with the eighteenth-century rioting and the events of the Arab Spring, different forms of media played a crucial role in both reporting riots and mobilising rioters in 2011.

5 Reading the riots from below: the radical case

In the previous section we saw the power of the national press which, combined with politicians and others with influence, can be authoritative voices. They provide valuable sources of information, can set agendas and provide a forum for discussion. As powerful influences, they are an important part of *how social scientists know* about riots. The need to sell newspapers often means that headline-grabbing topics are presented – in the case of tabloids in particular – in prejudicial and simplified forms. However, the independent media, which include unofficial blogging and podcasting, can often be illuminating in giving a 'voice' to the groups who were at the frontline of the disturbances.

Following the riots, a research study was commissioned by *The Guardian* newspaper in collaboration with the London School of Economics (LSE), funded by the Joseph Rowntree Foundation and the Open Society Foundation, entitled *Reading the Riots* (*The Guardian*/LSE, 2011). It was intended to take a similar approach to an earlier research study carried out by the *Detroit Free Press* newspaper and the Institute for Social Research in Michigan, which followed the 1967 riots in Detroit. What was missing was the view of the rioters themselves – the voices from below.

Reading the Riots (*The Guardian*/LSE, 2011) was therefore the first to look at the underlying causes of the riots and drew on accounts from significant numbers of those who were direct participants in the events. In all, 270 people were interviewed in London, Manchester, Salford, Birmingham and Nottingham by a team of 30 researchers who had the task of tracking down potential respondents, and reassuring them of anonymity and security at a time when police were still carrying out arrests in their communities. Most contacts were made locally, although 1000 people who had been arrested or charged were written to or visited. From the final sample, the majority of the 270 respondents (made up of 79 per cent men and 21 per cent women) had not been arrested.

Of the 270 people interviewed, 30 per cent were juveniles in the 10–17 age range; and 49 per cent were in the 18–24 age group, similar to the Ministry of Justice figures for those arrested. They interviewed a slightly larger proportion of ethnic minority respondents compared to the 37 per cent white, 40 per cent black and 6 per cent Asian who appeared in court according to official statistics. Their analysis of court records also found 59 per cent of rioters were from the most deprived 20 per cent of UK districts.

When the respondents were asked to identify the 'important' or 'very important' reasons behind the riots, poverty came top, followed by policing, government policy, unemployment and the shooting of Mark Duggan. Next came 'social media', 'media coverage' and 'greed', with moral decline and poor parenting well down on the list. At the bottom of the list, that is to say, least important, was 'gangs'.

When the researchers contrasted their findings with a Guardian/ICM poll (that is, a public opinion survey), there were marked differences, notably on 'poor parenting' (only 40 per cent of the riots sample as opposed to 86 per cent of the poll thought it was an 'important' or 'very important' factor), 'gangs' (32 per cent to 75 per cent), 'moral decline' (56 per cent to 82 per cent). The positions were reversed on other topics: poverty was viewed as more important by the riots study sample (86 per cent to 69 per cent), as were policing (85 per cent to 68 per cent) and the shooting of Mark Duggan (75 per cent to 51 per cent) (Glover, 2011).

The evidence from the respondents contrasts strongly with the reports in the national press and the explanations for the riots that accompanied many of them. It also contrasts with Cameron's conservatism. This is partly to do with methods, as the emphasis here is on interviews given by respondents. Rudé (1959) also drew on evidence from police reports, which gave some indication of the social composition of the rioters.

The ideas expressed by the 2011 rioters fit much more closely with arguments used by radicals and you might have identified similarities. For example, the view of the majority of the respondents that poverty, unemployment, social inequality and unacceptable government policy were much more significant than moral decline and poor parenting links closely to the radical perspective. These were structural socio-economic explanations that suggested that large numbers of young people had felt disenfranchised enough to take to the streets. These structural explanations, which also suggest that the causes of the riots are located in the way the society is organised, contrast with the conservative stress on morality and bad behaviour. A Trades Union Congress (TUC) report *Responding to the Riots* argued that Cameron and the government 'overlook(ed) the contribution that material conditions make to social exclusion and alienation' (TUC, 2011).

In contrast to the arguments of Cameron and conservatism, this would also give some credence to the radical view that the riots could be considered political. The more political nature of the riots is also apparent in dramatisations and documentaries made after the events. For example, in her 2011 play *The Riots*, Gillian Slovo adopted a style of verbatim theatre, which combined interviews from politicians, rioters and victims with a re-enactment of the events. The documentary film, *Riot From Wrong* (Fully Focused, 2011), made entirely by young people from communities affected by the riots in London, was a critical response to the coverage in the mainstream media. In making connections between cuts in youth services, the rise in university tuition fees, consumerism, the banking crisis and the parliamentary expenses scandal, it provided a critique of British society, the way in which riots were reported, and the links between the disorder and growing wider generational divisions.

In this radical interpretation, then, the rioters are seen not as a 'mob' or 'thugs', but as alienated youth, protesting against their lack of opportunities. In the words of one respondent in *The Guardian*/LSE study of the riots:

> I became involved in the riots in Salford because it was a chance to tell the police, tell the government, and tell everyone else for that matter that we get f***ing hacked off around here and we won't stand for it.
>
> (Unemployed man aged 22 who was present at the Manchester and Salford riots; *The Guardian*/LSE, 2011, p. 20)

Some of the places under attack could be considered symbolic of that division – the High Street, for example, as an image of consumerism and affluence for some, but beyond the reach of others at a time of economic crisis. Are their similarities between these protests and the Greek 'austerity riots'? You might also think back to. Thompson's 'moral economy' argument and apply it to the 'Blackberry riots' – could we say they occurred because austerity had undermined a collective feeling of fairness and equality for young people?

There could also be contradictions, too, in the attitudes of the protesters towards consumerism that do not fit easily with radical ideas. In the words of one respondent:

> I don't condone it [the looting] but like, it's like, it's helped me out financially ... I should look back on my values and my morals that my parents taught me ... but for that, snap, that night, I look back to my own 14 year old self. I wanna get it now. I want it now. That's what it was.
>
> (Business student aged 19 from London; *The Guardian*/LSE, 2011, p. 29)

How significant, in this regard, was the use of 'Blackberry' and other social media by the rioters? It could be compared to the 'unofficial media', which had roles in challenging power from below in earlier riots, while at the same time being indicative of the dominant consumerist values.

Summary

- The radical view of the 'Blackberry riots' emphasises structural factors such as social and economic roots and political disempowerment, and rejects moral decline as a convincing explanation for the causes of riots.
- The radical view of the 'Blackberry riots' is grounded in an expansive or broader view of politics in which the discontent of young people with their social conditions and lack of opportunities led to protests against institutions and values from which they felt excluded.
- There was a strong contrast between the participants' view on causes of the riots and official reports and explanations.
- Social media were an important influence on the riots, including the spreading of ideas and coordinating action, although it needs to be seen alongside the wider underlying causes of the riots.

Conclusion

This chapter started by asking what was meant by 'riot' and how to distinguish its meaning from other terms, some of which are used interchangeably. Baseline definitions gave some insight, but the question of what constitutes a riot requires a much deeper examination of its historical application, the nature of the society in which it occurred and the ideological agenda (including the role of the various media), which has sought to explain them.

Exploring the question of what constitutes a riot made clear the importance of understanding riots in the context of wider discussions about 'disorder', political and social protests. Are riots best understood as mainly irrational and destructive acts where the moral and social order has broken down, or should attention be on the social, economic and political circumstances? These different views of riots have been reflected in the different use of language (the 'mob' versus the 'revolutionary crowd'), while the different assumptions about riots underpinning such views tend to be associated with views *from above* (governments, those in power or authority) on the one hand; or *from below* (subordinate social groups) on the other.

The chapter explored two explanatory frameworks – ideologies – that provided competing interpretations of riots in quite different historical moments. It became evident that the debate between radicals and conservatives over the causes of riots was part of wider competing interpretations of society. For radicals, it was the social and economic inequality, undemocratic or oppressive regimes and the lack of rights that led to popular protests from below. The conservative view emphasised disorder, anarchy, moral breakdown, the threat to private property and claims to abstract rights. This contrast enabled us to look at the phenomenon of riots from different perspectives and assess the merits of each.

Burke and subsequent conservative thinkers would say that the 'terror' that followed the French Revolution demonstrates the strength of his thinking, while radicals would point to the further struggles for democracy and universal citizenship that were inspired by the events of 1789. Hopefully, this has helped your understanding of the causes of riots and their wider meanings. (Are you a radical or conservative, or sympathetic to aspects of both ideologies?)

Activity 5

In the following grid, jot down notes on the 'causes' of, and 'solutions' to, riots and disorder according to conservatism and radicalism.

	Conservatism	Radicalism
Causes		
Solutions		

It should also be noted that the two ideologies do not provide the last word on the matter, nor are their applications equally effective in different times and places. For example, were the political demands and social inequalities of the eighteenth century more evident than in the 2011 so-called 'Blackberry rioters', some of whom (on their own admission) were motivated by self-interest? Unlike the riots of the eighteenth century, no agreed fee was left in place of the goods taken. However, it was not only conservatives who could talk of morality (or the lack of it) as an important factor in the motives of the rioters. You will remember Thompson's (1991b) reference to the 'moral economy of the poor', which gave legitimacy to the actions of the rioters in the eighteenth century. Thompson also argued that although the riots were driven by social and economic conditions, part of their wider acceptance was because they were seen to act within a moral consensus of custom and tradition as a form of 'orderly disorder'. In fact, in that sense, they could be said to embody both radical and conservative ideas.

Finally, the role of the media was important in all the examples of rioting considered here. Though the media in the eighteenth century were very different in some forms, in the pamphlets, prints, art as well as printed newspapers, they had a similar function in providing ideas, mobilising opinion, reporting events and presenting images of the rioters, as did social media in 2011. Both forms of media faced censorship, though social media by their nature were less constrained in that way. The media, therefore, in different forms, are also important parts of the explanatory frameworks that help to make sense of riots and disorder.

References

Bohstedt, J. (1983) *Riots and Community, Politics in England and Wales 1790–1810*, Cambridge, MA, Harvard University Press.

Burke, E. (2003 [1790]) *Reflections on the Revolution in France*, New Haven, CT, Yale University Press.

Cameron, D. (2011) 'Fightback after the riots', speech to Witney constituents, 15 August, official website of the Prime Minister's office [Online]. Available at https://www.gov.uk/government/speeches/pms-speech-on-the-fightback-after-the riots (Accessed 23 July 2013).

France, A. and Flynn, B. (2011) 'Nail the Twitter rioters', *The Sun*, 11 August [Online]. Available at http://www.thesun.co.uk/sol/homepage/news/3741129/Cops-vow-to-nail-the-Twitter-rioters.html (Accessed 22 August 2013).

Fully Focused (2011) *Riot from Wrong* [Film/DVD]. Available at http://riotfromwrong.com (Accessed 9 August 2013).

Glover, J. (2011) 'Riots poll reveals public back police more than politicians', *The Guardian*, 12 August [Online]. Available at http://www.theguardian.com/uk/2011/aug/12/riot-poll-public-back-police (Accessed 5 November 2013).

Godwin, W. (2009 [1793]) *An Enquiry Concerning Political Justice*, Gloucester, Dodo Press.

Greenslade, R. (2011) 'How the newspapers headlined the London riots', *The Guardian*, 9 August [Online]. Available at http://www.theguardian.com/media/greenslade/2011/aug/09/national-newspapers-london-riots (Accessed 11 September 2013).

Huq, R. (2013) *On the Edge: The Contested Cultures of English Suburbia*, London, Lawrence and Wishart.

Kaplan, R.D. (2008) 'Those Greek riots', *The Atlantic*, 19 December [Online]. Available at http://www.theatlantic.com/magazine/archive/2008/12/those-greek-riots/307225/ (Accessed 9 August 2013).

Paine, T. (1971 [1791]) *Rights of Man*, London, Pelican Books.

Rudé, G. (1959) *The Crowd in the French Revolution*, Oxford, Oxford University Press.

Shenker, J. (2011) 'Mubarak regime in crisis as biggest anti-government demonstrations in a generation sweep across Egypt', *The Guardian*, 26 January [Online]. Available at http://www.jackshenker.net/egypt/mubarak-regime-in-crisis-as-biggest-anti-government-demonstr.html (Accessed 22 August 2013).

Slovo, G. (2011) *The Riots: From Spoken Evidence*, London, Oberon Modern Plays.

The Guardian/London School of Economics (LSE) (2011) *Reading the Riots* [Online]. Available at http://eprints.lse.ac.uk/46297/ (Accessed 9 August 2013).

Thompson, E.P. (1971) 'The moral economy of the English crowd in the eighteenth century', *Past and Present*, vol. 50, pp. 76–136.

Thompson, E.P. (1991a) *The Making of the English Working Class*, London, Penguin Books.

Thompson, E.P. (1991b) *Customs in Common*, London, The Merlin Press.

Trades Union Congress (TUC) (2011) *Responding to the Riots: A TUC Briefing* [Online]. Available at http://www.tuc.org.uk/tucfiles/80/respondingtotheriots.pdf (Accessed 23 July 2013).

Wollstonecraft, M. (2004 [1792]) *A Vindication of the Rights of Woman*, London, Penguin Books.

Chapter 9
Governing inequalities

Georgina Blakeley and John Clarke

Contents

Introduction

> Imagine the spread of incomes as an hour-long parade through a town, where the height of each individual corresponds to their salary. The first 40 minutes or so would witness a parade of dwarves, since the skewed spread of incomes towards the affluent few ensures that most people are below the average. After that, a fair few people of average stature would pass by, and then a few more who were somewhat on the tall side. But in the last few minutes, great giants would emerge, and during the last few seconds their heights would be measured in miles.
>
> (Clark, 2010)

Mile-high giants at one end and dwarves at the other paint an evocative picture of inequality as measured by income. Inequality appears to be an enduring issue despite being the subject of government action ever since the French Revolution in 1789 proclaimed all men (and yes, they meant men) to be born free and equal. Despite proclamations of equality as an ideal that's worth striving for, the world we live in grows more, not less, unequal. But why does this matter?

Perhaps it matters because of the consequences for people's lives: other things, such as health and life expectancy, are related to inequalities of wealth and income. Perhaps it matters because of the consequences of living in divided societies or a divided world. Some social scientists have claimed that all people, not just the poor, suffer from living in increasingly unequal societies (Wilkinson and Pickett, 2009). Perhaps it matters because inequalities sometimes produce social and political convulsions – as the poor and excluded rebel and demand that the economic and social order must change. Perhaps it matters to those who believe that societies should distribute resources more equally. There are many reasons for thinking inequality is a cause for concern, but evidence of increasing inequality within and between societies suggests that it is not necessarily a pressing public issue. Why might this be? Why might deepening inequality *not* be a matter of public concern?

Activity 1

Before we begin, we would like you to think about and make some brief notes on social inequality.

What, if anything, do you think should be done about social inequality? If you think something should be done, who should do it?

In this chapter, we will explore the different elements that are implied in this activity:

- What is inequality (and what is known about it)?
- What sort of problem is it?
- What is its relationship to social order?
- Who, if anyone, should act in relation to inequalities?

In Section 1, we explore what it means for something to become a public issue. In Section 2, we consider ways in which such public issues might be governed, giving particular attention to the role of the state. In Section 3, we look at some forms of inequality and examine some evidence about what has been happening to the social distribution of economic resources (income and wealth). In the fourth and final section, we compare two different views of economic inequalities: one that treats them as the natural and necessary condition of free-market economies; and a second that treats growing inequalities as social and political challenges (public issues) that require governing.

1 Governing public issues

Many political struggles begin by 'redefining what had previously been considered private, non-public, and non-political issues as matters of public concern' (Benhabib, 1992, p. 84). Much of political life therefore involves attempts by social groups and organisations such as political parties, professional bodies, non-governmental organisations, and so on, to make private troubles into matters of public concern. But what does it mean to make something 'public' and what might it mean to govern it? Consider first the following definition of private life as:

> ... the things that matter most to us as social beings: home, family, friends, sex and love ... the rhythms of leisure and relaxation, comfort, sadness and happiness.
>
> (Weeks, 1995, p. 131)

Jeffrey Weeks relates the 'private' to:

- things that engage our emotions
- things that relate us to particular others
- specific activities
- certain spaces.

The private is usually viewed as the opposite of public. But what, then, is public?

Activity 2

Consider the following and decide whether they are *private* or *public*:

- sexual relations between consenting adults
- relations between parents and children
- childcare.

Sexual relations between consenting adults and relations between parents and children are part of personal lives (or family lives) and therefore private – at least in terms of Weeks's definition above. But these relations are also regulated by law; indeed, state regulations govern many aspects of private life. Regulations determine at what age we can engage (legally) in some activities (from sexual relations to getting married); and they determine with whom we can engage in such activities (barring sexual relationships with close blood relatives – incest). The public authority – the state – regulates, and sometimes intervenes in, private spaces and private lives. For example, do you think that the state (in the form of police or child protection workers) should have the power to remove children from places where they are at risk of violence, cruelty or neglect? Should it have the power to remove vulnerable adults facing the same risks?

The third example in Activity 2 was childcare. In so far as it takes place within a family, it might similarly be said to be private, but the same activities carried out in a nursery school are public (even if the nursery is a private rather than a public organisation). But even the 'private' realm of the family is subject to various forms of public intervention and regulation: from midwife or health visitor inspections and assessments in infancy through to the scrutiny by social workers, police or teachers or carers who are thought to be putting children 'at risk' of physical, sexual or emotional abuse. Between these private/familial and public/nursery institutions there are a number of other forms of childcare. Would you say that a paid childminder is public or private? If a child is looked after by a grandparent, is that private? Does it make any difference if the grandparent is paid to look after the child? These examples show that there are always disagreements about where to draw the boundaries between public and private, and things move between being viewed as private matters and public issues at different times. Making something public is no simple matter.

Figure 9.1   Childcare carried out in a nursery setting – but is a paid childminder public or private provision?

But how and where the line is drawn is always a political process, and political choices always involve some construction of this public/private divide. Politics is the activity of arriving at collective choices, policies, regulations, and the like, in circumstances where there is always the possibility of doing things differently. Without some degree of cooperation, there is no collective choice and no politics; but without some conflict over alternative ways of drawing the distinction, there is no need for a political choice at all. So disputes continue over what counts as a public issue, or what should be left as a private matter. For example, since the late nineteenth century, various campaigns have demanded that forms of child abuse and domestic violence should not remain 'private' matters (kept within the home or the family). Instead, they argued that abuse and violence needed to be seen as matters of public concern and subject to intervention by public agencies (police, social workers, and so on). Issues or activities have to be made visible, named, defined and constructed in particular ways for them to become accepted as matters of public concern. This is one reason why the language and images used in politics matter alongside the material interests that may also be at stake. Questions of who speaks for whom and how issues are represented are central to political activity.

Activity 3

Can you think of other examples of things that have become public issues, or have been re-categorised as private matters?

As we were writing this chapter in June 2013, legislation was going through Parliament to allow same-sex couples to be able to marry. The passage of the legislation, however, was hotly contested. Those against the legislation argued that marriage should be reserved only for heterosexual couples while same-sex couples could enter into civil partnerships. Those for the legislation argued that equality could only be achieved if all couples, both heterosexual and same-sex, could marry.

Summary

- The distinction between private and public aspects of social life is an important one.
- The distinction between public and private is both changeable and complex in practice.
- Making issues into matters of public concern is a political process.
- Public issues can become matters to be governed.

2 How are public issues governed?

You will have noticed that in this chapter – and indeed in the module more generally – we have used some key words in ways that suggest overlaps and a lack of clear distinctions. Our list of connected and overlapping words about governing includes: govern, government, state, politics, political actors, politicians, parties, public, authority, political authority, legitimacy.

It would, of course, be easier for everyone if there was one simple and agreed definition of each of these terms that allowed clear differences to be drawn out. But that is not true in everyday speech where meanings shift, overlap and are contested. It is unreasonable to expect it to be true in social science writing (not least because social scientists use many of the same words as everyday speech, even if they then call them 'concepts'). Nevertheless, it may be worth trying to draw out some of the differences and connections a little more, as all of these words are important for this chapter.

Governments govern, but they are not the only agencies and institutions that attempt to shape collective choices and decisions. Social groups (both formal and informal) campaign on social issues such as poverty, migration and neighbourhood crime. Organisations such as churches, firms, trade unions, professional bodies and charities, as well as institutions beyond the nation such as the European Union or the United Nations, all attempt to govern aspects of social life. So, governing might be described as the process of trying to shape, direct or rule some areas of life. The process of governing – usually governing others – is undertaken by many sorts of agencies and groups who combine two things:

- A commitment to make things, or people, better (or to keep them the same in the face of threats that might make things worse).
- A claim that they have the authority to bring this improvement about.

(Li, 2007)

This double aspect of governing – improvement and authority – can be found in many practices of governing. For example, officially constituted governments claim authority (from elections or other expressions of popular support) to improve the well-being of the population. Religious organisations claim authority over their membership (or the faithful) and seek to guide their actions for their spiritual or material well-being. Schools are given temporary and conditional authority over children to shape their personal and social development. This authority, which is typically licensed by the state, is expressed in the Latin phrase *in loco parentis* (in the place of the parent), a reminder that parents have authority over their children. In exercising authority over their children, parents are expected to take proper care of them. Where parents fail to meet that expectation, their children may be removed from their authority and taken into public care.

But if there are so many types of authority, why do social scientists see states – what we called 'political' or 'public' authority – as so important? We want to suggest that states do more than 'connect' other sorts of authority. States order, organise and authorise types of authority. They establish who might legitimately claim to exercise authority over particular aspects of society, for example what kind of authority parents can exercise over their children; where the professions of medicine can exercise their authority (and what the limits are); over what aspects of personal and social life churches can claim to exercise authority. So, states tend to establish the legitimate reach or scope of many other types of authority.

The government of a state, therefore, has sources of authority and legitimacy that are highly distinctive. One of the most famous definitions of the state, which is regularly used in political argument today, highlights two elements of this distinctiveness. The German sociologist Max Weber, in a lecture given in 1918, defined **the state** as:

The state (as defined by Max Weber)
An organisation that successfully claims a monopoly of the legitimate use of force in a given territory.

> ... a human community that (successfully) claims the monopoly of the legitimate use of physical force within a given territory.
>
> (Weber, 1991 [1921], p. 78)

Territory is central to this definition – the state claims to be dominant (it claims to say what goes) within a defined territory or within a country's borders. Weber also argued that there was no point defining states by what they do – they do lots of different things. Better, he said, to define it by its means – 'how it does things'. Weber knew that states did things in various ways, but there was one way, one key characteristic of the state, that was unique: force. Institutions of coercion are crucial, as Weber suggests, and closely related to the defining idea of the state being the authoritative rule maker in the territory and among the people over which it rules. The idea here is that, in the end, it is only the state that can make and enforce laws legitimately; corporations, trade unions, universities and private citizens, for example, do not have that authority.

Governments claim political authority: that is, they claim to be the legitimate leaders, rulers or representatives of the people. 'Legitimacy' refers to a belief in the state's 'rightness', its right to rule, or the idea that its authority is proper. A state that is accepted as legitimate is more likely to succeed in governing than a state that is perceived as illegitimate. One of the main ways in which individuals express their acceptance or rejection of the state is through the ballot box. By and large, of course, elections do not tend to question the state's overall legitimacy: they provide a means for people to question and reflect on this or that government policy, the adequacy of this or that government agency, or the talents and policies (or lack of them) of this or that party, candidate or official. Nevertheless, in the contemporary world, legitimacy – the sense that the state is in some way rightful – is closely associated with democratic principles. One prominent democratic theorist, David Beetham (1992), suggests that **political legitimacy** can arise from:

- Legal validity – the government is formed, and state agencies operate, according to the rules of the constitution.

- The justifiability of those rules in terms of local values – the constitutional rules are themselves acceptable to the people who are ruled by them.

- Evidence of express consent – the people have regular opportunities to give or withhold their agreement with government and policies, especially, though not solely, through democratic voting.

Today, people often view free and fair democratic elections as the main, if not the only, reasonable indicator of whether people have given 'express consent' to those who hold state-derived power over them. Beyond groups of ideological and religious extremists, plus the rulers and defenders of isolated regimes such as that of North Korea, few would explicitly oppose **democracy**, even if they might disagree on what democracy is.

Political legitimacy
Arises in political orders that are rule governed, where the basic constitutional rules accord with the values of those who are governed, and the governed have opportunities to express their consent for how they are governed.

Democracy
Can be defined, minimally, in terms of procedures such as competitive elections, and maximally, in terms of ideas of participation, deliberation and the direct involvement of citizens in government.

Figure 9.2   Authority, even in coercive regimes, relies on consent

Authority, then, relies on consent from those over whom it is exercised. It is this feature that distinguishes authority from the direct exercise of power through force or coercion and thus makes the authority legitimate. Governmental authority is no different in this respect from, say, medical authority, parental authority or the authority of an employer: if it is misused or oversteps its agreed boundary, it may be called into question and need to be re-established, perhaps on a new basis. The authority to govern, like any other kind of authority, is justified in terms of the purpose it is intended to serve and the sources of its authorisation, and there is a delicate relationship between the exercise of authority and its ongoing need for authorisation. In fact, it can be argued that authority is the single biggest tool that governments have; after all, why do most people, most of the time, pay their taxes and provide the state with the information it seeks, if not because they recognise its authority to ask for these things?

Sometimes, and in some places, governments do govern through the use or threat of force, and all states have some machinery of coercion (armed forces, police, prisons, and so on) at their disposal. However, even the most coercive regimes need to maintain the loyalty of their means of coercion, such as the armed forces and police services. In general, it appears to be more economical and effective to govern through consent. By consent, we do not necessarily mean enthusiastic endorsement of the government or its policies. Consent can be passive, grudging or merely a matter of compliance. It may be consent to the 'rules of the game' in political terms, rather than consent to a specific government. But such varieties of consent contribute to, or enable, the exercise of authority.

Nevertheless, authority has to be earned and thus made and remade on a continuous basis. As political theorist Rodney Barker has put it, what characterises government generally 'is not the possession of a quality defined as legitimacy, but the claiming, the activity of legitimation' (2001, p. 2). The contemporary state is in a continuous process of legitimation – a claim that is never fully fulfilled and never uncontested. Two factors explain this constant search for legitimacy.

First, states are human constructions and not pre-given entities. They are artificially made and need to be constantly remade in numerous, regular ways. This can be seen by examining historical maps, which show how nation states have evolved. The idea of the United Kingdom would have been unintelligible from examining, for example, a map of Europe around 1000 AD (see Figure 9.3). This is because the UK is an artificial political unit that houses competing allegiances and identities. The borders of a state do not necessarily coincide with the borders of a nation, as in the case of the United Kingdom of Great Britain and Northern Ireland (the official title of the country since 1927) where one state houses three nations – England, Scotland and Wales. Wales, Scotland and Ireland all had their own independent parliaments in the fourteenth, seventeenth and eighteenth centuries respectively, before they were gradually brought under the political control of the parliament in Westminster in a process that was often violently resisted by those territories forced to give up their independent institutions. Northern Ireland is an interesting example: it is part of the state of the United Kingdom of Great Britain and Northern Ireland, but only some would consider it a nation or would describe their nationality as 'Northern Irish'. It is referred to variously as a 'state within a state', a 'province', the 'Six Counties' or 'Ulster'.

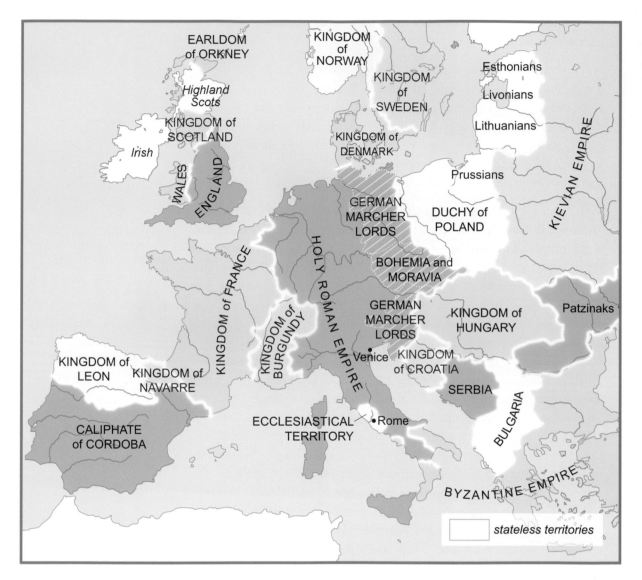

Figure 9.3   Europe around 1000 AD

Second, this ongoing process of making and remaking denotes that states are only ever partially and temporarily successful in promoting social order. All states succeed and fail to some extent. The artificial and temporary nature of social order means that states constantly seek legitimacy from their citizens through regular elections and other mechanisms. As a result, change is a constant factor in the life of states, even in those that appear to be more-or-less stable. The UK is generally seen as an example of a political system in which change has been gradual and evolutionary, and it has retained pretty much the same institutional political order over time. But in fact even in the UK the state has tended to be much more fluid and changeable than it might appear at first glance. New institutions have been created and existing ones revised. Malfunctioning institutions are repaired or replaced. The process of devolution in the contemporary UK in 1998, which resulted in a Scottish Parliament, a National Assembly for Wales and an Assembly in Northern Ireland, can be seen as part of this process of state renewal. Independence for Scotland, to be decided in a referendum in 2014, is another part of this process of making and remaking.

Summary

- Key words in relation to governing include: government, state, politics, legitimacy and authority. The question of authority is particularly important as it enables organisations and actors to shape or direct aspects of social life, and intervene to direct particular sorts of people or improve particular conditions.

- Authority is an important resource for governments, states and other social actors and organisations (from parents to churches) that seek to govern people's conduct. It needs to be legitimate (it can only be exercised with the consent of those being governed), and such legitimacy needs to be made and remade constantly.

- There is a relationship between the state, its territory and its people. This relationship is not pre-given or natural, but rather a product of constant claims.

- States have a unique role, being both sites of authority and institutions that distribute or license different social actors and organisations to exercise authority in specific settings.

3 Whose problem? The issue of social inequality

In 2010, a wave of protests challenging governments began in Tunisia and spread to many other countries, in what became known as the 'Arab Spring'. Inspired by this example, protesters soon took to the streets in Spain, Greece, the UK and the USA throughout 2011 and 2012. Although the political context was different in each case, protesters were united by a sense of outrage at the unfairness of the economic system (in Spain, the protesters were called *los indignados*, the indignant ones). This sense of unfairness became encapsulated in the slogan 'We are the 99 per cent', which highlighted the inequalities of an economic system where wealth has become increasingly concentrated in the hands of the 1 per cent at the top. This raises questions about the relationship between inequality and order and disorder, and the extent to which inequality helps to make and remake a certain kind of order, or as the protests suggest, the extent to which inequality might create disorder.

Figure 9.4   Protesting against inequality

In this section, we explore the issue of social inequality, putting some of the ideas from the previous sections to work in relation to the example of social inequality. For instance, we will ask what sort of problem social inequality represents (is it a public issue?) and what it might mean to govern social inequality (who should be responsible for governing inequality?). Inequality is one of the very long-running focal points of social science research and theorising. Studies have explored the forms that inequality might take, and how it persists or changes, and there are intense debates about what causes inequality and what its social consequences are. We do not intend to cover all of these in this chapter, but while you work through this section, you might want to reflect on why inequality is such a vital issue for the social sciences and why it has links to issues of social order and practices of governing.

Let us begin with a preliminary definition of inequality from a social science standpoint: social scientists are interested in the unequal distribution of valued social resources within a society and between societies. As you will see shortly, most studies of social inequality focus on the distribution of income or wealth, but it is important to recognise that income and wealth are particular sorts of valued resources. There may be others, for example power can be viewed as a social resource and may be unequally distributed; alternatively, happiness may be socially valued and also be unequally distributed. So, too, may life expectancy or good health. The point about stressing valued social resources is that different societies may value different sorts of resources (think about the significance of access to or control of land, for example). But in most contemporary societies organised around market economies, income and wealth command most social science attention – because income and wealth enable people to achieve desired goals, and may also be taken as a marker of an individual's or family's social standing, value or worth.

3.1 Inequality: globally and in the UK

Recent studies, at both the global level and at the level of nation states, point to a set of patterns and trends. By 'patterns', we mean the shape of the distribution of income and wealth and the relationship between different groups. By 'trends', we mean the ways in which those patterns change or stay the same over time. Let us begin by examining some sets of data that deal with changes in income and wealth distribution, and inequalities both within countries and between them. We examine data for both wealth and income: different aspects of economic inequality.

'Income' refers to the flows of money that households receive from various sources: employment, 'transfers' or benefits from public sources (disability benefit, state pensions, and so on) and income from investments (including private pensions). 'Wealth' refers to the property held by individuals or households. Property may be in the form of land, buildings, objects or financial items (shares, and so on).

Activity 4

Look at the 'wealth pyramid' in Figure 9.5. Describe the different segments and what the pyramid might tell us about the distribution of wealth globally.

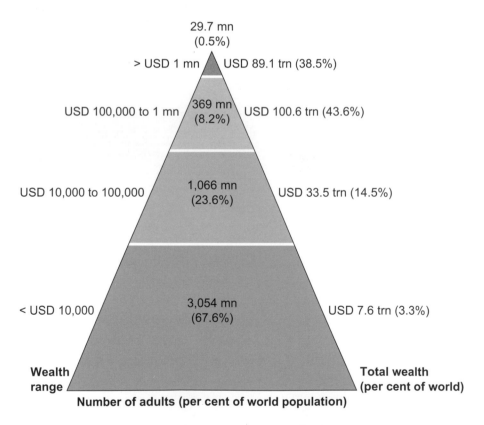

29.7 mn
(0.5%)

> USD 1 mn   USD 89.1 trn (38.5%)

USD 100,000 to 1 mn   369 mn (8.2%)   USD 100.6 trn (43.6%)

USD 10,000 to 100,000   1,066 mn (23.6%)   USD 33.5 trn (14.5%)

< USD 10,000   3,054 mn (67.6%)   USD 7.6 trn (3.3%)

Wealth range   **Total wealth (per cent of world)**

Number of adults (per cent of world population)

Figure 9.5   The global wealth pyramid (Source: Davies et al., 2011)

The *Global Wealth Data Book* (Davies et al., 2011) produced by the financial services organisation, Credit Suisse, provides an annual snapshot of the distribution of the world's wealth. Displayed in the form of a pyramid, the 2011 report shows that wealth is concentrated at the top, in a few hands, while the majority at the bottom owns only a small percentage of the world's wealth. The concentration of wealth is such that the top 0.5 per cent of the population holds 38.5 per cent of global wealth compared to the bottom 67.6 per cent holding only 3.3 per cent of the world's wealth. If we widen this lens, we can see that the top 10 per cent (approximately) holds 82.1 per cent of the world's wealth compared to the bottom 90 per cent (approximately), which owns a mere 17.8 per cent of the world's wealth. This inequality in wealth distribution has occurred at a time when global wealth, according to the *Global Wealth Data Book*, has increased by 72 per cent since 2000.

Here we can see an important distinction between patterns and trends. Patterns show the distributions (in this case, of wealth) at a specific point in time. Trends point to the way such patterns change over time. The pyramid reveals a pattern of distribution. The last sentence of the previous paragraph points to a trend: that the inequalities between rich and poor have been increasing globally during the decade 2000–10.

Activity 5

Below are some extracts from a newspaper report on a study about inequality, which was produced by the Organisation for Economic Cooperation and Development (OECD) in 2011. Can you identify the comments that refer to *patterns* and those that are about *trends*?

1   *The annual average income in the UK of the top 10 per cent in 2008 was just under £55,000, about 12 times higher than that of the bottom 10 per cent, who had an average income of £4,700.*

2   *This is up from a ratio of eight to one in 1985 and significantly higher than the average income gap in developed nations of nine to one.*

3   *Even in countries viewed as 'fairer' – such as Germany, Denmark and Sweden – this pay gap between rich and poor is expanding: from five to one in the 1980s to six to one today. In the rising powers of Brazil, Russia, India and China, the ratio is an alarming 50 to one.*

4   *The share of the top one per cent of income earners increased from 7.1 per cent in 1970 to 14.3 per cent in 2005.*

5   *Although spending on public services in Britain had gone up in the past decade, at the same time benefits to the poor were worth less and taxes were less redistributive. The effect has been a dramatic weakening in the state's ability to spread wealth throughout society. From the mid '70s to mid '80s, the tax-*

> *benefit system offset more than 50 per cent of the rise in income inequality. It now manages just 20 per cent.*
>
> 6 *Inequality in income is growing faster in the UK than any other rich country.*
>
> (Ramesh, 2011)

Extracts one and six describe patterns; extracts two to five describe trends. The extracts also include comparisons between countries (extracts two, three and six).

We might think about what this sort of statistical data tells us about inequality and, equally important, about what it does not. Such data enables us to assess national and international patterns and trends in the distribution of wealth and income. In particular, it informs us about the striking trend – across many countries – towards widening inequality. Such data does *not* tell us the causes of these patterns and trends: what makes inequalities deepen? Data like this also does *not* tell who is – or who becomes – poor: what economic, social or political processes shape who becomes rich or poor? What is the relationship between patterns of difference and patterns of inequality? Finally, data of this sort tells us nothing about the experience of wealth or poverty: how do these distributions of wealth and income shape social lives?

We should not expect a single type of evidence to tell us everything. Data about the changing distribution of wealth and income is important – and allows social scientists to ask and investigate some of those other questions. They are, however, not the focus for the rest of this chapter. Instead we focus on whether these inequalities are public issues that need to be governed.

3.2 What sort of problem is this?

Inequality is clearly a reality and growing, but is it a problem? And, if it is, what sort of problem is it? There are many different views of inequality as a problem for governing, but here we are going to concentrate on two of them. The first claims that it is not a problem at all: in this view, inequalities are both normal and necessary. They are normal because people are naturally unequal and all societies have some forms of inequality (see, for example, Gilder, 1985). They are necessary because unequal rewards create incentives and aspirations for people to work harder and be more innovative or entrepreneurial. This view – often associated with theorists of and enthusiasts for social organisation based on 'free-market' principles – has had a strong presence during the past 30 years or more. It has shaped approaches to the economic, taxation and social policies of many governments – towards combinations of lower taxes (individual and corporate), the privatisation of public services and industries, and the deregulation of economic activity, especially in the field of financial services. From this point of view, inequality is only a problem if politicians or governments think they should do something about it and engage in 'social engineering' (a term used to condemn political interference with the 'natural order of things' or the workings of the 'free market'). In this view, perfectly encapsulated in a comedy sketch that first appeared on the television programme *The Frost Report* in 1966, inequality is a crucial element of maintaining order because everyone knows their place.

Figure 9.6   John Cleese, Ronnie Barker and Ronnie Corbett – 'I know my place'

The sketch involved a six foot five John Cleese standing next to a five foot eight Ronnie Barker who in turn stood next to five foot one Ronnie Corbett, and used each man's height to illustrate their standing in society:

| Middle-class Barker explains: | I look up to him [Cleese] because he is upper class but I look down on him [Corbett] because he is lower class. |
| Lower-class Corbett: | I know my place. |

Although only a few minutes long, the sketch remains in the public memory because it accurately portrays, albeit in a simplified way, class inequalities in the UK and 'the natural order' of social and economic inequalities. More recently, the interest in class has been sustained by a BBC survey intended to establish how many classes there are in Britain (BBC, 2013).

This survey was discussed in Chapter 5.

The second view treats social inequality as systemic: as an integral feature of how a particular type of social order works. A society that values wealth and has means for distributing it unequally necessarily produces 'winners and losers'. Only by changing how the society works can the problem of social inequality be overcome. It is important to stress that this systemic view includes both the causes and the consequences of inequality. Where the first view tends to assume that the consequences of inequality are a problem only for the poorest, the systemic view sees a variety of social consequences that affects all members of society (even if they are affected differently). For example, a study for the Joseph Rowntree Foundation (2008) estimated that child poverty costs the UK £25 billion per year when direct public spending costs are combined with lost economic productivity. A series of studies by Richard Wilkinson and his colleague has demonstrated that the greater the spread of inequality in a society, the higher overall levels of sickness will be. That is, greater inequality does not just make poor people sick (although it certainly does that), but it makes all members of the society more prone to illness (Wilkinson and Pickett, 2009). The Marmot Review (2010, p. 9) demonstrated the link between social inequalities and health inequalities, and argued that reducing health inequalities, apart from being a matter of social justice, also made good economic sense because health inequalities accounted for 'productivity losses, reduced tax revenue, higher welfare payments and increased treatment costs' (2010, p. 18).

In the UK, the High Pay Commission noted that high levels of inequalities harm public trust, lower employee motivation, and distort the market by, for example, attracting individuals into the city rather than into science or medicine and, ultimately, can lead to social unrest and a breakdown in social cohesion (High Pay Commission, 2011, pp. 10–11). The High Pay Commission reported that:

> The public is rapidly running out of patience with a system that allows those at the top to enrich themselves while everyone else struggles to make ends meet. This has been thrown into stark relief by the economic crisis, but has been building for the past 30 years.
>
> (High Pay Commission, 2011, p. 7; see also Dorling, 2012, and the Joseph Rowntree Foundation, 2007)

It is worth remembering that a century ago many societies were embarking on social welfare programmes to reduce or at least mitigate the effects of social inequality. One recurrent reason given by politicians was the danger of social unrest or political rebellion. Introducing plans for unemployment insurance and old-age pensions, the British politician Joseph Chamberlain asked 'what ransom will property pay for the security which it enjoys?' (quoted in Saville, 1957, p. 13). The wave of protests about the unfairness of the economic system in 2011/12 would appear to support Chamberlain's claim that inequality may create disorder, in contrast to the first view where inequality is a necessary part of making the current order.

Figure 9.7   Joseph Chamberlain

Of course, these are very crude statements of different perspectives on social inequality, but they do indicate something of the range of social science views (and some of their echoes in politics and political ideologies: remember Chapter 8). We will explore below two different advocates of these perspectives and the issues that these conflicting perspectives raise for thinking about governing inequality.

Summary

- There is evidence of considerable inequality of wealth and income on a global and national scale.

- There is evidence that such inequalities are increasing on a global and national scale.

- Such evidence describes patterns and trends, but does not explain the causes of inequalities.

- There are disputed views of the relationship between economic inequalities and social order.

4 Governing inequality

In this section, we want to draw out some implications of the above discussion for the processes of governing that we discussed earlier in the chapter and for questions of ordering. Clearly, one of the critical questions is 'what sort of problem is this?'. If inequality is either natural or necessary, then it is not a public problem: it does not require governing. But if inequality is a matter of public concern, people may still argue that the governing processes that can deal with it should be private ones, rather than involve states or government agencies to avoid individuals, families and communities becoming dependent on the state.

The systemic view, however, tends to be associated with the view that social inequalities can only be reduced by purposive collective action, usually involving governments implementing policies to reduce or redress inequality. Here a public problem is to be governed by public means. So we could develop a simple typology in which the two views of the causes of inequality match with views about how it is to be governed (see Table 9.1). All typologies are by their very nature simplified pictures of a much more complex reality. It is worth thinking about the two views of inequality as representing opposite ends of a spectrum with various positions in between.

Table 9.1 Governing inequality

View of inequality	Natural	Systemic
Approach to governing inequality	No governing ('against social engineering')	Collective/public action to reduce or redress inequalities
Advocates of this approach	Friedman, Gilder, Hayek,	Keynes, Krugman, Stiglitz
Examples where some aspects of the approach were implemented	USA (under Reagan)	USA (New Deal)
	UK (under Thatcher)	UK (post WW2), Scandinavian countries (post WW2)
	Chile (under Pinochet)	

We are going to examine the views of two advocates of each of these approaches, Friedrich von Hayek (1899–1992) and Joseph Stiglitz (1943–), whose ideas have gained in popularity following the global recession and the resulting debates about who or what was to blame for the economic collapse, and the best way to solve it.

4.1 Hayek: the market and freedom

Figure 9.8   Friedrich von Hayek

Hayek's most famous book is *The Road to Serfdom*, which was first published in 1944, although it returned to popularity with the emergence of the New Right, symbolised by Thatcher's Britain and Reagan's USA in the 1980s, and again in the aftermath of the global recession in 2008. For all great thinkers, the context in which they write plays a key role in shaping their ideas. Hayek grew up in early twentieth-century Austria and was appalled by the fascist and communist regimes that developed in the 1930s. The totalitarianism of the communist Soviet Union and Nazi Germany is partly what Hayek was responding to when he wrote *The Road to Serfdom*. At the same time, it was also a response to the growth of economic planning in the wartime economies of countries like Great Britain. Against this backdrop, Hayek's work focuses on the damage that strong states can do to society, particularly in the ways in which they restrict the freedom of individuals. For Hayek, freedom is the absence of coercion and he is very specific that people can only be coerced by other people, and not by their circumstances. This concept of freedom is important to understanding his views on inequality. People who are unemployed or who are living in poverty do so because of the way the market functions, rewarding those with certain skills and penalising those without. But while these people might well be suffering, they are not coerced because the market is an impersonal mechanism. Constraint by people, not impersonal forces like the market, is what harms the kind of freedom Hayek values.

Hayek's central argument in *The Road to Serfdom* (1976a [1944]) is that any attempts to plan and regulate society, however well-intentioned the motives of those involved, inevitably lead to coercive government. This leads to a loss of freedom because it is coercion by people (government) not by circumstance. Although Hayek was talking about socialism as the road to serfdom, he argued in *The Constitution of Liberty* in 1960 that the interventions in the economy and society, which are typical of the welfare state, could also lead to serfdom.

Hayek seems to fear the gradual encroachments of the welfare state just as much as he feared full blown socialism in his earlier works. While the welfare state might not necessarily lead to the kind of totalitarian measures that socialism inevitably produces, the growing power of the welfare state produces 'the death of liberty of a thousand small cuts, each aiming at correcting some apparent flaw in the system' (Caldwell, 2011, p. 91). This is because '[T]he close interdependence of all economic phenomena makes it difficult to stop planning just where we wish … once the free workings of the market is impeded beyond a certain degree, the planner will be forced to extend his controls until they become all comprehensive' (Hayek, 1976a [1944], p. 117).

For Hayek, inequalities are natural because they result from the differences innate in human nature. Quite simply, some people are more gifted than others. These differences in human nature lead to the division of labour, with individuals concentrating on tasks to which they are most suited. For Hayek, although this division of labour inevitably leads to some people being better off than others, society as a whole is better off because the division of labour leads to more efficient economic outcomes. Making society as a whole better off is far better for improving the lives of those at the bottom than any redistribution of wealth that the state might engage in.

Thus:

> ... on the whole it would seem that the fact which, contrary to a widely held belief, has contributed most during the last two hundred years to increase not only the absolute but also the relative position of those in the lowest income groups has been the general growth of wealth which has tended to raise the income of the lowest groups more than the relatively higher ones.
>
> (Hayek, 1976b, p. 131)

Hayek claims that the overall expansion of wealth is not only a rising tide that 'lifts all boats', but disproportionately improves the lot of the poorest. (He was, of course, writing long before the data you were reading in Section 3.1.) Governments, therefore, should limit themselves to providing the necessary legal framework to permit markets to operate freely in order to increase overall wealth rather than trying to interfere in its distribution.

4.2 Hayek: what role for the state?

Hayek was particularly contemptuous of attempts to correct social inequality – because he thought it was impossible for governments to describe how merit should be judged and rewarded. Legislation that tries to change 'the material position of particular people or enforce distributive or "social" justice' (Hayek, 1960, p. 231) was a prime example of coercion. The only mechanism capable of determining the just deserts for each individual is the market because it is an impersonal mechanism. In this sense, he was echoing the view of the pioneer economist Adam Smith (1723–1790) who in 1776 argued that people should be left alone to buy and sell freely among themselves without government intervention because, in this way, markets produce positive outcomes for everyone as if guided by 'an invisible hand' (Smith, 1999 [1776]). Markets may not always produce perfect outcomes, but they are always more efficient than any government intervention.

Although Hayek recognised that all states intervene to some extent in the economy and our private lives, this intervention must be kept to a minimum and should largely consist of the provision of general rules and laws, which allow individuals to pursue their own ends without interference from others. This is often expressed as the idea of the *laissez-faire* state or the 'night-watchman' state, whose role is to secure the conditions for people to go freely about their business. When governments go beyond the provision of this minimal legal framework, coercive government always results because knowledge is inevitably limited. Hayek argued that it is impossible to know with any accuracy what those around us need or want; a problem which is only exacerbated if we try to know the needs and wants of the millions of individuals who make up society. Hayek constantly emphasised the limitations of our knowledge and it is this that led him to be pessimistic about attempts to improve conditions by state intervention in the economy because it generally had adverse results.

The workings of the free market would certainly result in inequalities, but for Hayek the only thing governments should do in response is to provide a minimum safety net. He acknowledged the necessity of 'some provision for those threatened by the extremes of indigence or starvation ... be it only in the interest of those who require protection against acts of desperation on the part of the needy' (Hayek, 1960, p. 285). Note, as the last part of the quotation indicates, a safety net should be provided not because the poor deserved help from the state, but because they might become dangerous without it. Only if the behaviour of the poor threatened the social order should the state act.

It should come as no surprise, then, that Hayek regarded the use of the tax system to mitigate inequalities as both inefficient and unjust. Inefficient because the state cannot process and communicate all of the necessary information to enable individuals to pursue their own ends as well as a market can, and unjust because if a government were to decide what reward each individual merits for his/her contribution, rather than the impersonal mechanism of the market, this would be tantamount to coercion. For Hayek, because government intervention always leads to adverse results, however well-intentioned such efforts might be, the only solution is minimal government.

Activity 6

How would you expect Hayek to respond to:

- concern about deepening inequalities?
- financial crises and recession?

Hayek's arguments continue to exert a profound influence on contemporary political thinking about the relationship between the state and the economy, and about the social and economic implications of a 'free-market' society. They were particularly influential in the efforts of governments (especially those in the UK and USA) to 'roll back the state' in the 1980s and 1990s; and they were profoundly influential in global organisations, such as the OECD and International Monetary Fund (IMF), for whom good governance usually meant minimal government. Certainly the popularity of these ideas coincided with the deepening of inequalities within and between nations that we have seen in this chapter. They also coincided with the increasing appearances of crises in lightly regulated global financial markets.

4.3 Stiglitz and the dangers of inequality

Figure 9.9   Joseph Stiglitz

If Hayek wrote *The Road to Serfdom* in the context of the rise of totalitarian fascist and communist regimes in the 1930s, Joseph Stiglitz's *The Price of Inequality*, published in 2012, is a response to the global recession that began in 2008. Even before this dramatic economic collapse, however, Stiglitz had become concerned about the unfairness of the global economic system, and specifically the sharp rises in inequality both within countries, in particular in the USA and the UK, and between countries. One of the most graphic illustrations that Stiglitz uses to convey the extent of inequality in the USA is the Walton family:

> … the six heirs to the Wal-Mart empire command wealth of $6.97 billion, which is equivalent to the wealth of the entire bottom 30 percent of US society.
>
> (Stiglitz, 2012a, p. 8)

Stiglitz uses the shorthand of the 'one percent problem' to highlight the extreme wealth of the 1 per cent who own more than a third of the nation's wealth and a fifth of its income (2012a, p. 2), while noting the racial and gender aspects to this inequality with large differences in income and wealth separating white men from women, African-Americans and Hispanics (2012a, p. 68). He claims, for example, that the average African-American household lost 53 per cent of its wealth between 2005 and 2009, 'putting its assets at a mere 5 percent of the average white American's', while the average Hispanic household saw its wealth reduce by 66 per cent (2012a, p. 13).

Stiglitz, however, is no radical. Like Hayek, he believes that free and competitive markets generally benefit society as a whole because:

> At their best, markets have played a central role in the stunning increases in productivity and standards of living in the past two hundred years – increases that far exceeded those of the previous two millennia.
>
> (Stiglitz, 2012a, p. xiii)

He would also agree that some degree of inequality is inevitable in market economies for many of the reasons that, for example, Hayek would affirm. However, today's extreme levels of inequality are, for Stiglitz, neither an inevitable by-product of a market economy nor necessary for its functioning. In fact, as we will see below, he claims that such inequalities have negative economic effects.

One of the problems for Stiglitz is not just that the information that any single individual can have is limited, which was the focus of Hayek's work, but that information is shared unequally among individuals.

Stiglitz labelled this 'information asymmetry'. Stiglitz was concerned with the fact that in any transaction, one participant has more or better information than the other. This imbalance of power in transactions, caused by the fact that information is not shared equally between those involved, means that transactions often fail, and indeed, that whole markets can fail. Stiglitz uses the concept of information asymmetry to illustrate the negative impact on society which results from some individuals having access to privileged knowledge that others do not. The overselling of mortgages in both the USA and the UK to those who could ill afford them is an example of a transaction where those selling the mortgages – the banks – had more information than the people buying the mortgages and were able to exploit this advantage accordingly.

At a global level, developing countries, which negotiate deals with institutions like the IMF, face a similar imbalance of information, which Stiglitz argues is exploited by the IMF to the detriment of the developing world (Stiglitz, 2002a). Indeed, Houseman argues that Stiglitz is at pains to emphasise that 'it is usually those without connections, education or influence – groups such as the working class, the poor and the consumer – who are most disadvantaged by the information gaps found in the marketplace' (Houseman, 2006, p. 57).

Hence, information asymmetry, which leads to market failings, justifies government intervention to correct the market. While economists like Hayek assume that markets are generally efficient, particularly if governments give them free rein, Stiglitz argues that this is generally true only under exceptional circumstances. Where information is imperfect and where information asymmetry exists, which for Stiglitz is generally the case, markets are inefficient. For Stiglitz, there is no such thing as the invisible hand of the market as thinkers like Hayek would affirm:

> Adam Smith's invisible hand – the idea that free markets lead to efficiency as if guided by unseen forces – is invisible, at least in part, because it is not there.
>
> (Stiglitz, 2002b)

Stiglitz also questions the idea of the market as an efficient allocator of rewards. He disagrees with the view that inequality is an inevitable and necessary feature of economies in which competitive markets are the best mechanism to determine the value of each individual's contributions such that those who work harder or who have a scarce and valuable skill will legitimately be rewarded more than those who do not. In this view, incentives are essential to a market economy and any incentive system will always produce inequalities, as some are naturally more talented than others and others will work harder than their colleagues. Pursuing equality, it is argued by those supporting free markets, can damage economic efficiency and entrepreneurialism because there is less incentive to strive. A popular version of this argument frequently used to defend large bank bonuses, for example, is that high salaries need to be paid to attract the best and the brightest. Stiglitz argues, however, that those 'who have made such large contributions to our well-being' such as Tim Berners-Lee, the inventor of the World Wide Web, or James Watson and Francis Crick who unravelled the mysteries of DNA, are not those most rewarded by the market (2012a, p. 41). Instead, it is the financiers 'who make up a significant proportion of the top one or 0.1 percent' (2012a, p. 41). Moreover, Stiglitz argues that much less is said about the need to provide incentives for ordinary workers. One key incentive is the perception of fairness, which is regarded as crucial to motivate workers, and 'while it is not always clear what is fair […], there is a growing sense that the present disparity in wages is unfair' (Stiglitz, 2012a, p. 103).

Wherever markets have been given free rein, Stiglitz points to the high levels of inequalities that have resulted. But Stiglitz also recognises the role of politics in producing today's extreme levels of inequalities. He quotes with approval the claim by Warren Buffet, the American billionaire and philanthropist, that 'there's been class warfare going on for the last 20 years and my class has won' (Stiglitz, 2012a, p. 180; see also Stiglitz, 2012b).

For Stiglitz, then, high levels of inequality have resulted not only from the ways in which information asymmetry leads to market failings, but also through the ways in which politics has shaped the markets to promote the interests of the 1 per cent rather than the wider society.

Stiglitz writes that:

> Much of the inequality that exists today is a result of government policy, both what the government does and what it does not do. Government has the power to move money from the top to the bottom and the middle, or vice versa.
>
> (2012a, p. 28)

In short, today's levels of inequality are not just a natural by-product of the market: 'inequality is the result of political forces as much as economic ones' (Stiglitz, 2012a, p. 30).

4.4 Stiglitz and the problem of politics

One example of the failure of politics to act in the interests of the majority rather than the 1 per cent, according to Stiglitz, is the government's abrogation of its role in ensuring the tax system is a progressive one. In other words, by failing to ensure that the rich pay more taxes than the poor, government has contributed to rising inequality. Stiglitz notes that:

> … the superrich actually pay on average a lower tax rate than those less well-off; and the lower tax rate means that their riches increase faster. The average tax rate in 2007 on the top 400 households was only 16.6 percent, considerably lower than the 20.4 percent for tax payers in general […] While the average tax rate has decreased little since 1979 – going from 22.2 percent to 20.4 percent, that of the top one percent has fallen by almost a quarter, from 37 percent to 29.5 percent.
>
> (Stiglitz, 2012a, pp. 72–3)

Such a regressive tax rate is not the result of market forces but of a failure of government to correct this inequality. Stiglitz notes that while the market generates inequalities, in part because politics gives it free rein to do so, what is also striking is that 'as the market-generated inequality has increased, our government has done less and less' in terms of addressing inequalities either through public expenditure programmes on health or education or through ensuring that the wealthy pay more taxes than the less well-off (Stiglitz, 2012a, p. 74).

If the origins of market inequalities are not just the result of impersonal market forces, but also result from the government policies that shape those market forces, it follows that governments have a role in mitigating inequalities. Stiglitz argues that government intervention is also justified because inequalities are not just harmful to those suffering them; they are also harmful in a broader sense. Inequalities of such magnitude lead to 'an economic system which is less stable and less efficient, with less growth, and a democracy that has been put into peril' (Stiglitz, 2012a, p. xii). Stiglitz shows how inequalities, far from being the price paid for efficient and competitive markets, act as a drag on economies for a number of reasons.

- Inequality reduces demand in an economy, and ultimately, economic growth because the very wealthy, despite their often very conspicuous consumption habits, are unable to consume all that they earn. Conversely, distributing wealth more equally would stimulate demand in the economy because those at the bottom spend all of their income (Stiglitz, 2012a, p. 85).

You read about conspicuous consumption in Chapter 5 of *Understanding Social Lives, Part 1.*

- Stiglitz claims that increasing inequality undercuts public investment in education and infrastructure, which also has negative economic effects, particularly in the long term:

> The more divided a society becomes in terms of wealth, the more reluctant the wealthy are to spend money on common needs. The rich don't need to rely on government for parks or education or medical care or personal security. They can buy all these things for themselves. In the process, they become more distant from ordinary people.
>
> (Stiglitz, 2012a, p. 93)

- Stiglitz argues that inequality means a growing sense of unfairness that makes it harder to motivate workers and ultimately leads to a breakdown of trust in both economic and political institutions, which ultimately damages social cohesion. The undue influence of the wealthy on the setting of economic and political rules damages the health of democracy. For Stiglitz: 'Economic inequality begets political inequality and vice versa [...]. One person, one vote becomes one dollar, one vote. That is not democracy. That is political decay' (cited in NPQ, 2013, p. 53).

Stiglitz represents one contemporary counter to Hayek's views of the free market and minimal state, based on a view of the social, political and economic risks of deepening inequality. He takes a different view of the market (emphasising its failings) and of how 'efficiency' might be understood. As a result, he identifies greater possibilities for states and other international organisations (such as the World Bank, of which he was once the director) to intervene to address market failure.

4.5 Hayek versus Stiglitz?

So, what unites and divides the two views of how to govern social inequality as represented by Hayek and Stiglitz? Hayek sees inequality as a natural and necessary element of a market economy while Stiglitz sees inequality as systemic and the result of both bad economics and politics. Knowledge is a central concept in the work of both of these economists. But if Hayek stresses the limitations of our knowledge, for Stiglitz it is the asymmetries of knowledge that are the problem. The way in which each views inequality and understands knowledge leads each to advocate a different role for governments. If inequalities are both natural and necessary, government intervention will only interfere with the natural workings of the market. Hayek, therefore, sees minimal government as the appropriate alternative to bad government. Stiglitz, however, sees good government as the appropriate alternative. If inequality results from market failure combined with bad politics, it is down to governments to manage economies better. Finally, while Hayek sees government intervention, however well-intentioned, as doomed to failure and ultimately likely to lead to a reduction in both economic and political freedom, Stiglitz is more optimistic about the potential of governments to intervene in positive ways and argues that greater inequalities, if left unchecked, will be bad for democracy, as it undermines the cohesion and social order on which society depends.

Summary

- Inequality is framed as a public issue in different ways and this section has considered two of these: inequality as normal and necessary; and inequality as part of the way that a social system is structured and organised.

- Different ways of framing inequality, especially different ways of understanding its causes, are related to different perspectives on how it might be governed.

- Making and remaking social order requires inequality to be governed – but it may be governed in different ways. Inequality might be seen as a natural and crucial element in making and remaking social order or as leading to disorder.

Conclusion

In this chapter, we have explored a connected set of issues. How do some issues come to be identified as matters of public concern that require active governing, while others are left to the actions of private individuals? This is a pressing question for the social sciences – not least in relation to the issue of inequality. If Hayek's view rules, then inequality is a private matter: it is the result of private choices, individual talents and unemployment, poverty and marginalisation are personal misfortunes. Inequality is only a problem for state action if the poor behave badly – and create social disorder. If Stiglitz's view is taken instead, then incquality is a pressing public issue and governments need to act to manage markets better, reduce gross inequalities, and encourage social integration and solidarity. Both Hayek and Stiglitz share assumptions about starting with the market, even if they disagree about how it works. Other views start from questions about whether economies can be ordered differently – but that, as they say, is another story.

References

Barker, R. (2001) *Legitimating Identities*, Cambridge, Cambridge University Press.

BBC (2013) 'The great British class survey' [Online]. Available at https://ssl.bbc.co.uk/labuk/experiments/class/ (Accessed 23 July 2013).

Beetham, D. (1992) *The Legitimation of Power*, Basingstoke, Macmillan.

Benhabib, S. (1992) 'Models of public space: Hannah Arendt, the Liberal Tradition, and Jurgen Habermas', in Calhoun, C. (ed.) *Habermas and the Public Sphere*, Cambridge, MA, The MIT Press, pp. 73–98.

Caldwell, B. (2011) 'Hayek on socialism and on the welfare state. A comment on Farrant and McPhail's "Does F.A. Hayek's road to serfdom deserve to make a comeback?"', *Challenge*, January–February, pp. 82–97.

Clark, T. (2010) 'Inequality in the UK: the data behind the National Equality Panel report', *The Guardian*, 27 January [Online]. Available at http://www.guardian.co.uk/news/datablog/2010/jan/27/national-equality-panel-inequality-data (Accessed 1 February 2013).

Davies, J., Lluberas, R. and Shorrocks, A. (2011) *Global Wealth Data Book* [Online]. Available at https://www.credit-suisse.com/upload/news-live/000000022231.pdf (Accessed 23 July 2013).

Dorling, D. (2012) 'On the rack of inequality: the gap between the richest and poorest in Britain is widening to new extremes', *SPERI Blog*, 15 November [Online]. Available at http://speri.dept.shef.ac.uk/2012/11/15/rack-inequality/ Full-text PDF (Accessed 23 August 2013).

Friedman, M. (1962) *Capitalism and Freedom*, Chicago, University of Chicago Press.

Gilder, G. (1985) *Wealth and Poverty*, New York, Basic Books.

Hayek, F.A. (1960) *The Constitution of Liberty*, London, Routledge.

Hayek, F.A. (1976a [1944]) *The Road to Serfdom*, London, Routledge.

Hayek, F.A. (1976b) 'The mirage of social justice', *Law, Legislation and Liberty*, vol. 2, London, Routledge.

High Pay Commission (2011) *Cheques Without Balances: Why Tackling High Pay Is in the National Interest* [Online]. Available at http://highpaycentre.org/files/Cheques_with_Balances.pdf (Accessed 7 February 2013).

Houseman, G. (2006) 'Joseph Stiglitz and the critique of free market analysis', *Challenge*, March–April, pp. 52–62.

Joseph Rowntree Foundation (2007) 'New poverty and wealth maps of Britain reveal inequality to be at 40-year high' [Online]. Available at http://www.jrf.org.uk/media-centre/new-poverty-and-wealth-maps-britain-reveal-inequality-be-40-year-high (Accessed 23 July 2013).

Joseph Rowntree Foundation (2008) *Child Poverty Is Costing the UK Billions* [Online]. Available at http://www.jrf.org.uk/media-centre/child-poverty-costing-uk-billions (Accessed 23 July 2013).

Keynes, J.M. (1933) *The Means to Prosperity*, London, Macmillan.

Keynes, J.M. (1936) *The General Theory of Employment, Interest and Money*, London, Palgrave Macmillan.

Krugman, P. (2008) *The Return to Depression Economics and the Crisis of 2008*, London, Penguin Books.

Li, T. (2007) 'Practices of assemblage and community forest management', *Economy and Society*, vol. 36, no. 2, pp. 263–93.

New Perspectives Quarterly (NPQ) (2013) 'The price of inquality', *New Perspectives Quarterly*, vol. 30, no. 1, pp. 52–3.

Ramesh, R. (2011) 'Income inequality growing faster in UK than any other rich country, says OECD', *The Guardian*, 5 December [Online]. Available at http://www.guardian.co.uk/society/2011/dec/05/income-inequality-growing-faster-uk (Accessed 23 July 2013).

Saville, J. (1957) 'The welfare state: an historical introduction', *The New Reasoner*, vol. 3, pp. 5–24.

Smith, A. (1999 [1776]) *The Wealth of Nations*, London, Penguin Books.

Stiglitz, J.E. (2002a) *Globalization and its Discontents*, London, Penguin.

Stiglitz, J.E. (2002b) 'There is no invisible hand', *The Guardian*, 20 December [Online]. Available at http://www.guardian.co.uk/education/2002/dec/20/highereducation.uk1 (Accessed 6 February 2013).

Stiglitz, J.E. (2012a) *The Price of Inequality*, London, Allen Lane.

Stiglitz, J.E. (2012b) 'The 1 Percent's Problem', *Vanity Fair*, 31 May [Online]. Available at http://www.vanityfair.com/politics/2012/05/joseph-stiglitz-the-price-on-inequality (Accessed 1 February 2013).

The Frost Report (1966) BBC, April.

The Marmot Review (2010) *Fair Society, Health Live, Executive Summary* [Online]. Available at http://www.ucl.ac.uk/marmotreview (Accessed 9 February 2013).

Weber, M. (1991 [1921]) *From Max Weber*, Gerth, H.H and Wright Mills, C. (eds), London, Routledge.

Weeks, J. (1995) *Invented Moralities: Sexual Values in an Age of Uncertainty*, Cambridge, Polity Press.

Wilkinson, R. and Pickett, K. (2009) *The Spirit Level: Why More Equal Societies Almost Always Do Better*, London, Allen Lane.

Chapter 10
Reflections on 'Ordering lives'

John Clarke

Contents

Introduction

In this third and final strand, 'Ordering lives', you have encountered another set of ways of thinking about the core social science questions:

- How is society made and remade?

- How are differences and inequalities produced?

- How do social scientists know?

The emphasis in this strand is on the processes and relationships of ordering. This reflects both everyday concerns (can society hang together or might it fall apart? How can order be maintained in the face of new threats?) and those of social scientists. Social order has been a key concern for the social sciences with much work devoted to defining it, explaining how it comes about, how it changes, and what sorts of processes, practices and relationships are involved in making, renewing, challenging and changing it.

1 The story so far … making, connecting and ordering

What does 'ordering' add to studying the processes of making and connecting social lives? At its simplest, it gives a central place to issues of pattern and repetition. How do social lives go on from day to day? How do people know how to act when they go to work, go shopping, or take part in political activities such as voting?

The idea of social order points to two particular things here:

1   The sense of a system, structure or shape within which people act. So, when we talk about a social order, we have a sense that there is something larger in which our actions take place. This might be a local social order (how does the neighbourhood work? Who lives here? What do they do? What do we expect of our neighbours?). It might be a specific society: the UK in the early twenty-first-century has a different sort of social ordering from twenty-first-century China … and a different sort of social ordering from early nineteenth-century Britain. It might even be a global social order: how are relationships between nations organised? How are they managed or governed? What happens when such relationships go wrong?

2   An issue about people knowing how to act – how to conduct themselves in particular situations (as neighbours, drivers, workers, citizens, parents and more). Order implies a sense of repetition: that people, in such roles, will behave in generally predictable ways. Predictable in the sense that they know what to do and others know what to expect of them. When they do not, social lives can get complicated very quickly. In both of these senses, the idea of social order points to the ways in which people enter into a pre-existing system or set of rules and expectations – even if, as you have seen, such social orders are constantly being made and remade.

Activity 1

Can you think of particular examples in the preceding chapters that exemplify these two aspects of ordering for you? Make a note of any examples.

For me, the first aspect of ordering – the idea of a system or structure – is best exemplified in Chapters 6 and 9 of the strand. Chapter 6 on neighbouring points to regular *patterns* in people's interactions with those who live close to them. These are patterns of habit and expectations (even if they differ between places). But Chapter 6 also suggests that there might be a gap between an image of social order and the way it works in practice. So there were tensions between how much closeness and distance people wanted or expected of their neighbours. There were also other rules or expectations that governed how people behaved in particular places (for example, the reluctance to interfere in 'family matters', or the suspicion about surveillance by government). As you think about ordering, you may want to consider whether people always think that the current social order is desirable.

The second example, the social ordering of inequality in Chapter 9, points to a larger-scale structure – inequalities of income and wealth on global and national scales. These too are orders as systems and structures: they persist (even while changing in some aspects); they shape the conditions in which people live their lives and have implications for those lives. Here it is also possible to see the ways in which a particular social order (the current distribution of economic resources) may be viewed differently. The dispute between Hayek's and Stiglitz's views of the causes and effects of inequality, and what should or should not be done about it, is not only a dispute among social scientists. These views both echo and inform public debates – and political choices – about inequalities and the sort of social order in which they are embedded.

The second aspect – ordering as rules of conduct – links Chapter 6's view of neighbouring to questions about disorderly behaviour in Chapters 7 and 8. Social order is marked by the sense of predictability that comes from people knowing how to act in a particular social role in a specific place. People learn how to be neighbours, workers, students, and so on, such that order emerges in their interactions. But sometimes people do not behave 'properly': they do not follow the rules, norms or laws. As Chapter 7 showed, social scientists have expended a lot of time on trying to explain why some people do not behave properly – why they become deviant, delinquent or criminal. Others, more interested in questions of control, have explored why some behaviours and some people become labelled and treated as deviant, delinquent or criminal. But in terms of ordering, there is another question here: what is the difference between people not behaving 'properly' and people refusing to 'know their place' – challenging an unjust or oppressive social order? I will come back to this question.

1.1 The puzzle of order and disorder

Social order – in the smallest and largest settings – involves these senses of shape/system and repetition. It is hardly surprising that social scientists have spent a lot of time and effort on studying social order: it is, for some, the most fundamental issue imaginable – social order provides a basis for *social* lives. Order in this sense involves a shape or pattern for the types of connections and relationships in which people live their lives. And yet, there is a deeper puzzle about social order. The starting point for studying social order (and for most public and political discussions that address it) is about stability: how is social order made and maintained? How do people do the same things and behave the same way over time? Stability and predictability are virtues from this starting point: they enable social lives. But stability is not only a virtue: both people in society and social scientists studying societies sometimes think that change is important too. So the puzzle of social order that emerges might be phrased as: how is social order made and remade?

Let me put this slightly differently. Stability and predictability are valuable conditions for social lives: we know what to do in our various social roles; we have expectations of what others will do and this means that much social activity and social interaction takes place as 'second nature' – things go as we expect, and we do not have to stop and think about how to conduct ourselves. But if we rephrased this sort of stability as being the product of 'people knowing their place', it might appear rather different. 'Knowing your place' summons a different set of images: people deferring to their 'social betters' in a *hierarchical* social order; women staying within the confines of kitchen, church and children (*die Küche, die Kirche, die Kinder* – a view attributed to the National Socialist Party in 1930s and 1940s Germany); children 'being seen and not heard' in the ideal Victorian home; or black people serving their white masters and mistresses in a variety of slave societies.

So, for many social scientists, the question of how social orders change is an issue that demands attention alongside how they are made and repaired. As you have seen, this brings social disorder into view in a number of ways.

Activity 2

What does the idea of 'social disorder' mean for you after your work on this strand? Make a few notes about what this phrase evokes.

I am going to suggest that the 'Ordering lives' strand contains at least three views of social disorder.

1   The first is that it is simply the opposite of social order – it is what occurs when order breaks down or becomes weakened. This sense is one that many social sciences share with much public and political discourse, and it becomes the driving force behind efforts to find out the causes of disorderly behaviour (from juvenile delinquency to rioting). This view of social disorder rests on a normative distinction between order (viewed as a good and virtuous condition) and disorder (viewed as a bad and dangerous condition). 'Normative' means resting on evaluative judgements about things – and social scientists should be wary of failing to recognise and take account of such judgements – not least because social science has produced much evidence that they vary across time and place.

2   The second view of social disorder treats disorder as part of the dynamics of social life, emerging from patterns of social difference and inequality. Conflicts arising from different experiences, expectations and even different 'local rules' create disorder. Some social scientists have been interested in disorder for what it can tell us about the form of social order that it interrupts. If some aspects of social order are unspoken, taken for granted, or practised as 'second nature', then seeing what counts as 'disorder' can reveal more about what is being 'taken for granted'. Here are some examples:

    ○   Some years ago, I heard several people being referred to as 'space invaders' because of their habit of standing too close to the people to whom they were talking. Sometimes, people would take an obvious step back from, or stretch out an arm – both to make a point and create some physical distance. It appears that these 'space invaders' were breaking unspoken assumptions about how close to stand in relation to others.

    ○   Digital technologies have increased our access to sources of information enormously, making it easier to 'cut and paste' to create documents (such as chapters for Open University modules or answers to tutor-marked assignment (TMA) questions). This has made it necessary for the academic world to be much more explicit about the 'disorder' of plagiarism (copying the work of others without acknowledgement). Previously, it was assumed that the unspoken or barely spoken norms of 'good scholarship' would be observed as normal conduct.

o   What are sometimes called 'eating disorders' throw light on two sorts of expectations: the expectations that govern how people eat; and the expectations that groups of people have about the relationship between eating and body shape or body image.

o   Protesters in the streets and squares of capital cities across the world have been accused of causing or plotting 'disorder' through their demands for changes of government or political regime. For some social scientists (and some protesters), the reactions to their disorderly behaviour have made important aspects of the existing regime, and the social order it tries to maintain, more visible.

These examples clearly differ in terms of scale and significance. But in each of them, the 'disorder' acts as a point of view on a particular sort of social order (and its often unstated or tacit assumptions and expectations).

From noisy and aggressive groups of young people in public places to people ignoring cries for help for what they feel to be good reasons; from people protesting inequalities and injustices to people rioting; this strand has contained many examples of how disorder might result from combinations of social difference and inequality. In this, disorder is the inextricable partner of order – they always coexist. For some social scientists, it is this dynamic of order and disorder that brings about social change – without disorder (or what is labelled as disorder), society would be static and ossified. Order without disorder may be a powerful political fantasy, but it is not an accurate description of most societies.

3   This points to the third significant aspect of disorder for social scientists studying social order, because it raises questions about who defines disorder. If we take the last example above, what are the implications of calling political protest 'disorder'? It might be in the interests of the existing regime to call political protest 'disorder' (or

'delinquency' or 'criminal behaviour'). They might think it discredits the protesters. By referring to political dissent as 'disorder' or 'criminal behaviour', it might undermine their challenge to the existing regime and the social order that it supports. The defining or naming of 'disorder' has been an important theme in the strand and it points to other central issues: the question of power (who has the power to successfully name things and people?); and the question of identities (who are protesters? Who are rioters? Who are criminals?).

2 Making and remaking society

All of these aspects of order and disorder are central elements of the contribution that this strand makes to the core question 'how is society made and remade?'. Indeed, for many social scientists it is impossible to think about 'society' as separate from the process of ordering. Social order is another way of naming 'society'. However, it refers specifically to the organisation of the relationship between individuals and between social groups: order is what enables social lives to take place. But there is one important proposition that emerges in what you have been studying: *social orders have to be made* – social order is not a naturally occurring condition (or a universal condition of society). How people are connected and the relationships between them arranged varies dramatically between societies, and across time within a specific society. It requires people to make and remake social orders. This is true at the micro-level of social interactions – think, for example, about changes in the ways in which parents and children interact. Writing this in 2013, I am struck by how different such relationships are in Britain in comparison with how they would have been a century before. Although some people might bewail the breakdown in discipline, the forms of discipline that were part of the social order in 1913 might now look like child abuse. Physical violence – in the home and school – was a much more frequent means of maintaining order in the relationships between children and adults (see, for examples, Humphries and Gordon, 1993; Humphries et al., 1988). What wider social and political processes contributed to this change? It has been claimed that wider movements towards democratisation and equality, a move away from unthinking deference to authority and societies becoming less violent, have contributed to changing family relationships (Gillies, 2003; Smart et al., 2001).

Activity 3

What sorts of processes of making and remaking society have caught your attention during your work on this strand? Make a note of the most interesting ones that you have noticed.

Several issues struck me about 'Ordering lives'. First, and possibly most fundamentally, processes of ordering seem to be essential to the making and remaking of society. Social order – the large and small patterns of social relationships – has to be made: order does not just happen naturally. Perhaps it would be better to say that, although human beings are social animals and have a propensity to find ways of living together, the *specific forms of social order* that organise particular societies have to be made and maintained.

Second, and following on from that last point, there is no one social order. Rather, social science studies reveal very different patterns of order – indeed, societies have found an astonishing variety of ways of organising relationships between people, between people and things, and between people and places. Societies differ in the ways that people relate to one another (from feudal hierarchies to more egalitarian patterns). They differ in how people's relationships to things (material objects) are organised – how ownership is structured; how people exchange things (for example through economic transactions, in gift relationships, through barter); how land is distributed, and so on. They also differ in how people relate to places: are people relatively immobile (attached to a particular place)? Do they move around freely or are they subject to constraints? Do people belong to places – or do places belong to people? Societies also contain different types of social order. Some are specific to particular places or social groups: hanging about on street corners may look aimless, but almost certainly involves a whole set of implicit rules about who can do it and about how it should be done. Such 'subcultures' exist alongside, and sometimes in tension with, a wider sense of social order, and may indeed lead to them being condemned as 'antisocial' or 'disorderly' (as we saw in Chapter 7). Other socially specific forms of order may be less visible (because they take place behind closed doors rather than in the street) or perceived as less dangerous because of the social positions and identities of those involved; what about the social orders of gentlemen's clubs, professional associations, or even economic cartels dividing up markets? Societies also, as we have seen, change over time, such that the prevailing patterns and rules that order social life would not be obvious, or possibly even comprehensible, to previous generations.

Third, social order tends to involve organising the relationships between different aspects of social life. In Chapters 6 and 9, we saw the importance of the distinction between public and private spheres – and the implications that follow from whether some issues (domestic violence, economic inequality) are judged to be private matters or public issues. The American sociologist C. Wright Mills once wrote about this distinction between what he called 'private troubles' and 'public issues', asking what might be involved in turning a private trouble into a public issue (1959). For example, for much of the eighteenth and nineteenth centuries in Europe, unemployment was viewed as a 'private trouble' (a personal misfortune). Only towards the end of the nineteenth century did a number of innovations (including social scientific research as well as the rise of trades unions) lead to a changing definition of unemployment in which social and economic causes came to be recognised. As a result, unemployment became a public issue, and a variety of efforts was made to govern it – from stimulating economic growth to create jobs, through the establishment of government-funded institutions to better match available jobs and available workers (originally known as Labour Exchanges in the UK), to the demand from trades unions for a guaranteed 'right to work' (Langan, 1985).

Activity 4

Thinking about unemployment in the present, would you say it is now viewed as a 'private trouble' or 'public issue'? How is it now governed?

The organisation of the relationship between different aspects of social life extends beyond the distinction between public and private spheres. It also involves conceptions of what should be the proper relationships between, for example, economic activity, political activity and social life. Thinking back to Chapter 9 and Hayek's view of freedom, it should be clear that for him, economic activity comes first – it should (as far as possible) be unconstrained by any political or governmental activity: the market should be free and individuals should be free to pursue their own (private) interests. This involves a rather 'thin' view of social life: people are not connected by much, except the market. They are driven by their own needs and interests, and possibly those of their family. This view of society tends to assume that people are pure individuals or live in families – a view strongly articulated by the then UK Prime Minister Margaret Thatcher when she asserted: 'And, you know, there is no such thing as society. There are individual men and women, and there are families' (Thatcher, 1987). There are, of course, other views, both within society and the social sciences. However, this view of the market combined with this thin view of social life has proved very powerful since the late twentieth century. In practice, its thin view of the social tends to be fleshed out with other claims about social order that centre on tradition, shared values and respect for authority. As we have seen several times during this strand, fears about social disorder are also often phrased in such terms.

This observation points to a final thought about the way ordering is important to the making and remaking of society – since any particular social order has to be made and remade. The turn towards a more Hayekian view of society as economic life did not just happen naturally – it was made and institutionalised by individuals and groups acting to remake aspects of the existing social order, and install new ones in their place. This involved political organisation and activity. It involved changing the shape and the role of the state (for example, reducing its responsibilities for social welfare). It involved encouraging new ways of thinking (for example, asking unemployed people to think of themselves as 'job seekers'). It also involved trying to establish new types of relationships between people, suggesting that they should think and act more like consumers – for example, in making choices of schools for children or in medical care. These point to processes of re-ordering – changing the expectations that people have of their lives and the world they inhabit; changing the rules that govern interactions; and establishing forms of authority that can, if necessary, enforce these expectations and rules. Perhaps most importantly, attempts at re-ordering often proclaim themselves both virtuous and necessary – virtuous because they represent a 'better way' of living together, and necessary because, in another phrase attributed to Prime Minister Thatcher: 'There is no alternative' (sometimes known as 'TINA'; see for example, Thatcher, 1980). Such re-orderings are successful to the extent that they can persuade enough people to believe that there really is no alternative, and that they can persuade people to take on these rules and expectations, ways of thinking, acting and interacting as if they were 'second nature' – the habits of everyday life.

In short, we might think of society being made and remade through different processes – some small-scale interactions as people find new ways of living together (as families, as neighbours and so on); and some large-scale processes involving formal or public authority. But, for social scientists, societies are fascinating because they involve the combination of order (its promise of stability and predictability) and change in which people find new ways of being together.

3 How are differences and inequalities produced?

In this strand, the question of inequalities has been important in several places. Most obviously, Chapter 9 focused on the governing of inequalities. It offered conflicting views of their origins and significance, and how societies could or should respond to them. Inequalities were mainly explored in terms of the distribution of both income and wealth.

Activity 5

Can you think of other points where inequalities – or differences – were important during your work on this strand?

I thought of several ways in which differences and inequalities featured. For example:

- Differences about neighbouring – and how people negotiate those differences – in Chapter 6.

- Differences in propensity to commit criminal/deviant acts in Chapter 7 (how do social scientists identify those most likely to break the law?).

- Differences (and inequalities) in vulnerability to policing and arrest in Chapter 7 (who is most likely to be suspected of being criminal?).

- Inequalities and injustices as motives for social and political disorder or riot in Chapter 8.

These examples point to very different social science issues, ranging from questions about how people find ways of living together across differences, to questions about which differences are connected to inequalities. Why, for instance, have gender differences (between women and men) been persistently linked to economic inequalities in many – but not all – industrial societies? In a similar vein, what enables the relationship between some differences and inequalities to be reduced? During much of the nineteenth and twentieth centuries in the UK, old age was associated with poverty for most people. However, as I write this, a report from the Institute for Fiscal Studies suggests that pensioner incomes have risen more than for other age groups in Britain during the past 30 years, while incomes of young adults have fallen dramatically (Cribb et al., 2013).

■ Age and gender are two types of difference associated with inequality: can you think of others?

Although there are many differences between individuals and groups, not all of them are connected with inequalities. For social scientists, the important questions concern which differences matter for inequality: how do some differences make inequality? There are some differences that seem to be systematically connected to inequality – recurring over long periods of time and occurring in different places. I have already touched on differences of gender: gender differences tend to affect access to income and wealth; and access to powerful positions (in both politics and the corporate world). Arguments go on about how this difference produces inequality – is it a matter of biological difference (over the years many have claimed that women's bodies and brains are inferior to men's)? Is it about a model of social order in which a gendered division of labour means that women tend to do unpaid work (in the private sphere) while men are associated with paid work in the public sphere? Does child bearing and childcare mean that women's careers are more interrupted and less well rewarded? How does that affect women who do not have children?

For this strand, the argument about social order is particularly relevant: there are certainly biological differences between men and women, but they can be and have been socially ordered in very different ways. From the nineteenth century, European societies have tended to develop divisions of labour (that is the distribution of social roles and tasks) that assumed men would be earning a 'family wage', which would enable women to stay at home and care for children (Land, 1980; Naples, 2005). Such a model has been challenged in various ways, not least because men could not always find work, or work that would pay an adequate wage to sustain a family. Since the industrial revolution, some groups of women went out to work, and indeed, often campaigned for equal access to and pay for work. But social orders have a way of persisting: gender assumptions about the care of children and domestic responsibilities continue (even alongside increases in women's paid work). Such assumptions and expectations shape both political and personal choices (who stays at home to look after children if men earn more than women?).

A second set of systematic connections between differences and inequalities is associated with ideas of 'race'. During the period when many European societies built empires, a whole set of would-be scientific theories were created to explain the superiority of white/European races – and therefore legitimate their control of other places and other 'races' (for example, Baker, 2010). Despite the breakdown of such empires, traces of such racial thinking have persisted as have the inequalities that they suggest are 'natural'. In many European and American societies, important inequalities in education, employment, income, wealth and life expectancy are linked to racial or ethnic identifications.

A third cluster of connections takes shape around class differences and divisions. Here, too, social scientists can trace systematic patterns of inequality – in education, employment, health and wealth (Dorling, 2011). They are systematic in the important sense that they are reproduced over time and between generations. The concept of class draws attention to social and economic divisions associated with wealth, income and power. Access to wealth is associated with power – it involves the ownership and control of things from land to companies. As you saw in Chapter 9, inequalities of income and wealth have not only persisted over time, but have deepened, both in the UK and globally.

These three sets of connection between differences and inequalities have been the focus of considerable attention from social scientists: they pose important questions about how differences and inequalities are linked; about how inequalities persist over time; and about how forms of difference and inequality are interrelated. Although I have presented them as separate patterns here, in everyday life they are interrelated. Nobody is just a member of a class; nobody is just a man or a woman; and nobody is without a racial or ethnic identification: so people live their lives as, for example, a Bangladeshi working-class woman; an African middle-class man; a white English upper-class woman, and so on. How would you identify yourself in this field of intersecting differences?

For me, the important point about these differences is that they are consequential: they have consequences for the sorts of opportunities, possibilities, problems and choices that are likely to come somebody's way. This does not mean that their position determines everything that happens, but that each position in this field of differences shapes the conditions and constraints in which people come to act. This is why attention to the intersecting forms of difference is important, and why others (political movements as well as social scientists) have drawn attention to how other forms of difference also connect and shape inequalities. For example, the difference between able bodied and disabled people; differences of sexual orientation; and differences of age. The connections between forms of difference and inequality are a vital and continuing focus for work in the social sciences.

4 How do social scientists know?

Across the 'Ordering lives' strand, you have encountered very different ways in which social scientists try to know about the social world:

- interviews (Chapters 6, 7 and 8)
- observation (Chapter 6)
- laboratory studies (Chapter 6)
- discourse analysis (Chapter 6)
- surveys (Chapters 7 and 9)
- longitudinal studies (Chapter 7)
- studies of what societies say about themselves (media studies, political statements, and so on) (Chapters 7, 8 and 9)
- quantitative data collection (Chapter 9).

The process of social science inquiry works through many different methods of gaining and analysing evidence. As a result, social scientists work with very different kinds of evidence. Probably the most familiar are those large-scale statistics about populations within societies: who lives longest or suffers the worst health? Who has greater or lesser amounts of income or wealth? You may remember from Chapter 9 that such evidence can tell us about two things:

- patterns (or distributions) such as how income is distributed
- trends (or changes over time) such as how relative shares of income have changed (as in the Institute for Fiscal Studies' report mentioned in the previous section).

Data of this sort has some limitations, of course. Such data cannot tell us about the experience or meaning of the condition being measured: what is it like to be wealthy or poor in this society? Nor does it tell us about the social relationships that are involved in such distributions: do the wealthy have obligations to the poor (think back to Chapter 8's discussion of a 'moral economy', for example); or do they enclose themselves behind protective walls, fences and security systems? Not surprisingly, other social scientists have tried to find methods that overcome such limitations – for example, by concentrating on getting closer to experience and meaning through observing or interviewing people.

Such methods may get closer to the way people feel and think about their lives and the social relationships in which they are lived, but they will have other limitations. They will tend to be small scale (by comparison with the statistical data collection above); they may only apply to a limited group of people (for example, it tends to be easier to observe or interview the poor rather than the wealthy). Observing or interviewing people have other problems attached to them: do people behave differently if a social scientist is watching them? This is sometimes called the 'observer effect' – the very presence of an observer can change the social situation being observed. For some social scientists, the solution to this problem is to take time – to become accepted as a part of the situation, either by being unobtrusive or by becoming a 'participant observer' (taking part in the activity being observed). Equally, in interviews, people may give responses that they think the interviewer wants, or the responses that portray them in a better light (you encountered this in the discussion of the Eysenck Personality Inventory in Chapter 7). It is a recurrent issue for studies that want to assess people's involvement in deviant or criminal activities: do people claim to be more 'innocent' than they are? Do some people claim to be more 'guilty' than they are (for dramatic effect)?

In some studies, social scientists are more interested in how people talk and think about an issue rather than whether they are telling the truth about themselves. Think back to Chapter 6 and the 'discourse analysis' approach to bystanders' perceptions of the situation (Levine's work). How people describe a situation and their relationship to it can provide evidence about how people understand particular forms of social order (and disorder). This is a different way of approaching the question of how people behave from the alternative that you encountered in Chapter 6, the laboratory experiment, a research method commonly used in psychological research to study different aspects of human behaviour. Experiments are not the only method used by psychologists, nor are they as dominant as they once were. Nevertheless, experiments occupy an important place in the history of psychology as a discipline and have provided many important insights into human behaviour.

The main feature of the experiment as a research method is that it involves the creation of carefully controlled experimental conditions in which the researcher is able to isolate, manipulate and measure specific aspects of human behaviour. This makes it possible, in certain circumstances, to try to identify the causal relationship between variables. For instance, in the case of Latané's and Darley's work, which examined, in a controlled environment, how the number of bystanders (the variable that was manipulated in the experiment) affects the likelihood of intervention in an emergency (a variable that was measured in the course of the experiment), researchers were able to determine that there is a causal relationship between the presence of bystanders and non-intervention. The 'bystander effect' is, in actual fact, a description of the relationship between these two variables.

Experiments are believed to uncover general principles about human behaviour, which are independent of the broader historical and social context, and which can therefore be extrapolated to any real-life event where the relevant variables (in this case an emergency and one or more bystanders) are present. For example, although Latané and Darley discovered the 'bystander effect' in the laboratory, using psychology students as participants, they treated it as a phenomenon that accounts for behaviour in any real-life emergency situation, including the murder of Catherine Genovese on a street in New York.

The main problem with experimental research is that the society in which people live their lives is not at all like a laboratory where experiments are conducted. In fact, the main advantage of the laboratory is that it is not like everyday life. By design, experiments involve greatly simplified, controlled simulations which hardly mirror the complexity of everyday life and social interaction. Thus, no matter how sophisticated, cleverly designed or well thought through an experiment might be, it is inevitably artificial, and lacking what is known as **'ecological validity'**. This is why we should not assume that findings yielded by experimental research always shed light on real-life situations.

Ecological validity
The extent to which a study reflects naturally occurring or everyday situations. Ecological validity is often low in laboratory experiments because of the artificial nature of the controlled environment created for the purpose of the study.

This was clearly revealed in Levine's (1999) study, which found that the bystander effect is too simple to explain the conduct of witnesses in the James Bulger case. In that instance, the responses of bystanders were mediated by an additional 'variable', namely the fact that the emergency was seen as being located within the family. Witnesses' assumptions about the perceived rights and responsibilities of the family were not merely a situational factor (like the number of bystanders), but a culturally specific, evolving, historically situated influence, which could not be manipulated and measured in a controlled laboratory setting.

This extended discussion of the laboratory experiment method of inquiry could be repeated for each of the methods of gathering and analysing evidence that you have encountered in this strand. But this is not a module about methods: our aim here is to indicate that you should be aware that all methods of gathering evidence have their own limitations.

Activity 6

Each method used by social scientists to produce evidence has a set of limitations associated with it. What conclusions should be drawn from this?

You might be tempted to think that the whole enterprise is flawed and should be abandoned! If social scientists cannot produce reliable evidence about such issues, then perhaps they should not bother … You might be tempted, but I would encourage you to think again. Across this module, you have encountered many things that social scientists have found out about issues and questions with relevance well beyond the social sciences. Here, I have concentrated on the limitations of particular approaches to producing evidence. I have stressed where particular approaches may have problems. But as will be clear from your work, knowing the limitations is not the same as saying the evidence produced in a particular way is worthless. Rather, all types of social science knowledge is necessarily partial – in several ways.

First, any particular social science study can only look at one aspect of the social world – whether that aspect is the distribution of wealth or the factors that make a delinquent. As a result, a lot of important work in the social sciences involves looking for possible connections: are there connections between economic inequalities and the pathways to being delinquent? Some might suggest the connections are clear-cut: poorer children are more likely to become delinquents (claiming an economic cause for delinquent behaviour). Others might suggest that the connections are more complicated: young people from relatively privileged backgrounds may be insulated against detection or being labelled as delinquents (even if they behave in a law-breaking way).

Second, social scientists have to confront the challenge of dealing with a moving target. People – and societies – change constantly in small and large ways. So, evidence of how things are or what people think at one point may be overtaken by changes in how things are or by changes in what people think. In mid-nineteenth-century England, women could not take degrees in English universities. This has changed (about 70 per cent of the people reading this chapter are likely to be women). The exclusion of women from universities was justified on a number of grounds: educating women was unnatural; it would undermine their womanliness and would endanger the family; it would bring severe health risks in its wake, pointing particularly to the impact of excessive mental stimulus on their capacity to bear children. Writing in 1874, physician and early psychiatrist Henry Maudsley argued that the demands of education would do serious damage to women's physical and mental health and disrupt their reproductive possibilities:

> The important physiological change which takes place at puberty, accompanied, as it is, by so great a revolution in mind and body, and by so large an expenditure of vital energy, may easily and quickly overstep its healthy limits and pass into a pathological change, under conditions of excessive stimulation, or in persons who are constitutionally feeble and whose nerve-centres are more unstable than natural; and it is a familiar medical observation that many nervous disorders of a minor kind, and even such serious disorders as chorea, epilepsy, insanity, are often connected with irregularities or suppression of these important functions.
>
> (Maudsley, 1874, pp. 207–8)

Both how things are – and how people think – have changed since the middle of the nineteenth century in terms of this issue and many others. For social scientists, this implies always having to bear in mind that what one is studying now may already be on its way to becoming history.

Third, what social scientists study tends to involve people – social actors – who think, form opinions, have feelings and reflect on the same situations. During the module, you will have encountered comments about the social or political significance of topics, issues and questions that social science studies address. That is part of the value of the social sciences: they engage with questions that matter to others. But it is also a problem: people talk back, change their minds, and quite often, think they know better. In one research study that I was involved in about 'choice' (a dominant theme in policy during the 2000s), the people interviewed presented subtle and complex thoughts about the ways in which inequalities might affect access to and uses of public services:

> Indeed, the discussions of 'inequality' in our interviews represent something of a masterclass in analysing dimensions of inequality and their implications for public services. Respondents deployed

different conceptions of inequality, reflected on how they intersected and puzzled about their likely interrelationship with choice. It was not that they saw the choice agenda as creating inequality, rather as creating a new terrain on which existing inequalities might be played out.

(Clarke et al., 2007, p. 79)

Social science inquiry is always in this complicated relationship with everyday life. It explores questions that people already think and argue about. Its aim is to generate evidence about those questions and enable new reflections about them. The evidence is, as you have seen, rarely definitive or decisive. Rather, the evidence creates the conditions for new thinking: for the identification of new connections and relationships about how things are and why they are that way. Evidence is important here in that it sharpens questions and acts as a discipline on assertions. But as Chapter 9 in the 'Making lives' strand argued, 'the facts do not speak for themselves'. They have to be analysed and explained, so that even when some facts have been collected, social science still involves competing views: analyses, arguments, explanations that try to best explain the evidence. That is why this module ends with an emphasis on the important – vital, even – skill of being able to compare and contrast different explanations and approaches.

5 Comparing and contrasting

Given that social scientists often disagree, it is important to be able to impose some sort of order on these competing approaches and the arguments they contain. There are many ways of organising such an order, for example studies can be allocated in a grid based on the disciplinary origins of each study: does study X belong to economics, geography, psychology, politics, sociology or some other field (criminology or social policy perhaps)? This can be helpful, and as you go on to further study in the social sciences, you will find much of it is organised in these disciplinary ways. But this dividing up of the field of social sciences has some problems. It is rather too clear-cut, missing approaches, issues and ways of studying that run across disciplinary boundaries. It also makes it harder to see how interdisciplinary work happens: are economists the only people with anything to say about studying economies, economic behaviour or economic thinking? Are political scientists the only ones with anything to say about politics? The answer is probably not!

A more useful way to think about the arguments within social sciences is to engage in an exercise of comparison: to *compare and contrast* different arguments and approaches. Throughout the strand, you have encountered particular studies offering explanations of particular issues. For example, Chapter 6 concentrated on two studies of bystander behaviour. But you have also explored contrasting approaches: approaches to thinking about deviancy in Chapter 7; ideological perspectives (also 'approaches') to interpreting riots in Chapter 8; different approaches to governing inequality in Chapter 9. When social scientists talk about 'approaches' in this way, they are trying to identify ways of looking and thinking at social questions that tend to be shared by a number of social scientists (rather than being unique to one particular study).

At one level, engaging in comparing things is an everyday activity. People find themselves carrying out comparisons in many situations: comparing schools when trying to choose one for their child; comparing holiday destinations when planning a holiday; comparing routes when doing a cross country journey, and many more. In doing so, people may consider the claims made by different schools or destinations; they might look at the evidence for the alternatives. For example, in choosing a school they may look at statistical data about a school's performance, Office for Standards in Education, Children's Services and

Skills (Ofsted) reports for schools in England, or ask other parents with experience of the schools. In making such comparisons, people will think about the similarities and differences (in this case, between different schools), and think about the relative strengths and weaknesses that they can identify.

Comparison in the social sciences shares many of these processes, but like many other aspects of social sciences, it needs to be done relatively systematically and explicitly. For example, it is important to compare the claims made by different social science studies – what do they promise to help their readers to understand? Another way of putting this is to say that it is vital to identify what *questions* a piece of social science is trying to answer. For example, in Chapter 7, the two approaches to studying delinquency were examining very different questions (what causes some young people to behave in a delinquent way? What leads to some behaviour and some people being labelled as 'deviant'?). So a comparison would have to start by recognising this extremely important difference.

Activity 7

Can you think of other examples you have encountered in this strand where the studies might be addressing different questions?

It is then a useful step to compare the *claims* that an approach is making. For example, we might summarise Hayek's approach in Chapter 9 as the claim that setting individuals free in the market is a more important policy than trying to regulate or control markets and the social inequalities they produce. This might be contrasted with the claim by Stiglitz that uncontrolled markets are causing increasing social and political disorders that need to be remedied.

In the process of making their argument, social science studies tend to draw on *evidence*. In comparing them, it might be useful to ask what evidence they use as well as what types of evidence they use. For example, in Chapter 6, even though the two approaches to studying bystanders shared the same question, they used very different methods of studying the issue (laboratory experiment and discourse analysis of witness statements) and thus produced very different types of evidence. The laboratory experiment produced evidence in the form of quantifiable observations – the number of times that people ignored the sounds of distress in specific conditions. In contrast, the discourse analysis approach provided qualitative evidence – the meanings that people attached to the event that they had observed and the identities they attributed to the people involved.

Finally, as you have seen throughout the strand, social science approaches to studying order differ in the arguments that they present. By 'argument', I mean the way that they organise questions, evidence, ideas (concepts) in a reasoned sequence to support the claims they are making. Mostly, social science inquiry works by making explicit these elements: the question(s); the evidence; how the evidence can be best explained. When comparing and contrasting two approaches, it is useful to be able to identify similarities and differences in each of these elements: do they share organising questions? Do they use or examine the same evidence? Do they present different explanations or arguments? It is often tempting to focus on the last point – the different arguments – but the other two are equally important. Being clear about how the argument is put together is a vital skill for engaging in social science inquiry.

In these ways, social science approaches can be compared and contrasted. But even where they differ in terms of their questions, claims, evidence and arguments, they share some common features by virtue of being social science studies:

- A commitment to work with evidence (rather than simply making assertions). They may disagree about what the evidence means, or even what the best evidence for this issue should be, but their explanations and analyses typically work with evidence.

- A commitment to making the reasoning of their explanation explicit – this is partly with the aim of being persuasive, but it is also about making debate and disagreement possible.

Social science proceeds through these shared commitments: to working with evidence; to making analyses explicit; and to making debate possible. These shared commitments also make it more possible to compare and contrast different analyses and arguments within the social sciences.

6 Moving on

We hope that you have enjoyed your encounter with the social sciences and that it has given you an interest or enthusiasm for going further. We have constantly stressed a way of thinking about the social sciences as a process – the view of social science as inquiry. It is always unfinished because the accumulation of evidence, analyses and debates is rarely settled definitively. But it is also unfinished because societies – and the people who make them – do not stand still. They make new connections. They imagine and make new types of social order. In the process, they sometimes draw on social science knowledge, but they certainly create new puzzles, questions and issues for social scientists to investigate.

References

Baker, L. (2010) *Anthropology and the Racial Politics of Culture*, Durham, NC, Duke University Press.

Clarke, J., Newman, J., Smith, N., Vidler, E. and Westmarland, L. (2007) *Creating Citizen-Consumers: Changing Publics and Changing Public Services*, London, Sage.

Cribb, J. Hood, A. Joyce, R. and Phillips, D. (2013) *Living Standards, Poverty and Inequality in the UK: 2013*, London, Institute for Fiscal Studies.

Dorling, D. (2011) *Injustice: Why Social Inequality Persists*, Bristol, The Policy Press.

Gillies, V. (2003) *Family and Intimate Relations: A Review of the Sociological Research*, ESRC Families, and Social Capital Research Group working paper, no. 2, London, South Bank University.

Humphries, S. and Gordon, P. (1993) *A Labour of Love: The Experience of Parenthood in Britain, 1900–1950*, London, Sidgwick and Jackson.

Humphries, S., Mack, J. and Perks, R. (1988) *A Century of Childhood*, London, Sidgwick and Jackson.

Land, H. (1980) 'The family wage', *Feminist Review*, vol. 6, pp. 55–77.

Langan, M. (1985) 'Reorganizing the labour market: unemployment, the state and the labour movement, 1880–1914', in Langan, M. and Schwarz, B. (eds) *Crises in the British State: 1880–1930*, London, Hutchinson in association with the Centre for Contemporary Cultural Studies, pp. 104–125.

Levine, R.M. (1999) 'Rethinking bystander non-intervention: social categorisation and the evidence of witnesses at the James Bulger murder trial', *Human Relations*, vol. 52, no. 9, pp. 1133–55.

Maudsley, H. (1874) 'Sex in mind and education', *Popular Science Monthly*, vol. 5, June, pp. 198–215 [Online]. Available at http://en.wikisource.org/wiki/Popular Science Monthly/Volume 5/June 1874/Sex in Mind and Education (Accessed 25 July 2013).

Mills, C.W. (1959) *The Sociological Imagination*, Oxford, Oxford University Press.

Naples, N. (2005) 'Family wage', in Ritzer G. (ed.), *Encyclopedia of Social Theory*, Thousand Oaks, CA, Sage Publications, pp. 267–69.

Smart, C., Neale, B. and Wade, A. (2001) *The Changing Experience of Childhood: Families and Divorce*, Cambridge, Polity Press.

Thatcher, M. (1980) *Press Conference for American Correspondents in London* [Online], June 25 at 10 Downing Street. Available at http://www.margaretthatcher.org/Speeches/displaydocument.asp?docid=104389&doctype=1 (Accessed 9 August 2013).

Thatcher, M. (1987) Interview conducted by Douglas Keay, *Woman's Own*, 31 October, pp. 8–10.

Acknowledgements

Every effort has been made to contact copyright holders. If any have been inadvertently overlooked the publishers will be pleased to make the necessary arrangements at the first opportunity.

Grateful acknowledgement is made to the following sources:

Chapter 1: *Figure 1.2* (left): Copyright © Bernard Gotfryd/Getty Images; *Figure 1.2* (right): Copyright © Morris Engels/Getty Images; *Figure 1.3*: Courtesy of Stephanie Taylor and Ralph Taylor.

Chapter 2: *Figure 2.1*: Adapted from Department of Health (2008) *Jubilee Line of Health Inequalities 2004–2008*, Department of Health. Crown Copyright ©; *Figure 2.2*: Sport England (2013) *Active People Survey 7*, Sport England; *Figure 2.3*: Copyright © Kevin Fraye/AP/Press Association Images; *Figure 2.4*: Copyright © Bob Daemmrich/Alamy; *Figure 2.5*: Copyright © Keith Morris/Alamy; *Table 2.1*: Sport England (2013) *Active People Survey 7*, Sport England.

Chapter 3: *Figure 3.1*: Copyright © Sefton Samuels/Rex Features; *Figure 3.4*: Copyright © Sinopictures/Joerg F. Mueller/Robert Harding Photo Library; *Figure 3.7*: Copyright © Frankie Quinn; *Figures 3.8, 3.9 and 3.11*: Copyright © Robert Kerr; *Figure 3.10*: Adapted from Mesev, V., Shirlow, P. and Downs, J. (2009) *The Geography of Conflict and Death in Belfast, Northern Ireland*, Annals of the Association of American Geographers; *Figure 3.12*: Copyright © Presseye.com; *Figure 3.13*: Copyright © Mark Ervine; *Table 3.2*: Copyright © Belfast Interface Project 2013.

Chapter 4: *Figure 4.1*: Copyright © Russell Pollard/Press Association Images; *Figure 4.2*: Courtesy of Promo Group; *Figure 4.3*: The Jewish Museum; *Figure 4.6*: Copyright © 2006 SASI Group (University of Sheffield) and Mark Newman (University of Michigan), http://www.worldmapper.org; *Figure 4.7*: Copyright © Ed Kashi/VII/Corbis; *Figure 4.8*: Copyright © Hulton-Deutsch Collection/Corbis; *Figure 4.9*: Adapted from Izady, M. (1992) *The Kurds: A Concise History and Fact Book*, Taylor and Francis Ltd.; *Figure 4.10* (left): Copyright © Time and Life Pictures/Getty Images; *Figure 4.10* (right): Courtesy of Sandhya Suri.

Chapter 6: *Figure 6.1* (top): Copyright © Andrew Fox/Corbis; *Figure 6.1* (bottom left): Copyright © Peter Durand/Arcaid/Corbis; *Figure 6.1* (bottom right): Copyright © Angelo Hornak/Corbis; *Figure 6.2* (top): Courtesy of Ronald Grant Archive; *Figure 6.2* (bottom): Copyright © ITV Granada; *Figure 6.3*: Copyright © New York Times; *Figure 6.4:* Copyright © Mercury Press/Sygma/Corbis.

Chapter 8: *Page 289*: From Kaplan, R. (2008) 'Those Greek riots', *The Atlantic Monthly.* Copyright © 2008 Robert Kaplan. Used by permission of Brandt and Hochman Literary Agents, Inc. All rights reserved; *Page 290*: Shenker, J. (2011) 'Mubarak regime in crisis as biggest anti-government demonstrations in a generation sweep across Egypt', www. jackshenker.net. Article originally published in *The Guardian*, 26 January 2011. Copyright © Jack Shenker. This file is licensed under the Creative Commons Attribution Licence, http://creativecommons.org/ licenses/by/3.0/; *Page 307*: Cameron, D. (2011) 'Fightback after the riots', speech in Witney, 15 August 2011. Crown Copyright ©; *Figure 8.1*: Mary Evans Picture Library/BeBa/Iberfoto; *Figure 8.2*: Mary Evans Picture Library; *Figure 8.3*: Mary Evans Picture Library.

Chapter 9: *Figure 9.1*: Copyright © Image Source/Corbis; *Figure 9.2*: Copyright © Ahmed Jadallah/Reuters/Corbis; *Figure 9.4*: Copyright © Mike Kemp/In Pictures/Corbis; *Figure 9.5*: Davies, J. (2011) *Global Wealth Databook 2011*, Credit Suisse; *Figure 9.6*: Copyright © ITV/Rex Features; *Figure 9.7*: Copyright © Hulton-Deutsch Collection/Corbis; *Figure 9.8*: Copyright © Bettmann/Corbis; *Figure 9.9*: Copyright © EPA European Pressphoto Agency b v/Alamy.

Cover image: Copyright © Ian Dalton/Getty Images.

DD102 Module team

Academic team

John Allen, Professor of Economic Geography

Geoff Andrews, Staff Tutor and Senior Lecturer

Georgina Blakeley, Senior Lecturer in Politics and International Studies (Module Team Chair)

Vivienne Brown, Emeritus Professor of Intellectual History

Jovan Byford, Senior Lecturer in Psychology

John Clarke, Emeritus Professor of Social Policy

John Dixon, Professor of Social Psychology

Umut Erel, RCUK Academic Fellowship

Ieman Hassan, Senior Faculty Manager

Catriona Havard, Lecturer in Psychology

Kevin Hetherington, Dean and Director of Studies

Steve Hinchliffe, Reader in Geography

Eluned Jeffries, Associate Lecturer

Juliet Landau-Pope, Associate Lecturer

Jenny Meegan, Senior Faculty Manager

Mel Nettle, Associate Lecturer

Rajiv Prabhakar, Lecturer in Personal Finance

Parvati Raghuram, Reader in Human Geography

George Revill, Senior Lecturer in Geography

Matt Staples, Staff Tutor (Deputy Module Team Chair)

Stephanie Taylor, Senior Lecturer in Psychology

Joan Vickers, Associate Lecturer

Kath Woodward, Professor of Sociology

External assessor

Professor Dale Southerton, University of Manchester

Production team

Roshni Amin, Sound and Vision Assistant Producer

Melanie Bayley, Media Project Manager

Katie Belcher, Media Assistant

Wendy Chalmers, Learning and Teaching Librarian

Sian Contell, Sound and Vision Assistant

Dale Harry, Copy Editor

Matthew Holley, Sound and Vision Media Developer

Joanna Mack, Sound and Vision Producer

Katie Meade, Licensing and Acquisitions Executive

Lesley Moore, Curriculum Assistant

John O'Dwyer, Editorial Media Developer

Eileen Potterton, Curriculum Manager

Emma Sadera, Editorial Media Developer

Ann Tolley, Curriculum Manager

Howie Twiner, Graphics Media Developer (Graphic Art)

The module team would also like to thank the following freelance staff: Mandy Anton (cover design), Julian Clark-Lowes (software), Isobel McLean (indexer), Joanne Osborn (proof-reader), Margaret McManus (copyrights) and Salia Nessa (book editor).

Video production

Mark Galloway, Series Producer, Evans Woolfe Media

Chris Guiver, Camera/Director, Evans Woolfe Media

Harvey Woolfe, Executive Producer, Evans Woolfe Media

Index